PREFACE TO CRITICAL READING

PREFACE TO CRITICAL READING

RICHARD D. ALTICK
Assistant Professor of English
The Ohio State University

New York
HENRY HOLT AND COMPANY

PRINTED IN THE UNITED STATES OF AMERICA

To My Mother

To The Teacher

THIS BOOK is designed to help teachers of English perform what is, in a very true sense, their highest social function—that of providing our democratic society with a fair number of citizens who will use their dispassionate intelligence in weighing and acting upon the appeals which are directed at them from every source of social and political pressure. Its primary objective is to teach those simple habits of critical reading and thinking which are indispensable to every intelligent man and woman in his or her constant role as a member of political and economic society.

Many careful studies have documented what every college teacher already knew from personal observation: namely, that possession of a bachelor's degree—marking the so-called "successful completion" of college work—is by no means *prima facie* evidence of true literacy. Many institutions, recognizing their failure to develop their students' critical intelligence, have required that the students be given formal guidance in how to read with actively questioning minds. For sound reasons, the responsibility for giving such training has been vested in the teachers of English, even though teachers in every department have a vital stake in the results.

Thus the basic one- or two-year college English course has recently developed a third objective in addition to the two traditional ones of cultivating a decent prose style and of encouraging an interest in literature. In *Preface to Critical Reading* I have attempted to relate the discussion to these two older concerns of freshman and sophomore English. I have tried everywhere to take full advantage of the intimate relationship between reading and writing. The discussions of such topics as denotation and connotation, diction, sentence structure, and rhythm, although here handled from the viewpoint of the reader, can always be applied to the problems of writing. Scattered by implication through the following pages, also, are hundreds of suggestions for stimulating theme-topics. Thus the book actually can supplement and illustrate in many ways that portion of the freshman English course which is specifically devoted to writing.

In the second place, courses in composition usually are followed by courses in the reading of imaginative literature. To prepare students for this sort of reading, I have included one chapter (that on "tone") which deals with some of the most important aspects of creative literature, and at many other points I have tried to relate the general principles of critical reading specifically to the understanding of literary material. Students going on to courses in literature will thus have had some preliminary training in the intelligent reading of poetry and imaginative prose.

The strength of a book of this kind lies largely in the wealth, aptness, and intrinsic interest of its illustrations and exercises. I have made every effort to select material that would arouse the interest of the average student and show him the vital relevancy of his classroom practice in reading to the affairs of his life in the world outside. I have included more exercises and illustrations than can be covered, even in a leisurely course. In selecting the ones to be discussed, the instructor may, of course, consult his own tastes and the particular needs and interests of his class. But the very best illustrative material is necessarily absent from these pages: it is the material which the teacher and the students bring to class on their own—excerpts from current newspapers, magazines, books, and broadcasts—examples which deal with topics and issues that are uppermost in people's minds at that moment. The illustrations printed here are merely suggestive, and the value of the book will surely not be lessened if they are constantly replaced by examples of immediate timeliness.

In planning for the use of this book, the teacher should not neglect to look through Appendix A, where I have printed a group of widely assorted illustrative texts for convenience in reviewing and testing. I have also prepared a brief Teachers' Guide, which lists the sources of all illustrations and examples contained in these pages and includes also some comments on various passages. This Teachers' Guide may be obtained by writing to the publishers.

Experience in teaching these chapters before printing has shown that many passages engender the liveliest sort of classroom controversy. Students often are deeply troubled to find their most ingrained habits of thought and their dearest prejudices called into question, and they eagerly rise to the defense of their established systems. Others of course take an opposite view. The result is an intellectual free-for-all, in which the very errors of thought and language which this book is designed to expose, as well as the proper methods of critical analysis, are given spontaneous practical demonstration. With the book itself furnishing the provocation, the students the heat, and the teacher the necessary tact and direction, classes in freshman English can well witness the birth of genuinely critical intelligence in numbers of college students.

The pleasant duty remains of thanking those who have contributed in one way or another to the preparation of this book. I must thank all the companies which have generously consented to my using their advertisements, as well as the owners of other copyright material, specific acknowledgments of which occur at the appropriate places in the text. All but one chapter of the book was used in preliminary form by a number of teachers at The Ohio State University, and I am grateful to them, and to their students, for many pertinent criticisms of my materials and methods. Professor William H. Hildreth, Director of Freshman Composition at Ohio State, has given me stimulating encouragement and advice at every stage of my work, in addition to allowing me to use material from his personal files. Another colleague, Professor Robert M. Estrich, has read my manuscript, chapter by chapter, and without the benefit of his shrewd criticism this book would have been much the poorer. My graduate assistant, Mr. Alfred Farrell, has helped with the proofs. Finally, I must record the debt I owe my wife, who not only served as typist, critic, and experimental teacher of this book, but during my months of preoccupation with *Preface to Critical Reading* was kind to me in innumerable ways beyond the call of duty.

R. D. A.

Columbus, Ohio,
July 26, 1946.

Foreword

THIS BOOK is meant to help you learn to read.

"Thanks," you say, "but I already know how to read. I learned in first grade."

Pardon us, we reply, but you don't know how to read: not really. And in telling you this, we imply no insult to your intelligence. The simple fact of the matter is that the great majority of college freshmen, for whom this book is primarily intended, do *not* know how to read. Yes, they have mastered the mechanical process which is called reading; they read constantly—the newspaper, *Life,* comic books, advertising cards on buses, even novels and textbooks; and in general they know what is being said. That is, they can usually give a report on the over-all sense of a passage of writing.

But reading is much more than this. True reading involves comprehension of material—comprehension far more penetrating and detailed than that required for a brief report on subject matter. True reading means digging down beneath the surface, attempting to find out not only the whole truth about what is being said, but also (and this is, in the long run, more important) the hidden implications and motives of the writer. When a reader finds out not only *what* is being said, but also *why* it is said, he is on the way to being a critical reader as well as a comprehending one.

It is in these two vital respects, comprehension and criticism, that college freshmen have been found to be seriously lacking. And in recent years there has been much discussion about it, both in and out of academic circles, because it is recognized that slipshod, careless reading frustrates the whole aim of college education. Unless you can read accurately for meaning, and at the same time are able to discriminate between the genuine and the false, the important and the trivial, you are wasting a great part of your time in college.

And thus the practice and advice we plan to offer you in this book has a vital bearing upon all the work you are now doing, or plan to do, in college. The work in reading happens usually to be assigned to the course in freshman English, perhaps on the theory that any study of what is written belongs naturally and properly to the English course. But actually, in how many college courses, excluding a few like physical education, can you get along without doing much reading? And in how many courses would your grades not be improved if you could do a better job in reading your textbook assignments and the collateral assignments you receive from time to time in the library? What this book is about to try to do for you has its application in every subject you will ever take in school. It will try to reduce the number of occasions upon which a student will complain to his instructor that he spends so many hours "reading" a certain assignment (as he probably does), but that when he is finished he has "got nothing out of it." Of course there is no short cut to intelligent reading; it is a long and arduous road to travel, and in the limits of this book we can at best give you only a few broad hints; but perhaps we can suggest, in a way that will make it impossible for you to forget, the most important things to look for when you read.

Many of you have already had some practice in intensive

reading, even though you may not have known it at the time. Mortimer Adler, in his book on *How to Read a Book*, says:

> If we consider men and women generally, and apart from their professions or occupations, there is only one situation I can think of in which they almost pull themselves up by their bootstraps, making an effort to read better than they usually do. When they are in love and are reading a love letter, they read for all they are worth. They read every word three ways; they read between the lines and in the margins; they read the whole in terms of the parts, and each part in terms of the whole; they grow sensitive to context and ambiguity, to insinuation and implication; they perceive the color of words, the odor of phrases, and the weight of sentences. They may even take the punctuation into account. Then, if never before or after, they read.*

But the necessity for close reading is not confined by any means to affairs of the heart or to the performance of college assignments. It is practically impossible to be a genuinely intelligent member of society without the ability to discriminate between the sincere and the fraudulent in all that is spoken or written concerning the affairs of society, and especially concerning politics. Most of you, by this time, have been made aware of the fact that there is such a thing as propaganda, which is an attempt by one group or another to persuade people to think and act the way in which that group wants them to think and act. Many of you feel confident of your ability to withstand propaganda appeals. Perhaps so; perhaps you can at least detect and reject a particularly blatant example of bad propaganda. But what of the more subtle kind, which is also much more prevalent? Can you distinguish between the statement of an idealistic "freshman" member of Congress, who is genuinely concerned with the larger issues, and that of the veteran Congressman Blabbermouth, who

* Quoted by special permission of Simon and Schuster, publishers.

is concerned only to keep his job and thus says only what no one could possibly take issue with? On the surface, the two statements may seem quite alike; it is only after some analysis that a reader begins to realize that one statement is sincere, meaty, informative, and that the other is composed of nothing but weasel words. Yet, since the second one contains nothing to offend, it will often succeed in winning more votes than the first, which, because it speaks out, will necessarily make enemies.

And since our democratic system of government is based upon representation, and representation in turn depends upon communication between candidate and voter, it is obvious that the success of our form of government hinges, in the last analysis, upon the use that is made of language. If voters are taken in by skillful politicians who know how to say what the public, in its uncritical way, wants to hear, they deserve the sort of representative they often get. If, on the other hand, voters can tell when they are being imposed upon—when a candidate is saying one thing and meaning another—then they can exercise their right to reject him in favor of one who talks to them honestly.

At a time when the very destiny of civilization depends upon the ability of the average citizen to understand the fateful issues which the free governments of the world—his elected representatives—must decide, it is superfluous for us to emphasize the urgency of this problem of intelligent communication. Not only national but international affairs are at the mercy of language. No small barrier in the progress of our relations with the Soviet Union is the great difference in language, a far greater one than exists between English and French, or English and German. We are not concerned here with that difference, but it is not without point to recall that a major question of diplomacy, one which had its very definite effect upon Anglo-American relations with Russia, arose in 1945 over the interpretation of the phrase "free and independent government" in connection with

Russia's Yalta guarantees to the post-war Poland. What does "free and independent government" mean? The words are "plain" English, and everyone was in favor of Poland's freedom and independence. But when the nations got down to brass tacks at the San Francisco Conference, it developed that the Russians had one interpretation of the term, the other nations a very different interpretation; and the ambiguity resulted in a serious misunderstanding among the powers. Multiply such an instance by many hundreds every year, on the level of governmental white papers and pronouncements by presidents, prime ministers, secretaries of state, chairmen of the Senate foreign affairs committee, and ordinary congressmen and members of Parliament—and you see why the state of the world demands so much more critical reading and listening habits on the part of the people who elect the governments. Because the use and misuse and abuse of words determine how people make up their minds, in a very real sense words are constantly shaping our destiny.

Or we can use another, perhaps even more potent appeal—to your pocketbook. Indolent, uncritical reading habits cost you money, and plenty of it. This is why. When you read an advertisement in a magazine or a newspaper, an attempt is being made to persuade you to buy something; and the chief means of persuasion are what the advertisers call "eye-appeal" and "copy." With "eye-appeal"—the illustrations, layout, and typography—we have nothing to do here; with "copy" we have much to do. The entire art of writing advertising copy is based upon the skillful, purposeful use of language: language that will subtly flatter you, whet your interest, entice you to buy. It is language specially chosen to do this job. You read, you believe, and you buy. But how many times are you being misled? How often do you buy a product, on the strength of the advertiser's sly persuasion, when you should have bought another brand, which is cheaper and better? We are prone too often to forget that the product which is most attractively and glibly advertised often is inferior to many other brands. If you question this, spend a half hour some time with *Consumer Reports,* which dispassionately ranks various brands on the basis of laboratory tests.

This book is planned, then, to develop your resistance to misleading persuasion, whether political or commercial, by showing you some of the tricks of language that deceitful writers and speakers use. But we also have another purpose, one which, if successful, should increase your profit in general reading. In these pages you will find suggestions that will enable you to derive more profit from all the reading you do, whether it be a story in *Red Book* or a factual article in *The American Magazine,* a best-selling novel or a commentary on the present stage of the world crisis. This is not a book specifically on creative literature; we shall make no attempt to show you the structure of a novel or a play or a poem, or to discuss the many problems confronting writers in these forms. Nor shall we attempt to develop "literary taste"—that is something which takes years of extensive and thoughtful reading. But we can point out some of the elements that distinguish good from bad writing: elements of style, of organization, of logic. When you reach the end of this book, you should be more impatient of shoddy, "hack" writing, of stuff that obviously is written for a market of undiscriminating people who read with their mental eyes shut; and on the other hand you should have a more acute sense of what is genuinely good writing.

At the present stage of your life, the great bulk of the reading you do is confined to material written especially for you. Newspaper reporters, magazine writers, popular novelists, the authors of textbooks and "popular" non-fiction works, all assume (necessarily) that the great reading public is made up of people who want to be amused or instructed without pain, cost, or obligation. They want what they read to be custom-made for them.

It must contain few words they do not understand, no allusions to anything they have not permanently learned early in high school, no ideas that force them to do some serious thinking. The "average" reader, including the college freshman, who is an "average" young American, is assumed to be quite indolent in reading habits. If he cannot have his reading spoon-fed, he wants none of it.

You can go through life quite easily without reading anything beyond this wide but still limited area of material specially designed for the "average" reader. But how much you will be missing! The fact is that most of the great writers of the past—the men and women who said things that still vitally apply to us today—have written for an audience of men and women of superior education and of cultivated reading habits. None of them has ever "written down"; they have written for their intellectual equals. And this is true of the contemporary writers whose work is most worth reading. They refuse to make concessions to the unambitious reader. And yet what these people say can make a tremendous difference in our lives—if only we will read them.

The only solution is for you to equip yourself to become a member in good standing of the superior audience to which the superior writers address themselves. You do not have to renounce your honest taste for popular magazine articles or Book-of-the-Month fiction; and there are plenty of highly intelligent and cultivated people who love detective stories, just as the late Justice Holmes is said to have been fond of a good earthy burlesque show. But you should also be *able* to read material that is several notches higher, both in content and in style. And although, as has been said, we cannot pretend to show you in detail how you can train yourself to do so, we can give you some useful hints.

There is a simple way by which you can measure your progress in the course. About halfway through the book, if you have done the exercises carefully and profited by class discussions, you should be worried because you no longer believe anything you read. Wherever you turn, you should be seeing clichés, "glittering generalities," fallacious reasoning, cunning manipulation of sentence rhythms; and you should be bothered. This is the healthiest possible sign, because it means that you have lost your faith in many false gods; you are wiser, even if, for the time being, you are sadder. You have been divested of lifelong prejudices, biases, implicit confidences in what has been proved to be fraud.

Don't worry. This is only half the process of becoming an intelligent reader. The other half, the constructive half, involves the establishment of positive critical standards by which you may detect what is good and credible and sincere in what men write. The establishment of this wiser faith is a slower process, but it will come. No one need be, or indeed should be, a mere scoffer, a cynic who maintains that nothing is written but to deceive. But in order to recognize the true you must first be prepared to recognize the false. And that is the first, and major, job confronting you.

And if you somehow regret the loss of those old prejudices which you so carefully cherished, remember the slogan of that cigarette ad campaign a few years ago: "It's fun to be fooled, but it's more fun to know." With that one advertising sentiment, at least, we can be in complete agreement.

It may be, also, that you will object to the great detail into which we shall go on occasion—to our insistence upon reading closely, sentence by sentence, phrase by phrase, word by word. "What's the good of doing all this?" you may ask. The answer is, Only by such close and admittedly time-consuming analysis can you hope to develop your critical faculty. It does no good at all to skim over the text of the exercises. You have probably been doing that all your life, and this whole book is designed to show you the pitfalls that lie in such superficial reading. We do not imply that henceforth, to the end of your days, you must read everything so minutely; but you must get into the habit of watching for certain tricks of style and rhythm and logic, and the only way to develop that habit is to practise it intensively for a while. Obviously, life being as short as it is, you cannot spend a fraction as much time in your general reading as you are expected to do in working the exercises in this book; but you must learn certain principles very thoroughly, and the only way to do so is to observe their operation in great detail.

This may sound rather forbidding; but to the conscientious student we can definitely guarantee a reward, one which is inevitably the result of close analysis of the ways of language and of thought. You will emerge from this work a more matured person. You will have had a glimpse into the way your mind works, and you will have had some exercise in making it work more efficiently and more critically. You will have made a start toward separating the vain illusions of this world from the substantial realities. You will have discovered the satisfaction of being able to expose the emptiness of much that is written for your personal consumption and at the same time to profit by what intelligent and honest men have written for other intelligent and honest men to read. In a word, these pages are designed to show you the direction in which intellectual maturity lies.

Contents

PREFACE TO CRITICAL READING

CHAPTER ONE

Denotation and Connotation

INCIDENTS like this are happening every day. A teacher in a college English course has returned a student's theme, one sentence of which reads, "All that week I walked on air, because somewhere I had acquired the delusion that Marge was in love with me." The instructor's red pencil has underscored the word *delusion,* and in the margin opposite it he has written "Accurate?" or whatever his customary comment is in such cases. The student has gone home, checked the dictionary, and come back puzzled. "I don't see what you mean," he says. "The dictionary says *delusion* means 'false belief; a fixed misconception.' And that's what I meant. I had a false belief—a misconception."

"Yes," replies the instructor, "that's what the word *means*—according to the dictionary." And then he takes down his desk copy of *Webster's Collegiate Dictionary* and turns to the word *delusion*. "Look here," he says, pointing to a passage in small type just following the definitions of *delusion:*

Delusion, illusion, hallucination agree in the idea of false seeming. *Delusion* is, in general, a much stronger word than *illusion.* It often carries an implication of being deceived, imposed on, or even consciously misled and bemocked. Further, *delusion* implies a false (often harmful) impression, commonly regarding things themselves real; *illusion,* an ascription of reality (often pleasing) to what exists only in fancy; as, to labor under a *delusion; illusions* of fancy. *Hallucination* emphasizes the groundlessness of the impression.*

The student studies the passage carefully and begins to see light. The word *delusion* carries with it a shade of meaning, an implication, which he did not intend; the meaning of his sentence would have been less ambiguous had he used *illusion* instead. He has had a useful lesson in the dangers of taking dictionary definitions too uncritically, as well as in the exceedingly vital difference between denotation and connotation.

The difference between the two is succinctly phrased in another of those small-type paragraphs in Webster: "The *denotation* of a word is its actual meaning; its *connotation,* that which it suggests or implies in addition to its actual meaning." The denotation of a word is its dictionary definition, which is what the word "stands for" to everyone. But note that according to the dictionary, *delusion* and *illusion* have the same denotation: both *mean* "false impression: misconception." Yet, as we have seen, they *suggest* different things. And that difference in suggestiveness, in shade of meaning, constitutes a difference in connotation.

Nothing is more essential to the process of intelligent, truly profitable reading than a sensitivity to connotation. Only when we possess such sensitivity can we understand not only what the author means, which may be pretty obvious, but also what he wants to suggest, which may actually be far more important than the superficial meaning. The difference between reading a book or essay or story or poem for gross meaning and reading it for implication is the difference between listening to the New York Philharmonic Orchestra on a 1923 crystal set and listening

* By permission. From *Webster's Collegiate Dictionary,* Fifth Edition, copyright, 1936, 1941, by G. and C. Merriam Co.

to it on a latest-model FM radio. Only the latter brings out the nuances that are often more important than the more obvious, and therefore more easily comprehended, meaning.

An unfailing awareness of the connotative power of words is just as vital, of course, to the writer. His eternal obligation is to select the word which will convey, not approximately but exactly, what he wants to say. He must remember that two words may be "synonymous" in respect to denotation; that is, they *mean* the same thing. But to the practised writer, as to the practised reader, few if any words are exactly synonymous in connotation; in a given context one word, and one word alone, will convey the precise implication the writer desires to communicate to his reader. The inexperienced writer, forgetting this, often has recourse to Roget's *Thesaurus,* where he finds, conveniently marshalled, whole regiments of synonyms; confronted by an *embarras de richesses,* he either closes his eyes and picks a word at random or else chooses the one that "sounds" best. In either case he is neglecting the delicate shadings of implication which differentiate each word in a category from its neighbors. To be certain that the word he has selected conveys exactly the sense he wishes to convey, he should check it in those invaluable little paragraphs in *Webster's Collegiate* or a similar dictionary.*

Exercise 1. By reference to *Webster's Collegiate Dictionary,* explain why the italicized words in the following sentences betray the writer's insensitivity to connotation, and in each case supply a more accurate synonym:

1. The principal reason why I didn't like him was that some of his mannerisms were *womanly*.

* If the definition of the word in question is not followed by a paragraph discriminating between its "synonyms" there is usually a cross reference to the place where this paragraph occurs.

2. Since he had to drive fifty miles in an hour and a quarter, he had to proceed with *dispatch*.
3. She is really a heroine; her *resignation* in the face of her husband's constant cruelty to her is marvelous.
4. When the boys finished shoveling the snow from her sidewalks, the woman *reimbursed* them.
5. Usually he was the liveliest member of the company, but this afternoon his *taciturnity* surprised everyone.
6. When the smoke began to seep in beneath the door and we could see the flames through the transom, we were filled with *dismay*.
7. After dessert was finished we *trifled* for half an hour over our coffee.
8. His stained, frayed old tie, his greasy, shapeless hat, and his filthy shirt combined to give him a *slatternly* appearance.
9. The child has been *petulant* all day; nothing seems to suit him.
10. What especially interests newcomers to the region is the absolute *smoothness* of the countryside.

Exercise 2. Explain the differences in connotation among the members of each of the following groups of words:

1. beautiful, beauteous, handsome, pretty, lovely, exquisite.
2. moody, cross, perverse, restive, cantankerous, intractable.
3. quail, skulk, flinch, sneak, slink.
4. poverty, indigence, pauperism, destitution, difficulties, need, privation.
5. unclean, dirty, filthy, grimy, soiled.
6. annoyance, grievance, irritation, mortification, worry, vexation, pique.
7. dextrous, adroit, handy, deft, proficient, accomplished, competent.

Not all words possess connotative powers. Articles, conjunctions, prepositions, many common adverbs (*well, badly, thoroughly,* etc.), lack connotative qualities because they are words used to connect ideas and to show relationships between them, or to modify their meaning; these parts of speech do not themselves stand for ideas. But all words which stand for ideas have connotations, even though they are often scarcely perceptible. That is because ideas themselves have connotations: they produce some sort of reaction inside us.

Connotations: Personal and General

There are two types of connotation: the personal and the general. Personal connotations are the result of the experience of the individual man or woman. The way in which we react to ideas and objects, and thus to the words that stand for those "referents," is determined by the precise nature of our earlier experience with the referents. The connotations that surround most of the words in our vocabulary are a complex and intimate record of our personal experience through life; that is, our present reaction to a word may be the cumulative result of all our experiences with the word and its referent. In the case of other words, our reaction may have been determined once and for all by an early or a particularly memorable experience with them. A student's reaction to the word *teacher,* for instance, may be determined by all his experience with teachers, which has been subtly synthesized, in the course of time, into a single image or emotional response. In it are mingled memories of Miss Smith, the first-grade teacher who dried his tears when he lost a trial bout in the schoolyard at recess; of Miss Jones, the sixth-grade teacher who bored her pupils with thrice-told tales of her trip to Mexico ten years earlier; of Mr. Johnson, the high school gym teacher who merely laughed when he saw the brush burns a boy sustained when he inexpertly slid down a rope; of Mr. Miller, the college professor who somehow packed a tremendous amount of information into lectures that seemed too entertaining to be instructive. Or, on the other hand, when the student thinks of *teacher* he may think of one particular teacher who for one reason or another has made an especially deep impression upon him—the chemistry teacher in high school, for instance, who encouraged him, by example and advice, to make chemistry his life work.

A moment's thought will show the relationship that exists between personal and general connotations as well as the fact that there is no line of demarcation between the two types. Since "the mass mind" is nothing more than the sum total of the individual minds that comprise it, general connotations result when the reaction of the majority of people to a specific word is substantially the same. The reasons why one word should possess a certain connotation, while another word has a quite different connotation, are complex. We shall spend a little time on the subject later. Here it need only be said that differences in general connotation derive from at least two major sources. For one thing, the exact shade of meaning a word possesses in our language is often due to the use to which it was put by a writer who had especially great influence over the language because he was, and is, so widely read. The King James version of the Bible, for instance, is responsible for the crystallization of many connotations. People came to know a given word from its occurrence in certain particular passages in the Bible, and thus the word came to connote to them on *all* occasions what it connoted in those familiar passages; it was permanently colored by particular associations. Such words include *trespass, money-changers, manger, Samaritan* (originally the name of a person living in a certain region of Asia Minor), *salvation, vanity, righteous, trinity, charity,* and *refuge.* The same is true of many words used in other books which, being widely read and studied, influenced the vocabularies of following generations—Malory's *Morte d'Arthur,* for example, or Shakespeare's plays (after they were printed), or the essays of Addison and Steele.

But general connotation is not always a matter of literary development. It can result also from the experience which men as a social group have had with the ideas which words represent. Before 1940, the word *collaborate* had a more or less pleasant connotation; it suggested the harmonious working together of two or more nations for some mutually desired end. But in 1940 the word became associated with the faction in conquered France whose announced purpose was to "work with" the Germans; and thus *collaborate,* together with its derivative words, was associated with a craven policy which the people of the surviving democracies looked upon with loathing. And though years have passed, the word still retains unpleasant suggestions of Pierre Laval and the Vichy government, and it is safe to say that no British or American official will use it in referring to an aspect of foreign policy for which he wishes to win public acceptance. Again, since most people in the non-Nazi countries reacted in the same manner to the deeds of Major Vidkun Quisling, the cumulative effect of those reactions was the establishment of a general connotation: *Quisling* came automatically to imply "traitor, fifth columnist."

All general connotations thus have their origin in private connotations—in personal, individual, but generally shared reactions to words and the ideas for which they stand. But later, after the general connotations have been established, the process works the other way: the individual, who may have had no personal experience with the idea in question, may acquire a personal attitude toward it through observing how society in general reacts to the word which symbolizes it. Thus in the future, men and women who were babes in arms when Quisling lived may react negatively to mention of his name because they will share the feeling implied in the general connotation.

Every writer is obliged to differentiate between general connotations and personal ones, and to rely only upon the former.

He can transmit his full meaning to the reader only when the reader can be depended upon to find in his words the same shade of meaning that he intended, and that is possible only when the commonly established distinctions among words are fully recognized. A writer who uses words which have special connotations to himself alone is writing in a private shorthand to which he alone holds the key; no reader can be expected to understand him, except imperfectly.

The Uses of Connotations

What forms do our reactions to words take? By no means all words evoke any distinguishable emotional response; our old friends *delusion* and *illusion,* for instance, probably do not do so for most people. Here the response is largely an intellectual one, a recognition that the two words are customarily used in different contexts, that they "imply" slightly different things. And this is true of many categories of words, such as those denoting abstract relations of various sorts, or referring to space or matter or intellect in the abstract.

But for our purposes the most important categories of words are the ones which touch the emotions of those who hear or see them. They are words that arouse people to a pleasant or unpleasant judgment—words that often stir them to decision. *Communist* arouses deep-seated prejudices for or against the ideas that the word is said to represent, for or against the people who are said to be communists. *Streamlined* connotes modern design, clean lines, efficiency, and thus has a generally pleasant suggestion. (On the other hand, like many words that become too fashionable and thus are overused and even abused, *streamlined* has come to have a negative connotation to many fastidious readers. Too often it has been loosely used as a means of apologizing for skimping and corner-cutting—as in *streamlined* education.) *Crucifixion* arouses in many persons certain well-defined religious sentiments. *Gardenia* may suggest to some a corsage sent to a girl before a high school prom—and to others a principal ingredient* in a funeral spray. Mention of *F.D.R.* evokes fervent sentiments, of very diverse quality, from both those who voted for him and those who did not. *Sub-deb* eases the selling of clothing to adolescent girls, of whom not one in a hundred thousand will ever have a debut. *Nigger* connotes very different things to a champion of white supremacy in Mississippi, a backer of the National Association for the Advancement of Colored People, and a Londoner whose only experience of Negroes has been in connection with jazz bands. *Draft* and *selective service* mean the same thing, but one term has a more unpleasant connotation than the other. And so on, *ad infinitum*.

EXERCISE 3. In Bliss Perry's *A Study of Poetry* (p. 140) is printed the following list of words which are part of the basic vocabulary of poetry because they possess particularly strong emotional appeal. Why are they so filled with suggestion? Are they also part of the basic vocabulary of today's popular songs?

> age, ambition, beauty, bloom, country, courage, dawn, day, death, despair, destiny, devotion, dirge, disaster, divine, dream, earth, enchantment, eternity, fair, faith, fantasy, flower, fortune, freedom, friendship, glory, glow, god, grief, happiness, harmony, hate, heart, heaven, honor, hope, immortality, joy, justice, knell, life, longing, love, man, melancholy, melody, mercy, moon, mortal, nature, noble, night, paradise, parting, peace, pleasure, pride, regret, sea, sigh, sleep, solitude, song, sorrow, soul, spirit, spring, star, suffer, tears, tender, time, virtue, weep, whisper, wind, youth.†

* Does the use of *ingredient* here seem inappropriate? Why?

† By permission of Houghton Mifflin Co., publishers.

Exercise 4. What are the present connotations of the following words, and why have they come to possess those connotations?

> realism and expediency (as applied to foreign policy), free enterprise, isolationist, labor leader, Russian, atomic scientist, underground, Pearl Harbor, patriot, radical, century of the common man.

Exercise 5. What reaction, if any, do you have when you hear the name "Gwendolyn"? Do you see any specific picture in your mind? How can you account for it? Try the same experiment with other Christian names: is there any general agreement on their connotation—and why?

Exercise 6. What do the following words connote to you personally?

> olive, G.I., caress, autumn afternoon, Abraham Lincoln, horsecar, willowy, intolerance, exotic, hoopskirt, high-hat (*adj.*), chocolate malted, sultry, librarian.

Exercise 7. What do the following words connote to you?

> appetency, kinkajou, Phaedra, recusancy, Bowdlerize.

Intimately associated with this emotional response, and often directly responsible for it, are the images that many words inspire in our minds. The commonest type of image is the visual: that is, a given word habitually calls forth a certain mental picture on the screen of our inner consciousness. Mention of places we have seen and people we have known produces a visual recollection of them. Of course the precise content of these pictures is determined by the sort of experience one has had with their referents. *Mary* may not recall the picture of one's childhood sweetheart, but it may evoke instead a picture of a pink hair-ribbon which Mary must once have worn. *Boston* may recall only the picture of a street accident, which was the most vivid memory one carried away from that city. And so on! It is a fascinating game to examine in this fashion the mental images thus spontaneously conjured up by words; equally rewarding is the effort to explain why many words evoke images which on first thought seem so completely irrelevant to their denotations.

It is not only words referring to concrete objects which have this power of evoking a visual response in the imagination. Our picture-making faculty also enables us to visualize abstractions in concrete terms—and, as we shall see, it gets us into a great deal of trouble on that account. *Capitalist* is an abstract word; it denotes a person who has a certain function in a certain kind of economic system. But to many people it connotes a definite picture, obviously derived from the cartoonist's stock figure, of a bloated banker in striped pants, cutaway coat, top hat, and spats; he is smoking a Corona-Corona cigar, on his fingers are rings with huge stones, and across his middle reposes a gold watch-chain with links as thick as frankfurters. To some, in a similar way, the noun *liberal* conjures up a picture of an intellectual-looking man with thick glasses, bushy hair, wrinkled clothes, and a wild, dreamy expression on his face. Thus abstractions are made concrete, and our reactions to the words that represent those abstractions are rigidly patterned in terms of that visual image.

Words evoke not only visual responses in the imagination but also responses associated with the other senses. Many words have connotations which appeal to our inward ear; for these, see the advertisements of radios, phonograph records, and electric organs. Other words appeal to our sense of touch—*stiff, smooth, velvety, sandpaper, bristle, resilient, Swansdown*. Another class invites palatal responses—*tangy, bittersweet, emetic, salty, flavorful, creamy, cod liver oil, sherry*. And a final group invites olfactory responses—*rancid, aromatic, piney, fetid, wet wool swim-*

ming trunks. Of course many words appeal to two or more senses at once—*talcum powder,* for instance.

Since our sensory experience may be either pleasant or unpleasant, the words which evoke their imaginative equivalents have the power to sway us to acceptance or rejection of an idea. "It's *precious* Persian, soft and supple, light in weight, flattering to every coloring because each tight, silky curl has the rich, blue-black lustre that only expert hand processing and dyeing can produce." Thus writes the man who wants his reader to buy a Persian lamb coat. "It's a foul, evil-smelling mess." Thus speaks a minority-party congressman who is dissatisfied with something the administration has done.

But sometimes men employ words lovingly, unschemingly, designing only to enchant:

> Season of mists and mellow fruitfulness,
> Close bosom-friend of the maturing sun;
> Conspiring with him how to load and bless
> With fruit the vines that round the thatch-eaves run;
> To bend with apples the mossed cottage-trees,
> And fill all fruit with ripeness to the core;
> To swell the gourd, and plump the hazel shells
> With a sweet kernel; to set budding more,
> And still more, later flowers for the bees,
> Until they think warm days will never cease,
> For Summer has o'er-brimmed their clammy cells.

Or:

> It is a beauteous evening, calm and free,
> The holy time is quiet as a Nun
> Breathless with adoration; the broad sun
> Is sinking down in its tranquillity;
> The gentleness of heaven broods o'er the Sea:
> Listen! the mighty Being is awake,
> And doth with his eternal motion make
> A sound like thunder—everlastingly.

And then we have literature.

We need to look a little more closely at these three main uses of connotation.

Connotations in Advertising

If it were not that many advertising copy-writers were such highly skillful masters of word-connotations, we should spend far less money than we do. They know how to cultivate our responses, always evoking pleasant pictures, making us yearn for what we lack—and all without our being aware of it. On the other hand they have a formidable list of taboos—words which must never be mentioned because they arouse negative connotations of one sort or another. In advocating the purchase of a product because (they say) it doesn't cost very much, they never use the word *cheap*: *cheap* connotes shoddiness, as well as penny-pinching. And so they appeal to our sense of *thrift,* which is more fashionable perhaps because it has the approval of Ben Franklin, an American folk-hero. In promoting a large-size package of their product, they have a tendency to call it the *economy* size—"You save when you buy it!" *Fat* is never used except in the reducing-course ads; you can never induce a woman to buy a dress or a corset by calling her fat. Instead there are dresses for *the larger figure*. And when it is a matter of selling pipe tobacco, perfume, or coffee, *smell* is absolutely interdicted.

It is not hard to find out for oneself exactly how advertising men work: a half-hour with one or two current magazines, keeping in mind the evocative powers of connotation, will supply abundant examples of the way in which a product is always presented in the most enticing light. Here are a few instances culled at random. In brackets are inserted alternative words which the writer of the advertisement may have considered and then rejected. Can you account for each rejection—or do you think some of the rejected words might have been more effective?

1. Frigidaire with the Meter-Miser brings [offers, affords, gives] you modern [up-to-date, new, advanced] frozen food storage, with a big [large, roomy, commodious], separately insulated Super-Freezer Chest. Unique temperature and humidity controls that safeguard vitamins, let you store foods uncovered. Famous Frigidaire Quickube Trays for trigger-quick [fast, immediate, convenient] ice service. [*Note how the catch-names* Meter-Miser *and* Quickube *were coined for their suggestive value.*]
2. Drinks mixed with Canada Dry Water or Ginger Ale are at the prime of life [height of their excellence, peak, zenith] . . . . stay that way to the last sip [drop, swallow]. That's because "Pin-Point Carbonation" insures drink-long [continuous, lasting, undiminished] zip and zest [effervescence, bubbling, life]. Both of these sparkling good mixers are made to exclusive [our own private, secret] formulae [recipes, directions]—scientifically controlled [carefully made]. Canada Dry water points up [improves, enhances] the flavor of any tall drink.
3. The eye-appeal [attractiveness, inviting quality] of appetizing [mouth-watering, tantalizing] dishes is set against a background of gleaming [bright, shining, polished] glass, stainless steel and immaculate [clean, spotless] new equipment, at the food counter of this ultra-modern [new, streamlined] Cafeteria Car.
4. [*With a picture of a lady in a hostess coat lounging in a red-quilted bird-house*] NEW WINTER PLUMAGE FOR YOU. Nestling-warmth to fly home to—Textron's quilted hostess coat in a nosegay print. With a slender [narrow] Princess back, a precious [conveniently placed] pocket. Tailored [sewed, built, made] with Textron's parachute-precision—of finest [top-notch, matchless, first-grade, the best] rayon satin . . . . dove-soft [baby-cheek-soft, velvet-soft] . . . . wing-smooth [satin-smooth, exquisitely smooth].

Obviously the exact choice of words a writer makes depends to a great extent upon the audience to which he is addressing his message. Confronted by four possible alternatives, all of which are pleasing, he selects the one which in his practised estimation will be most effective with the people he has in mind. Thus if he is writing an ad intended for the widely diversified readers of the *Saturday Evening Post,* he chooses words whose connotations would most affect them; but if he is writing an ad for *Harper's Bazaar,* let us say, or *The New Yorker,* his audience, having very different tastes, will be moved by a completely different set of words. We shall have more to say later of this matter of writing for a specific audience.

All this is very interesting; but is it important? The answer is a decided "Yes." Assuming, as we no doubt have a right to do, that your money is not unlimited and that you like to get as much as possible for it when you spend it: how many times in the course of a year do you buy something on the strength of the words some advertising agency magician has spoken to you, rather than on its own merits as a product? Perhaps you really do not need it, but the words of the advertiser (*luxurious . . . smart . . . efficient . . . delicious . . . figure-flattering*) have made you want it so badly that you buy it. Or perhaps you do need it; but why buy Brand A instead of Brand B, which is indisputably better? Because Brand A's advertising writer did a better job with words (*independent laboratory tests have proved . . . matchless flavor . . . super-swift . . . a little higher in price, but it's worth the difference . . . the best-groomed men everywhere . . .*). How much that is really worth knowing have you learned from Brand A's advertisements? Or has the writer been craftily playing upon your weak spots—your vanity, your envy of someone else, your desire for greater personal beauty or more leisure or more friends? You can find out, very easily, if you analyze his words for their connotative overtones. It is a salutary exercise to examine the advertisements in a single issue of a widely circulated magazine for content of genuine fact; you will learn that for every nugget of information you find, you must burrow your way through mountains of fine-sounding words. In the end you must decide whether it is sensible to let your emotions rule your pocketbook.

EXERCISE 8. The following advertisement appeared in *The New Yorker*—a magazine read by people in the "higher income brackets"—a year or two ago. From each group of alternatives, select the one which you think the copy-writer chose:

> Antoine, (cosmetician, make-up manufacturer, maker of beauty aids, artist sublime), (presents, announces, offers you, recommends) a new (adventure in beauty, idea, scheme, cosmetic, notion)—your own powder (expertly, professionally, carefully) (mixed, blended, put together) before your very eyes—in Antoine's own (machine, whirl mixer, gadget). (Personal as your initials, made to your own specifications, designed for you alone). (Deftly, Expertly, Cunningly, Admirably, Perfectly) (adapted, suited, adjusted, keyed) to your (coloring, complexion, hue, color) and (skin texture, skin graining, skin surface). (Perfumed, Augmented, Laden) with your favorite Antoine (odor, fragrance, aroma, scent). At (exclusive, expensive, fine, only the best) department stores.

EXERCISE 9. How honest is the use of language in this advertisement of Abercrombie and Fitch Company?

> Here is a featherweight rain coat of forest green nylon that rain simply cannot penetrate. It will not crack or become tacky. It has a fly front, raglan sleeves, balmacaan collar, two lined slash pockets.

EXERCISE 10. Make a list of the favorite catchwords in the present crop of advertisements—a good example would be the ubiquitous use of the word *modern*. What do these terms connote that makes them so precious to advertising writers?

EXERCISE 11. The following sentences are quoted from the menu of a Chicago restaurant. What is their literal, denotative meaning? Do they tempt you to order the dishes they describe?

> HOT MINCE PIE. A perfect symposium of harmony, a fusion of apples, raisins and citrus fruits, and real brandy. Ah, what ethereal essence!
> FRENCH FRIED SHRIMP. King Neptune and his court of beautiful sea nymphs lured these unsuspecting shrimp to their doom. Like a thing entranced, they blindly followed right into the snare of man.

Connotations in Political Persuasion

Now let us consider the reader not as a consumer, a buyer of things so cunningly advertised in the magazines and on the radio, but as a citizen of a free society, whose personal opinions, when joined with those of millions of other citizens, constitute public opinion. Every day, representative men and women of America are being interviewed for the public opinion polls. They are being asked what they think on this or that current issue, and most of them turn out to have a definite opinion. Where and how do they get their opinions?

Public opinion is being formed wherever and whenever one man expresses his opinion on a topic to someone else. Unless the hearer or reader has already made up his mind and refuses to change it (in which case his own opinion, whether in agreement or opposition, will be strengthened simply by hearing the arguments re-stated), he will be influenced by what he is told—and thus where before there was only one man who believed such-and such, now there are two. The medium of communication, of course, is words.* And just as is the case with commercial advertising, in persuasion designed to make someone think thus-and-so about a public issue, the emotion-producing powers of words are a vast force for good or evil. Used in one way, they are a means of perpetuating and intensifying the basest sort of prejudice and bigotry; used in another, they are a means of stirring the human spirit to heights of nobility and courage.

We wish at all costs to avoid the suggestion that words, used for the purposes of persuasion, are always either evil or empty. Mankind would never have risen from barbarism had there not constantly been men—poets, orators, preachers—to stir it to action. If you condemn persuasive language categorically as being delusive, designed to make men respond to empty symbols rather than to reality, you condemn a great body of our finest literature, from the Old Testament prophets with their sulphurous denunciations of a godless people to Winston Churchill's speech which rallied the British people to a defense of their island even after the catastrophe of Dunkirk. The Welsh hymn "Men of Harlech," Wordsworth's sonnet "Milton! thou shouldst be living at this hour," Milton's *Areopagitica,* Pericles' funeral oration, MacLeish's "Lines for an Interment," Hood's "The Song of the Shirt," John of Gaunt's speech in Shakespeare's *Richard II*—all are, in one way or another, pieces of persuasion. But they are all on a high plane; they are designed to stir men to positive, constructive action by appealing to their loftiest emotions, emotions of pride and honor and courage and pity. They inspire.

But much, indeed most, persuasion does no such thing. It strikes a much lower plane, reaching into those regions of men's

* Nowadays, to be sure, pictures have a great part in forming and spreading public opinion—as cartoons have had for almost a century and a half. Would hatred of the Nazi leaders have been so virulent had we not seen so many pictures and caricatures of them? But in this book we are concerned only with spoken and written language.

spirits which harbor their intolerance, their vanity, their hankering for superiority, their suspicion of the new or different, their jealousy, their fear. And words are the weapons which it uses.

Words, we have said repeatedly, have the power to evoke emotional response. The precise nature of that response too often is determined by prejudice. All of us are prejudiced; we dislike certain people, certain activities, certain ideas—in many cases, not because we have reasoned things out and found a logical basis for our dislike, but rather because these people or activities or ideas offend us somewhere in those lower regions of the spirit where we cherish our less noble instincts. Of course there are also positive prejudices, by which we approve of people or things—perhaps because they please our lower emotions (vanity, sense of superiority, etc.) or perhaps because we have always been taught that they were "good" and never stopped to reason why. In either case, it is these prejudices and biases, irrational and unfair though they are, which words can and do arouse. Two principal means by which this is accomplished are name-calling and the use of the glittering generality. They are alike in that they depend upon the process of association, by which one idea (the specific person, group, proposal or situation under discussion) receives emotional coloration from another idea which is placed close by.

Name-calling is the device of arousing an unfavorable reaction by such an association. There is a whole treasury of words which connote things unpleasant to most Americans: *un-American, alien, communist, fascist, bureaucratic, dictator, rabble-rouser, totalitarianism, politician, free spending, agitator, reactionary, radical* are a few of them. If, then, a speaker or writer wishes his audience to react against a person or party or principle, he will take pains to use such terms in his persuasion. "The bill now before Congress is un-American and will take us another long step on the road toward totalitarianism." "The Republican party is made up largely of smug, die-hard reactionaries." "The Democratic party is riddled with second-generation New Dealers and radicals." Name-calling is not confined to political discussion. It is found in every argument, on whatever topic, in which more heat than light is generated. "The preachers who want to padlock the movies on Sundays are strait-laced, bluenosed hypocrites who want nothing more than to spoil the poor man's only day of recreation." "The liquor dealers' association that is agitating for the emasculation of the state law is composed of racketeering saloon keepers and greedy proprietors of dives where every sort of sin and debauchery rages unchecked; every one of them is an agent of Satan." "The electric power rates are sky-high because of a corrupt alliance between the vested interests and a kept legislature." Every sentence we have quoted contains words loaded with unpleasant emotional suggestion. And inevitably their evil connotations spill over into the ideas with which they are associated.

The glittering generality, on the other hand, involves the use of good connotations. Most people automatically react favorably to such words and phrases as *American, freedom, democracy, national honor, patriotism, Constitution, statesman, human rights, peace, liberty, economy, equality of opportunity, prosperity,* and *higher standard of living*. Words like these therefore shed a pleasant glow upon the ideas with which they are associated. "The bill now before Congress is based on true principles of American democracy and will provide us with a strong bulwark against alien ways of life." "The Republican party is the party of men and women united for the preservation of private enterprise and the right to earn an honest living, unmolested by government or labor dictators." "The Democratic party is composed of practical idealists who are working for a better America—a land of peace, prosperity, and security." Nor is the glittering generality confined to political discussion. "The ministers who are urging Sunday closing are honest, unselfish servants of God and man, who are working for the best interests of the community." "The liquor dealers' association that is recommending the liberalization of the state law is composed of substantial taxpaying citizens who are well aware that their success depends upon the maintenance of order and decency in their establishments." "The electric power rates cannot be reduced without drastically curtailing the efficiency of the company's service and impairing the company's ability to pay dividends to the thousands of ordinary men and women—widows, clerks, young married couples, mechanics—who are its owners." In every sentence occur words designed to soothe the reader, make him feel good—and incline him to accept the idea which the words so agreeably clothe.

Be sure to note that these two categories do not by any means exhaust the methods by which words can be used to condemn or approve without reference to evidence or logic; you will be able to find many pieces of persuasion in which there is not a single example of name-calling or a glittering generality. These two devices have been singled out for notice because they are very common and because their unfairness is so patent. And so do not make the mistake of trying to fit every instance of abuse of connotation into one or the other of these two categories.

Next, the complete irrationality of such use of words and the injustices that result from it should be illustrated by a brief analysis of the actual process.

The speaker: "Mr. X [a high official of the government in Washington] is a communist."

The evidence: None. As a matter of fact, Mr. X, while a man of mildly liberal leanings in politics, believes firmly in the soundness and fairness of the capitalistic system, and disagrees completely with those who think Russia's economic system is better.

The innocent reader: "I don't like communists. They are a godless people, practice free love, have a low standard of living, speak a barbarous tongue, don't have freedom of the press, have the world's most ruthless secret police, send people to Siberia, and are trying to overthrow all the governments of the world. All these things are terrible; therefore communists are dangerous and diabolical. You say this man is a communist? All right then, THROW HIM OUT OF OFFICE!"

In other words: A (Mr. X) is B (a communist) [there is no proof that he is]; I don't like B [on no good grounds, because I am confused and misinformed on a number of important points]; therefore I don't like A.

To find all the lapses of logic in that simple statement would be the occupation of an hour—but never would an hour be more instructively spent. Yet the world rings with condemnations which are just as irrational, and people believe them because it is far easier to paste a label on a bottle than to analyze its contents.

Try the same procedure with the second device, the glittering generality.

The candidate: "We must protect our sacred heritage, the American way of life!"

First listener (a mechanic): "Good stuff! American way of life—high wages, profits of big business limited by taxation, monopolies forbidden, labor unions protected by law, equal opportunity for all, nobody too rich, nobody too poor . . . I'll vote for him!"

Second listener (owner of a small factory): "My sentiments exactly! American way of life—government keeps its hands off business, no excess profits tax, labor unions kept in hand by restrictive laws. If a man has the brains and the aggressiveness he can make a million dollars and it'll be his own . . . I'll vote for him."

Who is going to be disappointed after the candidate takes office and begins making decisions? He cannot serve two masters; yet both voted for him because he favored what they favored—a vague phrase which was bound to please them, *so long as it remained undefined*. The simple, devastating test to apply to every such word or phrase, so agreeable, so unexceptionably fine, is this: What *in particular* does it mean to the person who utters it? Is it as beautiful in practice as it looks on paper? Would you agree with the sentiment if it were put into operation in the way the man wants it to be?

The fatal fallacy in all such free-and-easy use of language is a lack of definition, which allows the emotions and prejudices untrammelled play. If words can mean what you want them to mean, then they can be used on both sides of an argument—and they often are. *The New Yorker,* a few years ago, printed a shrewd comment on the way in which the word *Fascist* can serve anyone who wants to smear anyone else:

> It is already apparent that the word "Fascist" will be one of the hardest-worked words in the Presidential campaign. Henry Wallace called some people Fascists the other day in a speech and next day up jumped Harrison Spangler, the Republican, to remark that if there were any Fascists in this country you would find them in the New Deal's palace guard. It is getting so a Fascist is a man who votes the other way. Persons who vote *your* way, of course, continue to be "right-minded people."
>
> We are sorry to see this misuse of the word "Fascist." If we recall matters, a Fascist is a member of the Fascist party or a believer in Fascist ideals. These are: a nation founded on blood lines, political expansion by surprise and war, murder or detention of unbelievers, transcendence of state over individual, obedience to one leader, contempt for parliamentary forms, plus some miscellaneous gymnastics for the young and a general feeling of elation. It seems to us that there are many New Deal Democrats who do not subscribe to such a program, also many aspiring Republicans. Other

millions of Americans are non-subscribers. It's too bad to emasculate the word "Fascist" by using it on persons whose only offense is that they vote the wrong ticket. The word should be saved for cases where it applies, as it does to members of our Ku Klux Klan, for instance, whose beliefs and practices are identical with Fascism.*

The obligation of the conscientious citizen is plain. He must be constantly on the alert for attempts to persuade him by the use of prejudice-stirring words or words whose connotations so charm the reader that he neglects to ask precisely what they mean. He must train himself to respond to ideas rather than to language—to demand arguments based upon reason and logic, arguments that have a hard core of truth.

Exercise 12. Examine the following passages for appeals to prejudice rather than to reason, and explain in detail why an intelligent reader would refuse to be swayed by such persuasion:

1. From this very platform, not so long ago, certain glib orators, henchmen of the power-happy administration, accused me of being anti-labor. This I deny with all the sincerity and fervor that God gave me. I am a friend of the working man. But I believe that his most precious possession, under our American democratic system, is his inalienable Right to Earn an Honest Living. Does he enjoy such a right? Look at the men who call themselves labor leaders—the Communist alien Bridges, who should have been deported long ago, but who has continued to stir up mischief and worse, protected by the shyster lawyers with whom the Washington bureaucracy is honeycombed; look at the czar of the musicians' union, a man with the good old American name of Petrillo, who wields more power than any dictator ever did, and from his luxurious suite of offices hands

* Permission of *The New Yorker*. Copyright 1943 by the F.-R. Publishing Corporation.

down edicts that tell all of us free Americans what to do! Can the working man enjoy any real freedom with such men at the helm of his unions, squeezing out his life-blood in the form of exorbitant dues, exacting tribute from him with the noble purpose of declaring strikes and thus *preventing* him from earning a decent living? Frankly, I shudder to think what the high-minded signers of the Bill of Rights of our Constitution would have thought had they been able to foresee the day when racketeers took over American Labor. Would Washington have countenanced such crimes in the name of human rights? Would Lincoln? Our finest American traditions are being trampled in the mud, and slowly but surely this great nation of ours is creeping toward collectivism.

2. As the people of this state search their hearts for new comfort and courage and resolve to pour their resources into the titanic struggle which has staggered both hemispheres with its cold brutality, they know that Pennsylvania's destiny and the destiny of the world depend upon leaders who will neither falter nor waver in their determination to preserve the bedrock of liberty, justice, and humanity.

   It is a generous Providence which provides us with men of steel in time of peril. The deathless spirit of other valiant Americans who fought against the yoke of tyranny must sustain us in facing the stern realities of this struggle and teach us never to forget that war is the perennial scourge of all free people. Pennsylvania, as the "Arsenal of America," must be the swivel on which this nation will turn its vaunted power full in the face of the enemy and lead civilization forever out of the cathedral woods of desolation, suffering and despair.

   As this nation turns its eyes to ever-widening battlefronts and resolves to pour its heart and hopes into the struggle to make the world forever safe from the hammerblows of organized war, Pennsylvania might well look to — as the soldier-Governor who can co-ordinate its far-flung resources and hurl them with smashing impact into the battle for world freedom and decency.

   His election will weld together the vital links of industrialism and give a powerful lift to civilian unity. His is the exacting discipline of a man who knows we cannot turn blindly from the brutal facts of war. His is the fighting heart of a man who has known the horrible carnage of armed conflict. His is the wartime doctrine which will open the floodgates of American patriotism so that Pennsylvania, in this zero hour, will not be found wanting.

A vote for him will be a vote for victory and enduring Americanism!

EXERCISE 13. Make a list of the catch-words and -phrases most in favor with propagandists at the moment. If a political campaign is going on, what are the terms most used to praise or damn a candidate or party?

Connotations in Literature

When we turn from these aspects of practical persuasion to creative writing—poetry, drama, fiction, and the rest—our duty as intelligent readers is quite different. Here the writer usually has no ax to grind, no product to sell, no vote to win, no policy to put over. His intention is not to deceive; on the contrary, it is to offer his readers a vivid experience, the essence of which is the transmutation of life, of actuality, into an imaginative adventure. He may wish to present before our inward eye a person or a scene that he himself has either actually witnessed or imagined, and to present it with as much color and credibility and meaningfulness as he can; or he may wish to play upon our emotions, so as to make us feel as he has felt concerning love or death or courage or religious devotion; or he may wish to communicate an intellectual idea to us in such terms that we cannot help apprehending its force and truth. Whatever the writer's precise intention, one of the major means by which he makes us see and hear and think and feel with him is the skillful use of word-connotations. And now, instead of being on guard against deception, we must make ourselves completely receptive to the subtleties of language, allowing them to sway us as their author desires.

A great part of the pleasure of reading poetry is due to the manner in which the poet is able to flood the reader's mind with a rapid pageant of impressions, which the poet may control and select in order to produce a single powerful effect. In the "Calais Beach" sonnet quoted on page 12, Wordsworth seeks to produce the single impression of quietness and serenity, and he does so by the conscious selection of words which connote those qualities. Sometimes, too, the poet relies upon the connotativeness of words to transport his reader from the world of actuality into a realm of the pure imagination, a never-never land of magical fascination created solely by language:

The moving Moon went up the sky,
And nowhere did abide:
Softly she was going up,
And a star or two beside—

Her beams bemocked the sultry main,
Like April hoar-frost spread;
But where the ship's huge shadow lay,
The charmèd water burnt alway
A still and awful red.

Beyond the shadow of the ship,
I watched the water-snakes:
They moved in tracks of shining white,
And when they reared, the elfish light
Fell off in hoary flakes.

Within the shadow of the ship
I watched their rich attire:
Blue, glossy green, and velvet black,
They coiled and swam; and every track
Was a flash of golden fire.

Often a single line or two may contain a wealth of suggestiveness. To one who knows the story of the fall of Troy, Marlowe's lines

Was this the face that launched a thousand ships,
And burnt the topless towers of Ilium?

contain all the emotional values implicit in the story of a beautiful woman for whose love a civilization was almost destroyed. Or take a minute to examine the manner in which the connotations of the separate words in such a passage as this merge to produce a simple but powerful emotional effect:

Your low voice tells how bells of singing gold
Would sound through twilight over silent water.

Of course it is not only the poet who makes constant use of word-connotations. The writer of imaginative prose uses them just as often, and for the same reasons. Here is a brief excerpt from Van Wyck Brooks' *The Flowering of New England,* in which the writer, by presenting a succession of connotative images, evokes the flavor of a particular time and place in history:

The Cambridge flowers had a moral meaning, as good New England flowers ought to have; but they had a poetical meaning that was even more apparent. So did the sounds one heard on summer evenings, the bells of the cows ambling home at twilight, the lullaby of the crickets in early autumn, the hymns of the frogs, in spring, in some neighbouring swamp, not to speak of the creaking of the winter wood-sleds, dragging their loads of walnut over the complaining snow. Every sound and odour had its value. One heard the carpenter smoothing his knotty boards, and the whips of the four-horse coaches rattling by; one heard the ticks in the joints of the old bedsteads; one smelt the salt of the sea in the summer breeze. What a store of allusions and similes, drawn from the homely facts of his daily living, a Cambridge boy might pack into into his poems! *

The importance of connotation in creative literature is admirably illustrated by a paraphrase of a familiar lyric by Lord Byron. Note that the paraphrase reproduces exactly the denotations contained in the original—it "means" the same. But the emotional qualities, supplied by words of rich and colorful suggestiveness, have completely evaporated. What is left is a dull, drab string of words.

(a)	(b)
There be none of Beauty's daughters	There are no girls in all the world
With a magic like thee;	Who have your power to attract;
And like music on the waters	And like an agreeable sound coming across a body of water
Is thy sweet voice to me:	Is the effect your euphonious voice has on me:
When, as if its sound were causing	When, as if the sound of your talking had the power
The charmèd ocean's pausing,	To make the fascinated ocean stop tossing around,
The waves lie still and gleaming	The waves keep motionless and shiny,
And the lulled winds seem dreaming:	And the quieted currents of air appear to be lost in thought;

* Quoted by permission of E. P. Dutton & Co., Inc., publishers.

(a)	(b)
And the midnight moon is weaving	And the 12 p.m. moon is being reflected
Her bright chain o'er the deep;	In a series of luminous patches scattered over the expanse of water;
Whose breast is gently heaving,	Whose surface is inconspicuously moving up and down
As an infant's asleep:	Like the chest of a sleeping baby:
So the spirit bows before thee,	So the non-physical part of me is humble in your presence,
To listen and adore thee;	In order to give an ear to what you say and show you how much I like you;
With a full but soft emotion,	With an abundant but unexcited feeling,
Like the swell of Summer's ocean.	Like the movement characteristic of the ocean in summer time.

What we are doing here is simply re-stating, from a new point of view, what is stressed over and over again in every course in English composition: avoid general, abstract words in your writing; select always words which are concrete and particular, which evoke vivid responses in your readers' consciousness. Only when you do this are you able to draw upon the powerful storehouse of word-connotations. When you neglect this advice, your writing inevitably is pale and dull; it fails to stir the reader. When you follow this advice, your writing can be so persuasive that the reader cannot help heeding what you have to say.

Exercise 14. Comment on the connotative power of the following passages:

1. Dark house, by which once more I stand
   Here in the long unlovely street,
   Doors, where my heart was used to beat
So quickly, waiting for a hand,

A hand that can be clasp'd no more—
   Behold me, for I cannot sleep,
   And like a guilty thing I creep
At earliest morning to the door.

He is not here; but far away
   The noise of life begins again,
   And ghastly thro' the drizzling rain
On the bald street breaks the blank day.

2. Press close bare-bosom'd night—press close magnetic nourishing night!
Night of south winds—night of the large few stars!
Still nodding night—mad naked summer night.
Smile O voluptuous cool-breath'd earth!
Earth of the slumbering and liquid trees!
Earth of departed sunset—earth of the mountains misty-topt!
Earth of the vitreous pour of the full moon just tinged with blue!
Earth of shine and dark mottling the tide of the river!
Earth of the limpid gray of clouds brighter and clearer for my sake!
Far-swooping elbow'd earth—rich apple-blossom'd earth!
Smile, for your lover comes.

3. It is common knowledge that water may exist in three very different physical states, namely, gaseous, liquid, and solid. Existence in all these three states is not peculiar to water but is the common behavior of the great majority of substances. Experiment has shown that every substance, whether element or compound, tends to pass into the gaseous state if its temperature is

raised sufficiently, although it is not always possible actually to bring about such a change. In some cases the temperature required is so high that it cannot be obtained by laboratory methods; in others, the substance decomposes before the required temperature is reached.*

4. But Herr Hitler is not thinking only of stealing other people's territories or flinging gobbets of them to his little confederate. I tell you truly what you must believe when I say this evil man, this monstrous abortion of hatred and deceit, is resolved on nothing less than the complete wiping out of the French nation and the disintegration of its whole life and future.

   By all kinds of sly and savage means he is plotting and working to quench forever the fountain of characteristic French culture and French inspiration to the world. All Europe, if he has his way, will be reduced to one uniform Bocheland, to be exploited, pillaged, and bullied by his Nazi gangsters.†

5. At length she came home one night after one of these saunterings and mounted to her bedroom. She took off her laced coat and stood there in shirt and breeches looking out of the window. There was something stirring in the air which forbade her to go to bed. A white haze lay over the town, for it was a frosty night in midwinter and a magnificent vista lay all round her. She could see St. Paul's, the Tower, Westminster Abbey, with all the spires and domes of the city churches, the smooth bulk of its banks, the opulent and ample curves of its halls and meeting-places. On the north rose the smooth, shorn heights of Hampstead, and in the west the streets and squares of Mayfair shone out in one clear radiance. Upon this serene and orderly prospect the stars looked down, glittering, positive, hard, from a cloudless sky. In the extreme clearness of the atmosphere the line of every roof, the cowl of every chimney was

* From McPherson, Henderson, Mack, and Fernelius, *Chemistry: A Textbook for Colleges,* by special permission of Ginn & Co., publishers.

† From *Blood, Sweat, and Tears,* copyright 1941 by Winston S. Churchill. Courtesy of G. P. Putnam's Sons.

perceptible. Even the cobbles in the streets showed distinct one from another.*

EXERCISE 15. The power of connotation is illustrated in the selection of titles for books. What value have the following titles? (It is significant that a number of them are quotations from poetry.)

Look Homeward, Angel.—After Many a Summer Dies the Swan.—Where Stands a Wingèd Sentry.—Nets to Catch the Wind.—For Whom the Bell Tolls.—Tender Is the Night.—Yankee from Olympus.—Bleak House.—Wind, Sand, and Stars.—Admiral of the Ocean Sea.—Kings and Desperate Men.—Midnight on the Desert.—The Stricken Deer.

How Connotation Changes

One of the chief difficulties students have in reading literature that was written a hundred or more years ago is that they encounter words which do not seem to make sense in the way they are used, even though they are words which are in daily use today. For example, the diarist Samuel Pepys, writing in 1660, described the execution of a leader of the Puritan rebellion of 1649. "I went out to Charing Cross," Pepys writes, "to see Major-general Harrison hanged, drawn, and quartered; which was done there, he looking as cheerful as any man could do in that condition." Immediately one stops short at that word *cheerful:* is it very probable that a man who was in the process of being hanged, drawn, and quartered maintained what we could call a "cheerful" countenance? Obviously Pepys meant nothing of the

* From *Orlando,* copyright, 1928, by Virginia Woolf. By special permission of Harcourt, Brace & Co., Inc.

sort; *cheerful* in his day connoted something unlike what it connotes today. To him it suggested "tranquil," "calm," "resigned," and had no implication of good feeling such as it now possesses. Such instances can be multiplied without end. We encounter them on every page of Shakespeare, Milton, Johnson, Pope, Wordsworth. What can we make of the lines in which Wordsworth is praising his wife for her manifold virtues—

> A Creature not too bright or good
> For human nature's daily food;
> For transient sorrows, simple wiles,
> Praise, blame, love, kisses, tears, and smiles.
>
> *And now I see with eye serene*
> *The very pulse of the machine.*

The word *machine* jolts nearly every reader who comes to it; what business has such a word, with its connotations of steel and gears and motors, in such a poem? What has machinery to do with Mary Wordsworth? The answer is that to Wordsworth and his contemporaries *machine* had a much more general connotation; the line might be paraphrased, "The very pulse [or heart] of her being." The word *engine,* incidentally, causes similar trouble to modern readers who run across it in older literature. What does "two-handed engine" mean in Milton's "Lycidas" (line 130) or "the fatal engine" in Pope's *The Rape of the Lock* (canto III, line 149)?

Connotations are in a constant state of flux; the writings of our own contemporaries will be as troublesome to readers a century or two hence as the English classics are to us. We have already seen the reasons why words acquire certain connotations which are agreed upon by all literate readers and writers: the practice of the most influential writers, and the attitude of society toward the ideas which certain words have come to represent.

But these general connotations are by no means permanently established, because no writer remains influential forever and no social attitude fails to undergo some modification. Although the usage of Addison and Steele "set" many connotations in their own day, the time came when other writers had more influence, and thus, gradually and almost imperceptibly, Addison and Steele began to seem old-fashioned in their use of words. The influence of social attitudes upon connotation is well illustrated by the history of *Roman Catholic,* which was brought into use when the older words used to designate a member of that faith, *Romanist, Roman,* and *Papist,* had acquired so heavy a stigma that a substitute was necessary—one which lacked the bad connotations that the other words possessed in Protestant England. The subsequent history of *Roman Catholic* is in effect a history of shifting winds of feeling. In England it gradually lost the stigma that it had inevitably acquired, in time, as a substitute for *Papist;* but wherever there is anti-Catholic feeling today, it retains its negative connotations. The histories of such words as *Methodist* and *Quaker* offer similar illustrations of the evolution of social feeling.

Suppose that a word with an established denotation acquires a new connotation which in time becomes as firmly established as the denotation itself. If it becomes customary to use the word only in the sense implied by this new connotation, the original denotation is forgotten, and the dominant connotation becomes the new denotation. In brief, change in connotation, if carried far enough, becomes change in actual meaning. Since there is no sharp dividing line between denotation and connotation, it is impossible to say just when change of connotation results in change of meaning. But it has happened in the case of thousands upon thousands of words, whose meanings have been completely revolutionized by a series of shifts in connotation. These changed meanings of course introduce further difficulties in the reading of the older literature. Take as an example of both types of change the opening sentences of Bacon's essay "Of Studies":

> Studies serve for delight, for ornament, and for ability. Their chief use for delight is in privateness and retiring; for ornament, is in discourse; and for ability, is in the judgment and disposition of business. For expert men can execute, and perhaps judge of particulars, one by one; but the general counsels, and the plots and marshalling of affairs come best from those that are learned. To spend too much time in studies is sloth; to use them too much for ornament is affectation; to make judgment wholly by their rules is the humour of a scholar.

One can grasp the general sense at a first reading; but that is because many of the words Bacon uses retain enough of the denotations they possessed in his day to give us clues. Yet no one will say that this is modern English, or even close to it. What if we are asked to rewrite the passage so that every trace of its late sixteenth-century origin is removed? *Delight* is too strong a word for this context; we should use *pleasure* instead. *Ornament* is no longer used in Bacon's sense of "social advantage"; *ability* stands for our modern "practical profit" or "usefulness." *Privateness* has gone almost completely out of use; taken together with *retiring* (people of Bacon's day loved to couple two virtually synonymous words) it means "our personal, or home, life." *Discourse* now means "talk by one person"; to Bacon it meant what we now mean by *conversation. Judgment and disposition* can be modernized as *conduct. Expert* to Bacon suggests "accomplished, competent" in general; in our time its use is restricted to suggest skill in certain techniques. And so on. Scarcely a noun of Bacon's could be retained if the passage were to be made intelligible to, let us say, a prospective student in a correspondence course.

It takes constant vigilance to pick up these changed connotations and meanings as we read, but the result is worth the effort, because when we read some piece of old writing with full understanding we have succeeded in cheating Time himself; we have received the message that the author, long since dead, intended for us. And that can often be a considerable satisfaction.

There is no royal road to such comprehension. The simplest way in which to improve one's ability to read material written in previous centuries is to read more of it. If a child has much contact with a very old great-grandparent, who uses English words in ways that were proper two or three generations ago, the child will gradually acquire a "feeling" for such usages, and they will seem entirely natural to him. Likewise if an adult reads more widely in the older literature than is customary nowadays, he will find himself gradually acquiring a similar feeling. His vocabulary habits will come closer to those of Malory or Shakespeare or Milton; such frequently-used words as *humor* will no longer perplex him by the oddness of their use. He will automatically think in the language of his author.

Shakespeare, because he made such audaciously original use of the English language, is somewhat harder to read than his contemporaries, and is nearly always read in annotated editions, with all the uncommon words glossed. But most of the other great authors of the past must be read without such easily available help. For the really inquisitive reader there exists the great *Oxford English Dictionary,* which is an encyclopedia of the history of the language. In the *OED* (or *NED*), as it is usually called, one can check up on all the shades of meaning which a word had at any given time in its history. Each shade is illustrated by passages quoted from the writings of the period. One's education is not complete until he has had the salutary experience of tracing the history of a few selected words in the pages of the *OED.*

EXERCISE 16. The italicized words in the following quotations have a meaning different from that which they possess today. Explain, if possible by context and in any event by recourse to the *OED,* what each meant to the writer's contemporary audience:

1. Weep not, my *wanton;* smile upon my knee;
   When thou art old there's grief enough for thee.
   (Robert Greene, 1589)
2. Tell me, where is *fancy* bred,
   Or in the heart or in the head?
   (Shakespeare, 1596)
3. Perhaps my *semblance* might *deceive* the truth
   That I to manhood am arrived so near.
   (Milton, 1631)
4. He went out of my chamber, and I thought seemed to have a little *heaviness* upon him which gave me some disquiet.
   (Steele, 1709)
5. Authors are partial to their *wit,* 'tis true,
   But are not Critics to their judgment too?
   (Pope, 1711)
6. Come, my Celia, let us *prove,*
   While we can, the sports of love.
   (Jonson, 1606)
7. The Trout is a fish highly valued both in this and foreign Nations; he may be justly said . . . to be a *generous* fish.
   (Walton, 1653)
8. Get on your *nightgown,* lest occasion call us,
   And show us to be watchers.
   (Shakespeare, 1606)
9. . . . I have found, by trial, Homer a more pleasing task than Virgil, though I say not the translation will be less *laborious;* for the Grecian is more *according to my genius* than the Latin poet.
   (Dryden, 1700)
10. Bossu is of opinion that the poet's first work is to find a *moral,* which his *fable* is afterwards to illustrate and establish.
    (Johnson, 1779)

The Importance of Context

We were able to understand the general sense of the passage quoted from Bacon because some of the words it contained had not shifted so radically in meaning as to conceal Bacon's thought, and they threw light on the words whose meaning had changed more completely. Thus we had a brief glimpse of the meaning and usefulness of context, which is the reciprocal relationship between a given word and the words which surround it in any passage. Think of a sentence as a row of highly polished vases (the important words—nouns, verbs, and modifiers). What we see when we look at each of those vases includes not only the form of the vase itself but also reflections of the adjacent vases. Those reflections are what we mean by context. Each word has a meaning in and of itself, but as we read along, we find that that meaning is affected by the meanings of the words which precede and follow.

The use of context for the clarification of individual words and phrases can, when the process is understood, be the most entertaining and instructive of mental exercises. The reader should try to solve as many as possible of the riddles confronting him without recourse to a dictionary. In many cases the meaning of a certain word is hinted at by the words that surround it. The momentum of the preceding thought carries us right to the explanation we require. Or if we are still mystified, it often pays to go past the word in question to see what follows; perhaps the sentences immediately following it will throw light on its meaning.

In any event, the most powerful aid to context is some knowledge of foreign languages, especially Greek, Latin, and French, from which so many thousands of our English words are derived. A student who has had as little as a year or two of foreign languages in high school or college has a tremendous advantage over those who have not. His native ingenuity is strengthened by a knowledge of word-roots which can help him over innumerable obstacles in his everyday reading.

Of course the method of trying to guess the meanings of words is by no means foolproof; mere ingenuity can lead one far astray, inviting him to interpret passages in a way the author never intended. Therefore the dictionary should always be kept close at hand for the resolution of difficulties. Under the word in question, the dictionary lists a number of definitions (usually in chronological order—the original meaning first, the newest meaning last). The trick then is to select from the list the meaning which best fits the context. Often it may be a difficult matter to decide which of two or three meanings, each of which apparently fits the context, the author intended. Then the reader should return to the context, rereading the whole passage more carefully, until he is able to reject certain definitions as not being *precisely* what the author meant and to emerge with the one meaning which, he feels, adequately conveys the author's intention.

Here is part of the conclusion of Henry James's essay on Emerson, which took the form of a review of Cabot's biography of the essayist:

> It has not, however, been the ambition of these remarks to account for everything, and I have arrived at the end without even pointing to the grounds on which Emerson justifies the honors of biography, discussion, and illustration. I have assumed his importance and continuance, and shall probably not be gainsaid by those who read him. Those who do not will hardly rub him out. Such a book as Mr. Cabot's subjects a reputation to a test—leads people to look it over and hold it up to the light, to see whether it is worth keeping in use or even putting away in a cabinet. Such a revision of Emerson has no relegating consequences. The result of it is once more the impression that he serves and will not wear out, and that

indeed we cannot afford to drop him. His instrument makes him precious. He did something better than anyone else; he had a particular faculty, which has not been surpassed, for speaking to the soul in a voice of direction and authority.*

As was the case with the selection from Bacon printed above, we are probably able to apprehend the general sense on first reading. James is saying in effect that the test of a great man's permanent worth is whether his fame can survive a biography like Cabot's, and that Emerson triumphantly passes the test. (The fourth and fifth sentences say as much.) But a careful reader will wish to know more. Since James presumably wrote each sentence for a particular purpose, to advance and add to his earlier argument, to clinch a point, to prepare for a new idea—each sentence should be considered and understood. And upon closer examination we find a number of words and locutions which need explanation:

Ambition. "Remarks" are not usually thought of as having ambition; normally we think only of people as having it. But the meaning is clear from context: "design," "purpose," "intention."

Illustration. Since James has already used the word in the same sense earlier in the essay, the careful reader will already have discovered its meaning: "quotation," "the selection of examples to clarify certain aspects of the subject."

Continuance. By "importance and continuance" James means "his present and future importance," or, as we should say, more simply, "his continuing importance."

Gainsaid. The context suggests the idea of opposition. The conjunction *and* implies agreement or similarity between the two parts of the sentence; therefore the second part should be in essential harmony with the first. "I have thought so-and-so," says James, "*and* others will probably agree with me." *Gainsaid*

* From Henry James's *Partial Portraits*. By permission of The Macmillan Company, publishers.

is more commonly used to mean "denied" ("The assertion will not be gainsaid") but its meaning here ("I shall probably not be opposed") is plainly similar.

Revision. This can be attacked in two ways. Obviously the word does not mean "change [of opinion]" or "new edition." The reader with a smattering of Latin will recognize the prefix *re* (again) and the root *vis* (seeing, looking—as in *vision, visual, visionary*). He then realizes that James is using the word in its original, literal sense of "looking over again." And if he reviews the context, he will find that the preceding sentence had already explained the word to him!

Relegating. Latin is of some help here, but again the context is sufficient; "putting away" in the preceding sentence is the literal meaning of *relegating*. In other words, in the preceding sentence James has said in Anglo-Saxon-derived words what he now says in Latinized diction.

Serves. Definition 6 under *serve* (verb, intransitive) in *Webster's Collegiate Dictionary:* "to answer a purpose." But the meaning can be inferred from the following, "and will not wear out."

Instrument. This is explained by what follows. "Not *what* he said so much as *how* he said it."

Direction. Definition 2 in the *Collegiate:* "That which is imposed by directing; command; also, authoritative instruction." Definition 4: "The line or course upon which anything is moving or aimed to move, or to which anything is pointing." The latter meaning is more familiar to us; but the context, especially the proximity of "authority," shows plainly that the former meaning is intended.

It is by such a combination of methods as this that the full purport of a passage can be arrived at. Analyzing a few paragraphs, word by word, for complete, rather than superficial, meaning will impress you with the importance of each individual word in context. In the best writing there are no superfluous words or sentences; each small brick in the structure has its own particular function and cannot be removed without loss.

Exercise 17. Here is a good opportunity to measure how much you have learned in this chapter. The following quotation is from a work written almost two hundred years ago; but the ideas it contains are essentially the same as those we have set forth in this chapter. With this hint, read carefully through the selection, sentence by sentence, relating each idea which the author discusses to points already covered in this book. Some of the words (*e.g., passions, eloquence*) have changed connotations; substitute for them the equivalent modern words used in the preceding discussion. You will thus be testing two things: (1) Your comprehension of the subject-matter of pages 8-33 (the fundamental importance of word-connotations), and (2) your ability to read non-contemporary writing.

> *How Words Affect the Passions.* Now as words affect, not by any original power, but by representation, it might be supposed that their influence over the passions should be but light; yet it is quite otherwise; for we find by experience that eloquence and poetry are as capable, nay indeed much more capable, of making deep and lively impressions than any other arts, and even than nature itself in very many cases. And this arises chiefly from these three causes.
>
> First, that we take an extraordinary part in the passions of others, and that we are easily affected and brought into sympathy by any tokens which are shown of them, and there are no tokens which can express all the circumstances of most passions so fully as words; so that if a person speaks upon any subject, he can not only convey the subject to you, but likewise the manner in which he is himself affected by it. Certain it is, that the influence of most things on our passions is not so much from the things themselves, as from our opinions concerning

them; and these again depend very much on the opinions of other men, conveyable for the most part by words only.

Secondly, there are many things of a very affecting nature, which can seldom occur in the reality, but the words that represent them often do; and thus they have an opportunity of making a deep impression and taking root in the mind, whilst the idea of the reality was transient, and to some perhaps never really occurred in any shape, to whom it is notwithstanding very affecting—as war, death, famine, etc. Besides, many ideas have never been at all presented to the senses of any men but by words, as God, angels, devils, heaven and hell, all of which have however a great influence over the passions.

Thirdly, by words we have it in our power to make such *combinations* as we cannot possibly do otherwise. By this power of combining, we are able, by the addition of well chosen circumstances, to give a new life and force to the simple object. In painting we may represent any fine figure we please, but we never can give it those enlivening touches which it may receive from words. To represent an angel in a picture, you can only draw a beautiful young man winged; but what painting can furnish out anything so grand as the addition of one word, "the angel of the *Lord*"? It is true, I have here no clear idea; but these words affect the mind more than the sensible image did; which is all I contend for. . . .

Now as there is a moving tone of voice, an impassioned countenance, an agitated gesture, which affect independently of the things about which they are exerted, so there are words, and certain dispositions of words, which, being peculiarly devoted to passionate subjects, and always used by those who are under the influence of any passion, touch and move us more than those which far more clearly and distinctly express the subject-matter. We yield to sympathy what we refuse to description. The truth is, all verbal description, merely as naked description, though never so exact, conveys so poor and insufficient an idea of the thing described, that it could scarcely have the smallest effect, if the speaker did not call in to his aid those modes of speech that mark a strong and lively feeling in himself. Then, by the contagion of our passions, we catch a fire already kindled in another, which probably might never have been struck out by the object described. Words, by strongly conveying the passions, by those means which we have already mentioned, fully compensate for their weakness in other respects.

CHAPTER TWO

Diction

LET US now do a little detective work.

1. "Listen, slip me a fin, will you? I'm in a jam. I'll pay you back Saturday." What sort of person is writing? (Or is he speaking?) In England or America? At the present time, or at some time in the past?

2. "If I were you I'd inquire at the ironmongers' in King Street. They probably stock spanners. Take the first turning to your left." What is the nationality of the speaker?

3. "She don't think much of him, but believe me, if I ever got near to him, nobody else wouldn't ever have a chance at him." How well educated is the speaker? To what social class does she belong?

4. "So we were making up our sacks that morning when in came the chief with the latest scuttlebutt." What is (or has been) the occupation of the speaker?

5. "The present meteorological pattern permits us to infer that the next forty-eight hours will witness substantial precipitation, together with a decline in temperature readings." How much of a gift for clear communication has this writer?

6. "Her kinfolk came from up in the mountains." From what section of the United States does the speaker come?

7. "His style normally is clear, incisive, vigorous; but under the stress of emotion (or, it may be, the pressure of publishers' dead-

lines), it often becomes involved, circuitous—sometimes, indeed, almost chaotic." What can you infer about the education, professional interests, and writing skill of the author?

8. "They took the cars late that evening, and at ten o'clock the next forenoon they arrived in San Antonio." When was that sentence written?

9. "Her singing that night was divine." What is the sex of the speaker?

10. "In the allegro vivace slow movement, the 'cellos blended magnificently with the brasses to form a climactic cadenza." How much does the writer know about music?

If we have a moderately sensitive feeling for words, we should have no trouble answering these questions somewhat as follows:

1. That this passage was spoken, not written, is suggested by the form of the sentences, especially the free use of contractions and the slang. The slang itself is contemporary; "slip me a fin" (give me a five-dollar bill) and "in a jam" (in trouble) would have been incomprehensible not many years ago. The speaker is probably young or middle-aged (older people usually do not pick up and use the latest slang), and he probably is American, although the British take over much American slang from the movies.

2. An Englishman is talking. *Ironmongers'* is the American *hardware store; stock* is the American *keep* or *carry; spanners* is the American *wrenches; turning* is the American *corner* or *intersecting street;* and British usage speaks of a house or store as being *in,* rather than *on,* a street.

3. The speaker is not well educated; *she don't* is grossly ungrammatical, as is the double negative (*nobody . . . wouldn't*). The use of such conspicuously bad grammar probably indicates a fairly low social level, although it would be perilous to be dogmatic about it.

4. The speaker is, or has been, a sailor; *sacks* is nautical slang for *beds* or *hammocks,* and *scuttlebutt* is the sailors' word for *rumor.*

5. This writer has no gift at all for clear communication. What he says in twenty-four words could be boiled down to six: "Rain and colder tomorrow and Wednesday."

6. The speaker is probably from the South, where *kinfolk* is characteristically used for *family, relatives.*

7. The writer is well-educated, has a greater-than-ordinary interest in literary style, and writes well. He may be a professional critic. The adjectives he uses to describe another's style (a notoriously difficult thing to describe) are well chosen; the sentence itself is maturely constructed.

8. The sentence must have been written many years ago—or, possibly, it was written lately by someone who is now very old. *The cars* used to be the ordinary term for a train, but it went out of common use long ago. *Forenoon* too is old-fashioned.

9. The sentence was probably written (or spoken—no sure evidence) by a woman. The adjective *divine,* in its popular, loose sense of "wonderful," "excellent," or "good," is characteristically feminine. Most men would rather be caught dead than utter it.

10. The writer is either simply deceiving himself or else deceiving himself that he is deceiving others; in either case, he knows nothing at all about what he is saying. A slow movement in music would scarcely be marked *allegro vivace,* and a cadenza is a passage for a solo instrument, not for groups of instruments.

From these examples we can draw one extremely important conclusion: that words not only connote shades of meaning, but also contain valuable clues to the background, the personality, and often the intention of the writer or the speaker. Thus it is possible to supplement what we are told outright with data shrewdly inferred from the *manner* in which the information is given.

Some of the following material is found in college textbooks of composition under the heading of "Diction." There it is intended primarily to help you achieve a good writing style by the selection of words and idioms appropriate to such writing; here it is intended primarily to show the technique by which we can extract more information from what we read. Of course the two purposes are closely associated. Just as we hope that the chapter on denotation and connotation has made you more aware of the necessity for accuracy in the selection of words when you are doing your own writing, so we hope the present chapter will enable you to avoid some of the other common pitfalls in writing.

Elementary Clues of Diction

1. *Geographical clues.* There is a vast difference between the British and American vocabularies, even though both are called "English." No American reader of British novels can long remain unaware that our *fall* is the Englishman's *autumn,* our *day-coach* is his *railway carriage,* our *mailbox* is his *pillar-box,* our *weather forecast* is his *inference,* our *radio tube* is his *valve,* our *ashcan* is his *dust-bin,* our *store* is his *shop,* and so on.*

Similarly there are vocabulary differences between the various sections of the United States. A *hit-run driver* in the East is a *hit-skip driver* in the midwest; a *town* in New England is what a *township* is elsewhere; a Southerner's *poke* is the Northerner's *paper bag* or *sack.* What is a *block* (the distance between two street intersections) in one part of the country is a *square* in others.

2. *Occupational clues.* Every profession and occupation has its own slang as well as its own technical vocabulary. If a man speaks of his being on "O.B." duty he is probably a young interne, on duty in the obstetrical department of a hospital. (However, someone else using the same abbreviation may turn out to be a school teacher—"O.B." is also a polite abbreviation for "orthogenic-backward", *i.e.* "problem" children.) Mention of *accessioning* or *analytic cards* identifies the librarian; *of posting,* the bookkeeper; of *jamming,* the short-wave radio operator; of

* Long and interesting lists illustrating this difference are printed in H. L. Mencken's *The American Language,* 4th edition, pp. 233–237, and *Supplement One* thereto, pp. 457–487.

dead-heading, the railroad man; of *makeup,* the newspaper editor; of *double-clutching,* the truck driver.

Often, however, what began as a term peculiar to one occupation or another ends as a member in good standing in the common vocabulary. *On the nose,* which in the sense of *on time* originated in the broadcasting studio, now is common slang; *top kick,* originally an Army term, is widely used for *head man, boss, executive;* the noun *complex,* recently the possession of the psychologists, has been taken over and manhandled by the general public. Sometimes, therefore, what seems at first glance to be a clue to a man's occupation actually has no value as such.

3. *Educational clues.* Patently bad grammar, such as the use of the double negative, the use of the nominative case with the object of a verb, and the mismatching of verb and subject ("he don't"), marks the man or woman who either has never had an opportunity for education or has failed to profit by his advantages. It would not do, of course, to go farther and say that a person using such poor grammar is obviously a member of the lower classes. In practice, however, this is often true, if only because there is a certain amount of social pressure in the upper reaches of society which requires people to speak correctly.

It must be remembered that modern standards allow the genuinely literate person quite generous leeway in English usage. Only those who have been reared in outmoded, unnaturally rigid traditions of language censure the splitter of infinitives or the supposed ignoramus who ends a sentence with a preposition. Probably no reputable grammarian will deny that "It is me" is perfectly good colloquial English or that there are many situations in which it is conspicuously awkward *not* to split an infinitive. Only when a writer or speaker indulges in errors which are not condoned, even by the most liberal judges, are we justified in calling him uneducated. In the case of the lady in Example 3 above, we are amply justified.

Grammar is the most obvious clue to a person's educational background. Another, equally important, clue is vocabulary. The writer or speaker who uses words accurately and appropriately, as does the writer of Example 7, is well educated beyond question—whether formally, in college or university, or informally, by wide and thoughtful reading, is immaterial. On the other hand, the person who strays beyond the confines of his established vocabulary and misuses words, either by mistaking their meaning or by insensitivity to connotation, is not soundly educated, because one of the first principles of education is to teach a man to use his native language with *accuracy*. Again, the verbose weather prophet in Example 5, although he uses words correctly, is just as ignorant as the man who uses words of whose meaning or connotation he is not sure, for he fails to understand that stilted language is entirely out of place in a simple statement addressed to an ordinary audience. The only way in which we can be fair judges of another person's use of language is to be accurate users of it ourselves. Only when we are ourselves certain of the meaning and connotation of a word can we justly call someone else to account for his clumsiness in expression.

4. *Time clues.* We have already seen, in Chapter One, how words shift in meaning through the years. Many other words, once in common use, have disappeared, either because the object they designated disappeared (*growler, crossing-sweeper, end-seat hog*) or because other words took their place (*antimacassar, phthisis*). The occurrence of a word whose meaning has changed, or of a word that is obsolete, is a clue to the date of the passage in question. If we know approximately when the word was current, we have an approximate dating for the passage. The *Oxford English Dictionary* and its American counterpart, the *Dictionary of American English,* are the standard sources of information on this subject.

The occurrence of slang or colloquialisms is a particularly important clue to the time-background of a passage. A letter in which a young man speaks of a fraternity stag party or a musical comedy as having been "bully" can be dated with fair accuracy about fifty years ago; Theodore Roosevelt, one recalls, was particularly addicted to the use of the word as a general mark of enthusiastic approval. A young lady's characterization of a picnic supper, for instance, as "elegant" would probably belong to the nineteenth century—or to one who dates from that period; *elegant* once served all the purposes which *swell* or *super* serves today. *Baloney, banana oil, tell it to Sweeney, oh baby!, the cat's pajamas,* and *chin-music* date from a slightly later period, but any piece of writing containing them is still not contemporary. It would be an interesting exercise to gather a list of all the words which have been used, at one time or another, to designate the activity once known as *sparking* or *spooning,* and at a later date as *pitching woo.*

Clues to Personality and Intention

These types of clue are all fairly simple. Used discreetly, and always with the realization that they are nothing more than indications, they often throw valuable light upon the social, occupational, and educational background of the writer or speaker. But language also contains subtle clues to the writer's character, personality, and intentions. "Style is the man," once remarked a famous critic; and it is true that a person's habitual manner of speaking or writing, or the manner he assumes for a particular occasion, reflects more of him than he is aware.

The language which the speaker in Example 1 chose to convey to his friend his urgent need of five dollars, suggests that he was the sort of person to whom slang was the normal mode of expression. (With that clue, you can fill in the details of the portrait for yourself.) But what if he had said, instead, "I'm awfully sorry to bother you, old man, but I wonder if you could possibly lend me five dollars. I'm in a sort of predicament. I will repay you on Saturday"? Plainly the meaning is the same: he still wants the five dollars. But the language in which he couches the request is very different. The speaker is no longer the unabashed borrower of the example; he is more diffident in his approach. His personality, one is tempted to say, is as different from the one reflected in the example as *predicament* is different from *jam,* or *repay you* is from *pay you back*.

"Poor Elsie treats him rather frivolously, I'm afraid. I confess I have a different feeling about men like him. I find them quite fascinating." This is essentially what the speaker said in Example 3; but what a difference between the two women, at least on the surface! The girl quoted earlier, whatever her grammatical frailties, is blunt, outspoken: let her once get that man into her clutches . . . The second girl, however, tries to disguise her eagerness for the man by a studiedly light, offhand manner of speaking. She does not even come right out and say she wants *that* man—she merely is fascinated by his type! One could conclude, then, that she places more store upon outward appearance; she does not want to admit her feelings as candidly as does the girl in the example. The *rather* and the *quite,* for their part, suggest that she is of a different social class from the other girl; they are affectations characteristic of a certain upper stratum of society, or of what would like to think of itself as being an upper stratum.

Again, our demonstration that the statement in Example 5 could be reduced from twenty-four words to six shows that the writer cared nothing for economy or clarity in communication. Why didn't he? Either through sheer ignorance or through desire to appear more important than he was. Sometimes, as we shall point out later, such addiction to excess verbiage is an indication that the writer is trying to put something over on his audience. Here, however, since the subject is merely the weather, deception is not to be suspected.

In Chapter One we showed how connotations are used to influence others to pass judgment upon a given idea or person. Connotations also reveal the writer's or speaker's own judgment, often without his knowledge or desire. This is one of the most valuable phases of intelligent reading—the analysis of a person's language to discover his true feelings about a matter. We often find that even though a man asserts he has no prejudice in a certain matter, his choice of words betrays his bias; and we may find too that his true feelings on a question, as reflected by his diction, are the direct opposite of his alleged feelings. Examination of diction, therefore, helps us strike toward the truth despite a writer's attempts to conceal it.

Consider the "kinfolk" mentioned by the speaker in Example 6. What if she (or he—it could have been either) had added that they were "simple, good-hearted mountain people"? Quite plainly she would have been patronizing them—acknowledging their humble goodness while implying (by what she leaves unsaid) that they were, after all, a pretty uncultivated lot, whatever their rough native virtues. In other words, by casting emphasis upon the traits of simplicity and good-heartedness she avoided expressing a judgment, which would have been by no means flattering, upon their intelligence, social charms, cleanliness, and other characteristics. From her choice of words, therefore, we can infer something of her own personality: she has a definite sense of personal superiority but at the same time she wants to *appear* tolerant. But what if, on the other hand, those same kinfolk had been spoken of by a writer as being "one generation removed from the baboons, and they still feel uncomfortable when they sit in a chair"? Here the writer is making no effort to disguise the revulsion which these people breed in him; he even magnifies it by humorous exaggeration. He also is prejudiced, but at least he does not conceal his bias. He is an honest, if intolerant, man.

It is impossible to lay down any rules for this sort of character-reading through diction. It requires, far more than rules, two gifts: a sense of the implications of words—in what situation they would most likely be used, and by just what sort of person, and for what purpose—and, equally important, a shrewd sense of human nature. And it is always a dangerous game to play; there is always the possibility of serious error. We are dealing here with probabilities, never with certainties. But the attempt to read deeper into a passage of writing—to discover, by a careful consideration of the way in which the writer expresses himself, more than he chooses to tell you—often pays rich dividends.

EXERCISE I. Use clues of diction to infer what sort of person wrote (or said) each of the following statements:

1. (a) She's a dear.
   (b) She's quite a heifer.
   (c) She's the cream in my coffee.
   (d) She is a very charming, well-behaved girl.
   (e) My own observation of her has been that she is a young woman of exceptionally pleasant personality; she is unusually well adjusted to life and she makes and keeps friends.
   (f) She is a girl who cannot help attracting many beaux.
2. We scooped the whole city on that story. Our extra hit the streets half an hour after Bill phoned in the first flash.
3. Harry and I motored to our country place for the Bank Holiday. We plan to have a shooting party there this autumn.
4. I regard such an escapade as you plan with complete disfavor, and I do not propose to accompany you.
5. So I says to him, "Nobody is going to say that to me and get

away with it. I'm going to tell my mister when he gets home from the job."

6. It is really *most* annoying to be disturbed by these constant appeals for assistance, especially in view of the fact that we made what we consider a very handsome contribution to the Community Chest. I suggest that you transfer your application to one of the agencies which are prepared to deal with cases like yours.
7. He made a humble start indeed, his first situation being that of an errand boy in a counting house.
8. Well, well, how's the boy! Haven't seen you for a coon's age. Where you been keeping yourself?
9. And thus when misfortune visits us, we must keep our countenances turned toward that radiant source whence springs all our comfort and our help.
10. I don't have a thing to say against her. She's not my type, that's all. I mean, she and I don't have the same interests in common, or anything. Please don't misunderstand me. I wouldn't criticize her for the world. It's only, well, it's only that sometimes we don't see eye to eye. I don't know if I make myself clear.
11. Nothing doing. Much as I want that suit, I'm not going to pay such an absorbent price.

Exercise 2. The following letter was written by a prisoner in a state penitentiary to the police officer who had been largely responsible for his receiving a long-term sentence for robbery. How much can you infer about the prisoner's degree of education, his personality, and his outlook?

My dear Mr. Kauffman:

Another Christmas is about here and I am still in the process of social rehabilitation. Honestly John, do you think that I am so harden against the susceptibilities of reformation that all of these years are necessary for society to realize her objective? Some times while in one of those characteristic moods of retrospection I think of the true prophesy I made in regards to my present plight. Doubtless, you may also be able to recall the pronastication I made in regards to that magazine article, "Life begins at sixty-five." It is unnecessary for me to say I was not at all serious but somehow I have conceived the idea that his honor was. What do you think?

Well, John, as in Dante's "Inferno," I am at present enjoying that state of re-segration. Upon the termination of my quarantine period in May, I asked permission to go to school, which was granted. I was making good progress in my clerical work until I aspired to the more academic subject of geology. Naturally, I wished a little practical experience; therefore I made a couple of explorations into the more subterraneous cavaties of the institution for that purpose, and can you imagine my consternation upon being apprehended and having a misinterpretation taken of my geological propensities. During the earlier part of my incarceration I found a profound necessity for the sake of mental stability to accept some medium of philosophy which would make a partial alleviation of such a invariable routine of monotony. What would be more appropriate than for me to become a student of the old stoic Socrates? In accepting such a medium of philosophy I took their misconception with placid resignation, as I realize that they do not understand such an aspiration.

John, I wish to apologize to you for my conduct in court. Possibly I am presuming too much in thinking that my actions in any way affected you, but I remember the conversation we had on the road from Philadelphia to Lancaster and the magnanimous treatment I received while under your care; therefore I have no reason to doubt your integrity. Because of my negligence in writing as I promised is not that I in any way hold you responsible for such a sentence or any one, as I realize that I am the vicitim of my own avarice and jackass philosophy. I do not wish a misinterpretation taken of this letter. I wish only to express my appreciation for what you would have done and my admiration for you as a man.

Before ending this idiotic epistle, as I see paper is getting short, I wish to take this opportunity of wishing you a Merry X-Mas and Prosperous 1936. So until next Christmas, good luck and health.

Gratefully yours,

—— ——

Exercise 3. Who wrote (or said) each of the following statements, and why?

1. On behalf of the Board of Trustees and all the potential beneficiaries of your generosity, permit me to extend to you our heartfelt gratitude for this unexpected largesse. Let us hope your fine example will be emulated by others who desire to erect living monuments to themselves.
2. Generous, hell; if he didn't give it to the hospital he'd have to pay it out in taxes anyway. And he'd give it to anybody, just so's the government didn't get it.
3. It is just like Father, you know; so impulsive always. He never said a word about it to any of us; the first we knew of it was what we read in the newspapers. I do wish he'd have said something to me, though; I know things about the way that hospital is run that he probably hasn't heard.
4. It's all the same to me. Let him shoot his roll that way if he wants to; he made the money in the first place. I can always go on relief—isn't that what we pay taxes for?
5. The casual observer would perhaps never realize that under the rather brusque exterior of this man lies a heart that is extraordinarily sensitive to the sufferings of humanity. His manner is curt and perhaps offends some who do not realize that it is but a defense mechanism to cover his real shyness. Yet after Tuesday's gift no one can deny his great-heartedness.

Exercise 4. What is the difference in attitude implied in each of the following words?

1. Negro, colored man, nigger, nigra, nig, Aframerican, gentleman of color, eight-ball, jigaboo.

2. Jew, Hebrew, non-Aryan, kike, sheenie, Hebe.
3. The President, the Chief Executive, the Man in the White House, the helmsman of the ship of state, Mr. Truman, Truman, our great leader.
4. this city, this urban locality, this great marketing area, this sprawling metropolis, this Babylon.
5. village, community, cross-roads, whistle-stop, jerk-water town, Podunk, rural settlement.
6. my parishioners, my flock, my congregation, the souls with whose care I am entrusted, my brethren.
7. kid, boy, lad, urchin, brat, young person, member of the rising generation, future citizen.

Talking the Language of the Audience

In Chapter One we pointed out that every writer who wishes to be understood must take care to select words that connote the same thing to his audience generally that they do to him personally; otherwise his message will not be received as he sent it. Although we did not say so at the time, this is but one phase of the larger truth that the writer's or speaker's diction must be accommodated to the diction of the audience. Not only must words be used whose connotations can be depended upon to convey shades of meaning across the communication-bridge between writer and reader; in addition, the writer's vocabulary must be that of his audience, and the way he says things—his use or avoidance of slang, for example—must accommodate the habits of his audience. Only then can he be certain that he is establishing successful rapport with those whom he wishes to inform or persuade.

The way in which diction is modified to suit the experience and limitations of the audience can be illustrated by the obvious differences between history books written for fourth graders, for high school students, for college students, and for historians. In these four examples we note a sharply ascending scale of complexity, from the very simple diction required to communicate ideas to a ten-year-old, through the somewhat more difficult diction (necessary to convey more complex ideas) of the books addressed to adolescents, to the diction of highly educated specialists. Each book is written for one particular audience, and no other audience could be expected to profit very much from reading it.

To appeal to the audience for which it is designed, every magazine must be carefully edited so that its language is the one with which its readers are most at home. *Boys' Life,* the Boy Scout magazine, must avoid the use of difficult, unusual words because its audience is composed largely of teen-aged boys. *Vogue* may perhaps allow itself more freedom in this respect, but on the other hand it must be careful always to use the diction most natural to women—such things, for instance, as the adjectives that appeal most strongly to feminine tastes, *pert, charming, sophisticated, youthful, alluring,* and so on. (One can imagine the results were the *Vogue* style to be transferred to *Boys' Life*—or *Esquire.*) The diction of a writer for the *Saturday Evening Post* must differ from that of a writer for *The American Scholar.* An article written to the specifications of *The New Yorker* would be out of place in the pages of *True Detective.*

This constant requirement, that the writer adapt his style to the tastes and habits of his audience, is even more important when he is attempting to move them to a course of thought or action. Now he not only has to tell them something: he has to change their minds. And there is no more effective device for doing so than speaking to them in their own language. "He speaks my language" is no empty formula of compliment; it means that one likes a certain person because his manner of expression identifies him with one's own group. Suppose a college professor addresses a meeting of a steelworkers' union. If he speaks to them in the language in which he is accustomed to speak to his classes or to his colleagues, his chances of success with the steelworkers are desperately slim. If, however, he has the knack of talking their own language—without their even feeling that he is deliberately "talking down" to them—he can be a great success. As they leave the hall, they will be saying that he is a swell guy, even if he is a college prof—he didn't put on the dog but talked to them straight from the shoulder. And (and this is the important thing) they will be inclined to react favorably not only to his manner but to what he was saying to them. He may have been all wrong; the union perhaps would seriously jeopardize its strength if it were to act on his suggestions. But the members are in danger of being converted by his use of language alone.

Thus the use of appropriate diction to establish rapport between the writer or speaker and his audience can often become abuse of the worst kind. Just as is the case with words of highly emotional connotation, the employment of words and idioms designed to promote a fellow-feeling between the two parties can divert attention from the reasonableness of any argument. "We're pals, we see eye-to-eye, and of course you'll believe what I'm telling you."

WE WOULDN'T LIKE IT OURSELVES!

A lot of men we know are leery about using scents. "What do you think we are, anyway?" they say. "Would *you* go around smelling as if you'd just come out of a barber shop where Tony had given you the works, and we do mean the works?"

Frankly, no. We wouldn't want to be caught reeking with ten different heavy aromas of hair tonic and cologne and all that stuff. We know people who would, but we don't like them. A man's a man, not an itinerant perfume bar.

But Ad Club is different! In fact, it makes all argument silly. Because Ad Club was thought up by men, real men—and designed for use by men like them. Tabu and My Sin and Mais Oui and all those fine perfumes are wonderful—in their place. You know what they do to you when your best girl or your wife uses them. But men want a delicate scent, something that's scarcely noticeable, yet adds a definite dash of personality to them, tops off the combination of bracing shower and fresh shave and crisp new shirt and perfectly tailored suit. And that's just what Ad Club gives you. Pantywaist nothing! It's a real man's fragrance. Next time you go out, on a very special occasion, use a tiny bit of it. Then ask Her what she thinks of it—and unless we're very, very wrong (and we don't think we are), her eyes will light up, and—well, we *know* what she'll say. Wanna bet?

The advertiser is obviously trying to talk to the doubting Thomas (the reader of a men's magazine) in his own language. "A lot of men" (not "many") . . . "the works, and we do mean the works" . . . "thought up by men, real men" . . . "pantywaist nothing!" . . . "wanna bet?": this is not the usual prose of the advertiser; it is prose especially designed to suggest oneness with the reader. The logic is: (1) I talk like you. (2) Therefore(!) I'm really like you. (3) If I'm like you, I'm a pretty nice guy. I know what I'm talking about, too. And like you, I wouldn't deceive anybody. (4) So listen to what I tell you—man to man!

The chain of logic is weak in every link. Confidence men take pains to talk like their prospective victims, too, but they can scarcely be trusted. A moment's thought should convince you that the advertiser's manner—his chumminess, his assiduous attempt to say his say in just the tone of voice that will make you feel most at home with him—has nothing at all to do with the merits of his product. Maybe his product *is* the best; but has he *proved* to you that it is—or, indeed, given you any sound reason for *believing* that it is? And do you really need it—or has the advertiser made you *think* you do? Homey, face-to-face talk can often be a device for evading the issue, for inducing the reader to relax his vigilance. When it is, the rapport of language is being abused.

The same device is dear to all politicians, and for exactly the same reason. No candidate who cherishes votes can afford to allow himself to be thought of as several notches loftier than the common run of men. He therefore takes pains to convince his prospective electors that he is wood from the same fine block from which they themselves were carved. The baby-kissing expeditions, the "front porch" campaigns, the clam bakes, the publicity given to the simple, affectionate, moral domestic life of the candidate—all are designed to encourage the people's conviction that he is one of them, has the same tastes and hobbies—and therefore (that long-suffering word!) must be wise and honest, too. His language is designed to serve the same end, especially when he is meeting the electorate face to face. Public education has progressed to the extent that every politician above the rank of ward-heeler is expected to be reasonably grammatical in his public utterances; but his choice of words, his use of local idiom and current colloquialisms, must convince the audience that this man talks their language (and thinks their thoughts).

The most famous example in recent history of the careful cultivation of rapport between speaker and audience is President Franklin D. Roosevelt's fireside chats. The magic of those radio talks lay not merely in the inspired name that was given to them (analyze the connotations of *fireside* and *chat*); it lay in the way in which Mr. Roosevelt's whole manner—his invariable use of simple words, his homely illustrations and analogies, his frequent use of the pronouns "you" and "I" instead of the impersonal diction of the statesman—fulfilled the promise of the name. Time after time he won public support for his side of a controversy by talking "with" the people, in their own language.*

* Although in this book we are concerned primarily with the language and the logic of communication, we should add a word on the actual mechanics of spoken communication. Another very important reason for

EXERCISE 5. What requirements of diction should be observed by a person writing the following items?

1. A birthday letter to a seven-year-old niece.
2. A booklet to be enclosed in a home first-aid kit.
3. An advertisement of a new sulfa drug, to be published in the *Journal of the American Medical Association.*
4. A factual article written for *Scholastic* (a news periodical for high school students).
5. A letter to a college professor, explaining why one missed the final examination in his course and asking to be given a make-up.
6. An article on a new type of circuit in a magazine read by radio repairmen.
7. The text of an illustrated leaflet issued during the Community Chest campaign.
8. A talk to be delivered to a Women's Republican Club.
9. A talk to be delivered to the local teamsters' union.

EXERCISE 6. Comment on the following revised versions of the opening sentences of a well-known American historical document. For what audience and for what sort of medium (popular magazine, book, etc.) might each have been designed? How does each version compare in effectiveness with the original?

Mr. Roosevelt's success as a public speaker was his spoken diction, which suggested cultivation without ostentation, and the peculiar quality of his voice, friendly but also authoritative. Another man, reading the same fireside chats, would have been a dismal failure. Since the radio is all-important in modern persuasion, a man's "radio voice" and his habits of speech have a great deal to do with his success or failure as a persuader of the public. The late Wendell Willkie, despite his honest Hoosier manner of speech ("Amurrikuh"), could not compete with Mr. Roosevelt as a radio spellbinder. When Alfred E. Smith was at the height of his career, his careful retention of Lower East Side inflections was political capital in his native state; elsewhere it was of doubtful value. How do the "radio personalities" of the present crop of high government officials and candidates for important offices impress their hearers?

ATTENTION, KING GEORGE III!

1. According to international etiquette, when a nation wants to break up housekeeping with another, it must give due notice of its intentions.

   Well, here you are.

   Effective immediately, we are quitting. Cold.

   Here's why:

   We think that everybody has the right to be free and happy.

   We think that the big job of government is to protect that right.

   We think that if a government can't, or won't, do that job, the people should set up one that will.

   Your government has failed to do that job.

   So out we go. We hope you miss us!

2. According to the standards of conduct prevailing among civilized nations, any nation which contemplates separation from one with which it has been politically connected is obligated to issue a manifesto setting forth its grievances against that other nation.

   The reasoning followed in the case now under discussion runs thus: (1) All human beings possess equal capabilities, and in addition they are entitled to certain basic life-values, such as physical security, freedom of action, and freedom to seek fulfillment of their personal wishes. (2) The institution of government exists primarily to guarantee these rights, such government being based upon the right of the persons which it affects to direct its course of action. (3) When a government takes a course antagonistic to the best interests of the persons affected, those persons are entitled to modify or terminate it and, if the latter alternative is adopted, to establish in its place another government which more nearly conforms to their desires and needs, especially as these relate to the life-values referred to in (1) above.

3. Friends, I'm sure I don't need to repeat at this time the reasons why we've decided to break with the British and strike out for ourselves. But you know as well as I do that there are always

people who will shake their heads and say, "Why did they do it?" And so for the sake of the record, maybe I'd better say once more just why we're taking this stand. I know you'll bear with me, even if it is old stuff to you.

It goes without saying that to all right-thinking men, everybody is born with certain rights, such as the right to live, the right to do as you please, the right to go out and find happiness. You know also that that's why we have government—to guard those rights. And since we're the people who make the government, we're the people to decide whether or not it satisfies us. If it doesn't, then we've got to make changes. Maybe the existing government just needs a little tinkering. But if it's too far gone for that, then we have to wipe the slate clean and start all over again. And that's just the position where we find ourselves today.

Exercise 7. How accurately does the author of the following passage imitate the characteristic diction of the audience to which he addresses himself?

SMILE—WHEN YOU SAY THAT ABOUT MY RAREBIT!

Just wait . . . you'll eat those words.
And my rarebit, too. It's terrific.

Oh, we believe you. A good rarebit is a feast any day. Body-building and smooth-as-cream. But there you go again, eating soft food.

Sure I eat soft foods. So what?

So *this*. Today's creamy, soft-cooked foods are too easy on the chewing—exercise that Nature intended your gums to have.

Back to Nature for my GUMS?

You're catching on. Modern gums are often tender. You may even notice a warning tinge of "pink" on your toothbrush. So massage, brother, massage—with Ipana Tooth Paste. Help put new life in your gums—and your smile.

Come again? Massage for my SMILE?

Sure. It's this way. A bright, snappy smile comes from teeth that sparkle . . . sound, bright teeth that depend so much on firm, healthy gums. And Ipana with massage is specially designed to help the health of the gums. So get going!

EXERCISE 8. From one of the volumes of *The Public Papers and Addresses of Franklin D. Roosevelt,* select one of the fireside chats (or several of Mr. Roosevelt's informal speeches to people along the route of his train tours) and analyze the means by which he kept "the common touch."

EXERCISE 9. The following excerpts are from a campaign biography of a recent candidate for governor of a large and important state. How do the facts recited bear on his qualifications for this office? What consideration has governed the writer's choice of words?

> To better understand the present-day philosophy of this vibrant personality, one must trace his lineal history to the lush and rolling hills of Greene County, where on September 18, 1879, near the village of Ten Mile, Edward —— was born in an unprepossessing, weather-bludgeoned log cabin. His father, the late Joseph Thomas ——, was a farmer and sheep herder. His mother, Hannah M. —— ——, was a descendant of a pioneer family which had helped to hack a pathway through the Pennsylvania wilderness so that the course of the empire might flow ever westward. Edward —— is a direct descendant in the tenth generation of John and Esther ——, American progenitors who joined the Colonists in the middle of the 17th century.
>
> Even today, General —— regards his father with awe and devotion; his mother with the all-consuming love a son places first in the temple of filial worship.
>
> "My father was a fine man; a very careful planner of things," he says, his voice betraying the fierce pride he has always expressed toward his forebears. "He was a very rugged man, severe in discipline, but always benevolent in his love for his family. My mother was more sympathetic toward me and extremely active. I inherit my discipline from my father; my activity from my mother."

Here, in exquisitely simple language, is the basis for the homespun philosophy of the man his army of friends and admirers predict will be the next Governor of ———.

The period of adolescence for Edward ——— was fraught with the same intense hardships historians tell us were endured by Abraham Lincoln in his insatiable quest for book learning. As a boy, straight and lean as a sapling, Ed——— used to trudge for miles over sprawling, timber-studded hills to reach the single-room schoolhouse which was to be his first citadel of golden enlightenment. He was an observing lad with a practical mind and those who knew him as a boy recall his ability to analyze problems clearly and with straight-from-the-shoulder sincerity. Likewise, the call of the Church impressed itself on his eager young mind and so deeply ingrained were his contacts with the Scriptures that even today he is a devoutly religious man.

The experiences of his boyhood were to become a strong breastwork against egotism and selfish paternalism in his later years. His schooling was punctuated by the prescribed demands of farming, clearing the land with broad ax and hacksaw and using his hands to build as frontiersmen have built since time immemorial. His schedule of work and study was a hardy, sun-up to sun-down regimen.

It seems incongruous now in analyzing the whirl-wind, work-a-day career of this amazing, high-spirited man that romance could intrude on his carefully sculptured life. Yet, in 1908, exactly three years from the time he was admitted to the bar, he married winsome —— ——, whose ancestors were of proud Revolutionary stock. They have two children, —— ——, born May 2, 1914, and —— ——, born February 19, 1916. Their son is now a First Lieutenant with the 28th Division.

Through all the mutations of his civil and military career, Mrs. —— has been the General's light and hope; his Rock of Gibraltar. A woman of kindly wisdom and genteel bearing, she has been friend and counsellor, as well as wife and mother. One of his proudest possessions is a Bible given to him by Mrs. —— when he entered the Spanish-American War. He has carried it

> with him ever since. He used it when he was sworn in as Auditor-General and State Treasurer and his friends anticipate that he will complete the trinity when he uses it to take his oath as Governor of ——.

At this juncture we had better clear up an important point. We have just remarked that every author, if he is to succeed in communicating his ideas, must address himself to his chosen audience in its own language. This fact may suggest to you that the obligation is all on the writer's side; that all you have to do is allow him to impart his information and his arguments to you, in your own terms. This is not true. You must go halfway to meet your author, whoever he is; as should be abundantly clear by now, reading is in no sense a process of passive absorption.

Furthermore, do you belong to the audience to which the greatest writers have addressed themselves, and to which they continue to address themselves? As we have already said in the foreword to this book, the supremely rewarding writing of our civilization has been addressed to an audience which possessed reading talents not found among the great majority of men and women who are products of modern mass education. Those talents can, however, be cultivated; and possession of them will enable you to be enrolled in the true audience of the great writers of this and preceding ages.

It would be a mistake, therefore, to infer from the preceding pages that the writer must come to the reader; the reader has just as great an obligation to seek the writer—to place himself in the audience for which the writer intended his message.

The Clues of Unnecessarily Difficult Language

Every reader, however, has a perfect right to expect that a writer will express himself as clearly and directly as he can.

Whenever he encounters language which seems unnecessarily difficult, he should follow this procedure:

1. Find out what is said—by use of context, dictionary, and brains.

2. Try to re-state the idea in simpler language, without using much more space—using less, if possible—and without sacrificing the essential idea. If this experiment is successful, two preliminary conclusions may be made: (a) The difficult language is not justified because it saves space. Sometimes oversized words are used because the ideas they embody otherwise can be expressed only by awkward, space- and time-consuming clauses or sentences. Rightly used, this is a perfectly legitimate sort of shorthand. But if the big words can be replaced by short synonyms, obviously no space has been saved. Furthermore, if some words or phrases can be omitted without loss, space is being wasted. (b) The difficult language is not called for by the complexity of the idea. In a complex culture like ours there are many ideas which cannot possibly be expressed by the familiar, short words of our everyday vocabulary; they require the use of longer words, many of which were created expressly to stand for such ideas. If, however, you can be sure that your paraphrase in simpler language does preserve the sense of the passage, you have demonstrated that the language is unjustifiably complicated.

If, on the other hand, after conscientious effort you have failed to simplify the language of the passage, you probably have proved that the difficult language which the author used was justified—and you have no choice but to dig in and try to understand him by learning his terminology. He cannot come any farther to meet you, so you must work toward rapport with him by equipping yourself with his vocabulary.

But if your experiment has proved that the author's use of difficult language was not justified—what then? Several possible conclusions may follow:

1. The writer's mind does not function clearly and precisely, and this lack of clarity and precision is reflected in his attempts at communication. As we have implied time after time, language and intellect are intimately connected. If a man is a muddled thinker, his writing is likely to be muddled, too.

2. The writer may be a fairly incisive thinker, but he honestly thinks that he can convey his ideas only by the use of outsized language and roundabout expressions. He should be listened to with respect, because his ideas may be valuable; but he should be pitied for his ignorance of the art of communication.

3. The writer knows better than to clothe his ideas in language that is too big for them, but he goes ahead and does it anyway because he thinks he will impress his audience. He may be right. The uncritical reader will think, "Gosh, what complicated language; he must be a brilliant man to be able to write like that." But the critical reader will be impatient and suspicious: "Who do you think you are? I can write like that too, but I have more sense."

4. The writer is deliberately using such language, not to display his own talents (which may be pretty dubious anyway) but to hide something—perhaps his own ignorance, perhaps an idea of which his audience would not approve were he to express it so that they would immediately recognize it.

There is also a fifth conclusion, which may well accompany any of the preceding four. That is, the writer who uses an unnecessarily wordy or obscure style may have little sensitivity to the beauties of language. Writing that is full of polysyllabic words and hard knots and clusters of phrases is likely to affront not only the intellect but also the ear. We shall say more of this matter of the rhythm of language in Chapter Four. But as you read the examples of bad writing in this chapter, notice how jagged, heavy, cacophonous, the sentences often are, and try to discover the cause of this unpleasantness.

This brings us to the important topic of jargon, which is defined by a noted English critic of language as "talk that is considered both ugly-sounding and hard to understand; applied especially to the sectional vocabulary of a science, art, class, sect, trade, or profession, full of technical terms . . . and the use of long words, circumlocution, and other clumsiness." Or, to put it in terms familiar to you from your handbooks of composition, jargon is that kind of bad writing which prefers the roundabout expression to the direct one, the long word to the short, the high-sounding word to the plain one, the abstract term to the concrete, the noun to the verb, and the "weak" passive to the "strong" active voice.

Jargon: (1) *Dead Wood*

In every handbook of composition at least one section is devoted to directions for expunging so-called "dead wood" from one's writing. Dead wood—words and phrases that add nothing to the sentence or that could be drastically simplified—is the most obvious form of jargon. Strewn carelessly across the straight highway of thought, it forces constant and perfectly unnecessary detours. "The condition of redundancy that exists in such a great number of themes produced by college undergraduates should be eliminated by every means that lies at the disposal of the person who teaches them."—There is a sentence full of dead wood. Such phrases as *the condition of, the quality of, the state of, the nature of,* can nearly always be expunged without loss. *That exists* and many similar locutions are nearly always redundant. *Such a great number of* is a roundabout way of saying *so many. Produced by* is unnecessary, and *that lies at the disposal of,* like the concluding clause, can be greatly condensed. Thus the sentence could be revised to read, "The redundancy found in so many college undergraduates' themes should be eliminated by every means known to the teacher." This sentence, though much improved, is still not perfect; we shall return to it before long for further simplification.

It is a profitable exercise to make a list of the most common stereotyped phrases that clutter up our government documents, our newspaper articles, our business letters, our student themes. Among the most common and indefensible space-wasters are *due to* (or *in view of*) *the fact that* (= *because*) and *despite the fact that* (= *although*). The simple *the fact that* often is equally superfluous (*the fact that he was ill* = *his illness*). Here are some other chunks of dead wood, selected almost at random, together with their simple equivalents:

in the matter of (in respect to)	about
a long period of time	a long time
in the capacity of	as
resembling in nature	like
in some instances	sometimes

One especially useless sort of dead wood is that which provides a whole verb phrase where one single verb could do as well, or better:

make an attempt	try
reach a decision	decide
met with the approval of Jones	Jones approved
signed an agreement providing for	agreed to
announced himself to be in favor of	said he favored
it is the belief of	he believes
will be hostess to . . . at a dinner party	will give a dinner for
paid a compliment to	complimented
is in the process of being	is being
exhibit a tendency	tend

Such circuitous expressions seldom cause much confusion; their principal offense is that they waste space and the reader's time and eyesight. (Note that we might have said, "Circuitous expressions of the nature of those cited just above do not cause a great deal of confusion except on a few occasions; the chief respect in which they are the cause of offense is the way in which they result in the wasting of space and of time and eyesight on the part of the reader." The sense would not have been much obscured, but your patience would have been tried.) And when we observe that a writer or speaker habitually clutters up his discourse with unnecessary words and phrases, we are well justified in concluding two things about him: (1) He is inefficient; zealous though he may be to have things accomplished with the utmost dispatch and the least possible waste of motion, his language cries out for the attentions of a so-called time- and motion-study expert; (2) he is a slave to custom; he has absorbed these stereotyped expressions from his associates and from his routine reading—and he has never stopped to examine and criticize them. What an exhilarating experience it would be for him to break with hallowed custom and insist on saying things simply, tersely, directly!

Jargon: (2) Big Words, Stock Words

A more serious enemy of clarity is the jargonist's predilection for big words where shorter ones would do as well. Because so many people are superstitiously afraid of *all* big words, it will not hurt to repeat here what we said on page 70. It is not true that short words are always better than long ones. There are many ideas which cannot possibly be conveyed in words from the common vocabulary; and in addition, although two words, one short and one long, may seem to be synonymous, the practised reader and writer knows that their connotations are substantially different, and therefore that if the longer word conveys the idea more precisely than does the shorter, it must be used. It is a foolish reader indeed who shies away from a book that contains long words because he thinks they are always merely ostentatious. Perhaps they are; but in the use of language, as in the eyes of the law, a man is presumed innocent until he is proved guilty. If the reader resents a writer's use of big words, he must prove that he, the reader, could say the same thing more simply.

The jargon-addict, however, is fatally fascinated by the unnecessary polysyllable. He is the sort of person who during the Second World War enthusiastically adopted and propagated the imposing Latinized vocabulary by which Army, civil government, and business alike beclouded simple ideas. He says *activate* instead of *form* (as in referring to a new army division), and *inactivate* instead of *disband;* to him, workers or employees are always *personnel;* the business of buying something is *procurement* (and that of hiring someone is *personnel procurement*); an order is a *directive;* to manage or to direct is *to coordinate;* to carry out is *to implement;* to hurry up is *to expedite;* to attend to is *to process.*

Jargon of this kind is not a byproduct of war alone. It has been a barnacle on the keel of business and government for many years. And closely associated with it is a vocabulary of stock words which presumably save the harassed businessman from having to find the exact word he needs to fit each contingency. Such a word is the grossly abused *set-up,* which rushes in to fill the gap whenever one is too busy (or too lazy) to select *situation, scheme, arrangement,* or *plan.* Another is *picture* ("Do you get the picture?" = "Do you understand?"; "Let me give you an over-all picture" = "Let me give you a general account"; "What's the picture?" = "What's the situation?").

The picture here is that in many organizational set-ups the personnel, particularly on the junior executive level, show a trend toward acting like automatons when they are contacting other personnel—and to treat those whom they contact as automatons, too. Language like this is language of the machine: it is language as standardized and impersonal as something stamped out by a die. Individuality, freshness, even humanity itself are rigidly excluded from such discourse. It suggests that the human touch has no place in business; that people who write and talk in the course of their duties must be as mechanized as the products they make and sell. There is as little excuse for robot-language in business as there is for a man who, in "contacting" his "junior partner" by telephone late in the afternoon, says, "Darling, I regret very much to inform you that the termination of my day's responsibilities will be somewhat delayed. A cutback in the secretarial staff has resulted in unavoidable pyramiding of dictation for Miss Jones, who is therefore unable to process my interoffice communications as per schedule. Will you please convey my best regards to the younger members of our organization, and promise them I will contact them before they are transferred to bed? By the way, was Jackie upgraded in school? And will you please send me information as to whether you have succeeded in procuring a replacement in our kitchen personnel for Lizzie?"

Jargon: (3) Overworked Nouns

Another constant element of jargon is the gross overuse of nouns and the accompanying neglect of verbs. In all written and spoken discourse, verbs, and verbs alone, furnish the power by which the sentence moves. They are like truck-tractors: their function is to pull along the nouns (trailers), which have no power unit of their own. But even the strongest tractor stalls if it is given too heavy a load to pull—and that is exactly what happens in jargon. "The EFFECT of the OVERUSE of NOUNS in WRITING *is* the PLACING of too much STRAIN upon the VERBS and the resultant PREVENTION of MOVEMENT of the THOUGHT." One verb—and you can count the nouns for yourself! Forms of the verb *to be* are hard workers, but they cannot possibly do everything that is demanded of them by people who apparently know few other verbs. As in the sentence above, the copulative (*is,* etc.) is too often required to pull a subject loaded down with nouns and noun phrases and at the same time to push a predicate that is also loaded down with them. The result is a sentence that creaks and groans when it moves; and you can hear it groaning, too. For the presence of so many nouns requires one to use many prepositional phrases, especially *of*-phrases, to the detriment of smooth rhythm. Any intelligent writer, if he has committed a sentence like the one quoted, will immediately replace some of the noun phrases with clauses, thus adding verbs which will help share the load: "One who overuses nouns in writing places too much strain upon the verbs and as a result prevents the thought from moving along."

Good judges of English style strongly object to the overuse of nouns in modern writing not merely because their cumulative weight can overtax the single verb or two that the sentence may contain. They also point out that many of the favorite nouns used by businessmen, lawyers, and other kinds of learned writers end in *-tion, -ity, -ment, -ness,* and *-ance*. These suffixes are not notably lovely in sound, and if used to excess they grate upon the ear. Listen to this sentence from a professional educators' journal: "Merely to enumerate these five outstanding characteristics of an urban community, namely, chaotic stimulation, mechanization, impersonalization, commercialization, and complexity of organization, suggests many implications for the city school." (It is too bad the last word was not *education*.) And here is an order ("directive") issued by the Office of Civilian Defense early in 1942:

> Such preparations shall be made as will completely obscure all Federal buildings and non-Federal buildings occupied by the Federal Government during an air-raid for any period of time from visibility by reason of internal or external illumination. Such obscuration may be obtained either by blackout construction or by termination of the illumination.

According to press accounts, President Roosevelt himself paraphrased the order thus:

> Tell them that in buildings where they have to keep the work going, to put something across the windows. In buildings where they can afford to let the work stop for awhile, turn out the lights.

(One hopes that the faulty syntax was a newspaperman's, not Mr. Roosevelt's.)

Furthermore, such nouns are nearly always undesirably abstract. They fail to stimulate our senses, to suggest a picture; and they therefore lack vividness. Which is the more effective term—*illumination* or *lighting? obscuration* or *blackout?*

When we discover a man coupling a four-noun subject to a four-noun predicate and expecting a single copulative to pull the whole train, we may suspect him, like his fellow-jargonists, of inefficiency and of neglecting the principal rules of lucid communication. In addition, he is particularly to be pitied for his insensitive ear—the ear that allows him to pile up *-ations* and *-nesses* and *-ities* regardless of their unpleasant sound. He may have something to communicate, but he cannot say it in a manner that will delight us to hear.

Jargon: (4) *The Overused Passive*

Another prominent ingredient of jargon is the overuse of the passive construction. The passive voice is nearly always less effective than the active; that is, it is less vivid to say that "a letter is dictated" than it is to say that "Mr. Barnes dictates a letter." In the first instance, attention is fixed upon the act itself, which is hard to visualize, since apparently no one is around to perform it; the letter is just there, being dictated. But in the second instance, attention is fixed not upon the abstract idea of the act itself but upon the concrete presence of someone who is performing it. You will recall that we had not finished correcting a sentence upon which we were working on page 72. We had left it in this form: "The redundancy found in so many college undergraduates' themes should be eliminated by every means known to the teacher." We now get rid of ("eliminate") the weak passive, and the sentence becomes much more vigorous: "The teacher should use every method he knows to get rid of the redundancy found in so many college undergraduates' (students') themes."

Like all legitimate grammatical constructions, the passive voice has its uses. In particular, it allows one to express ideas without attributing them to a specific individual source. That is why it is so widely used in government communications, in which decisions and opinions are presumed to be those of the bureau or agency as a whole and not of individual officials. But legitimate use can easily turn into abuse. While the convention by which governmental edicts come from an impersonal entity can be defended, the indiscriminate use of the passive as a grammatical camouflage can also be a sign of moral weakness. Anyone who does not wish to assume personal responsibility for his statements finds an "out" by writing "it is directed that" instead of "I direct that," or "it is the opinion of the firm" instead of "I think." Readers must distinguish carefully between those writers who use the passive because of well-established convention, as in the Army and Navy, and those who use it because it is a convenient way out of a tight spot.*

* At least one governmental agency has been conducting a heroic campaign against jargon in all its forms. The humane and witty guides issued for the employees of the Social Security Board admirably illustrate and summarize what we have been saying about business jargon and "governmentese." We reprint in Appendix B three of the Board's "Better Writing" leaflets.

The Uses and Abuses of Technical Language

We are far from wishing to suggest that unnecessary complication of language is a sin confined to businessmen and government employees. We have chosen to speak first of business and "bureaucratic" jargon because it is the most commonly encountered of all types and because, in addition, it can be most easily analyzed to show the folly of over-affection for long, abstract nouns, for circuitous expressions, and for constructions dominated by nouns and *of*. But we must turn now to another vast field in which jargon flourishes—jargon of a much wilder species. Many of you will encounter it, to your sorrow, in your professional lives; but we hope that you will do nothing to propagate it. We are speaking of the jargon of the various professions.

Here we must inject another word of caution, to reinforce what we said a little while ago about the necessity for discriminating between necessary and superfluous use of oversize and involved language. Since every trade and profession has its own special ideas, methods, materials, and tools, obviously it must have a special vocabulary to designate these things. The doctor's professional vocabulary, which may seem completely barbarous to the layman, is absolutely essential to him, for it enables him to speak concisely and accurately of such things as medicines, surgical procedures, courses of treatment, and clusters of symptoms which could otherwise be described only by most indirect and time-wasting paragraphs. And similarly with all other men and women who have their own special occupational vocabularies—the radio engineer, the dress designer, the psychologist, the food chemist. Their special vocabularies enable them to think more precisely when they are at work and to communicate with their fellow-workers with the greatest possible ease and exactness. This is, after all, but a logical extension of our earlier principle that men must address their hearers in a language intelligible to both parties.

But by the same token, the use of technical language in addressing a non-technical audience is not only inappropriate but also inefficient and, it may be, actually dishonest. When a physician speaks to a patient in the scientific terms in which he habitually thinks or in which he speaks to his fellow physicians, he is not achieving rapport with his listener, even though he may not be consciously trying to prevent understanding; but another, unscrupulous, physician may deliberately employ such language to confuse a patient—perhaps to impress him with the magnitude of the miracle he has performed and thus to prepare him for the magnitude of the bill. The wilful use of technical double-talk is important to the success of quacks in every field. Every man who sets himself up as a psychologist catering to the emotional ills of newspaper readers and the buyers of popular books, cultivates the glib use of such terms as *complex, neurosis, frustration, personality, sublimation, fixation, compensation, phobia* —terms which have immense prestige value with the public because they are associated with the "mysteries" of the psychological science. Actually, nobody but a highly trained psychologist or psychiatrist is entitled to use such terms, because they represent exceedingly complicated ideas which cannot be grasped by the layman; but they have become part of the popular vocabulary, even though their meanings are grossly distorted in common usage.

Thus the use of technical jargon can often be a danger signal to those who would escape deception; but much oftener it serves simply to expose the ignorance or the conceit of the user. For we must remember that by no means all technical jargon is justified, even when used by experts in addressing other experts. If the idea can be communicated just as well in simple, everyday terms, it should be. Technical language should be reserved for occasions when there is no other way of concise, exact communication. It should not be used as an elaborate disguise for the simple thoughts of those who wish to impress the layman, or as an easy escape for those who are too indolent to express themselves simply.

The exact scientists have a crisp, clear professional language which seldom deserves to be described by a word with the negative connotations of *jargon.* In scientific writing, certain nouns and verbs which look strange and meaningless to the unpractised eye actually convey meaning with the utmost exactness and economy. But in an effort to emulate the physical scientists, the social scientists have evolved a language bedecked with pseudo-scientific terminology which often degenerates into the worst kind of jargon. Of course there are many terms in these fields which are absolutely necessary for an adequate expression of meaning. To the sociologist such words as *status, ethnic, mobility, institution, disorganization,* and *culture* are indispensable, because they embody basic sociological concepts; and while the student may feel affronted by the constant use of such terms in his textbooks, he has no alternative but to learn exactly what they mean—otherwise he will know nothing about sociology. But many writers in these fields go to unwarranted extremes, preferring to describe the phenomena of human behavior in inhuman language. The sentence "People have lately been moving to the cities" states in plain English the idea which many sociologists would prefer to set forth in these terms: "The tendency in recent years has been for the population to shift toward urban areas."

The following sentences appeared in a recent article, published in a sociological journal, on the problems of readjustment faced by the returning soldier:

> This discrepancy between the uniqueness and decisive importance that the absent one attributes to his experience and their pseudo-

typification by the people at home, who attribute to them a pseudo-relevance, is one of the biggest obstacles to mutual establishment of the disrupted we-relations. Yet the success or failure of the home-coming will depend on the chance of transforming these social relations into recurrent ones. But, even if such a discrepancy did not prevail, the complete solution of this problem would remain an unrealizable ideal.

A painstaking examination of the context of the passage suggests to us that the writer meant:

The soldier has had experiences which are of supreme emotional importance to him and which he thinks the home folks can't possibly understand. The home folks, on the other hand, *think* they know what he's gone through, because they have seen war movies which to them represent (falsely) the real thing. Thus the two groups—the veterans and the home folks—can't see eye to eye. But if they are to get along together as well as they did before the war, they must understand each other. But even if they do understand each other there are still obstacles in the way of complete readjustment.

The "educationists" are as infatuated with jargon as are the sociologists—if not more so. The situation in which every child and adult finds himself, a hundred times a day, of being confronted with two choices (to do homework or not to do homework, to run for the bus or wait for the next one) is designated in educational jargon as the "Policy Determination Problem Question." We have found writers for educational journals speaking of "instructional personnel" when *teachers* would have been just as good a word, and of "homes of low socio-economic status" when *poor homes* would have adequately embodied the meaning. Professional books and articles are filled with such terms as *acceleration, integration, activity, instructional, skill, tool, orientation, relatedness, situation, experience, evaluation, frame of reference.* Use of these words would be justified if they stood for more or less well-defined concepts—concepts which could not be described in simple language. In many cases, however, the meaning of the term in any given context remains nebulous at best. Even when an attempt is made to define terms, the results are often less than satisfactory, as in this excerpt:

> This article will attempt to point out the part played by personality maladjustment as a causative factor in reading disability . . . For the purposes of this article "personality maladjustment" will be defined as any behavior that deviates from what is considered the normal behavior of children in the school situation.

The examples of sociological and educational jargon already quoted show that while an unnecessarily complicated vocabulary is a constant "factor" in such jargon, the writers in these fields, like businessmen and bureaucrats, love to complicate their syntax and to load up a single weak verb or two with noun-phrases galore. One or two more illustrations will clinch the point:

> In addition to the inclination to overstatement of the problem [of the older workers in industry] in the fight for social reform, we find employers and employees alike looking for excuses and rationalizations, if confronted with the necessity of explaining the termination of employment in the case of an elderly worker. . . . Satisfactory continuity of pupil development is indicated when the pupil's understandings of life are being constantly broadened and deepened and when his responses to life-situations are becoming increasingly mature, constructive, and skilful. Basic considerations in determining the sequence of a series of experiences that will contribute most to the unity of development are the interests of the pupils as affected by biological and psychological growth, together with the complexity of the processes involved. A pupil's background of experience, which may be conditioned by nearness in time and space, influences his readiness for, or interest in, a new experience.

Can you paraphrase each sentence in readily understandable English?

EXERCISE 10. Use the test of the simpler paraphrase to determine whether or not the following passages can be called examples of jargon:

1. Colleges may not only add to a student's knowledge and skills but also help him change his former evaluative attitudes and develop new patterns of values in general harmony with those which a particular college champions and for the implementation of which it provides a distinctive curricular and extra-curricular program. In a democratic social organization, with reasonable freedom for the organization and carrying out of differential educational programs, and within the permissive latitude of cultural norms, the development of distinctive value patterns among the graduates of different colleges is possible. A democratic theory of education would, it seems, demand the maintenance of differential educational programs with the consequent distinctive patterns of value, just as a dictatorial theory of education would enforce a uniform educational program resulting in a uniform set of values for all.

2. The period of adolescence in a small rural community in the period antedating the introduction of modern recreational facilities in such areas was one in which the individual's field of choice in respect to opportunities for recreation was rigidly circumscribed. The possible alternatives for such activity included only participation in aquatic sports at a locality which was only superficially suitable for such activities, having neither sanitary precautions, supervision by adequately trained protective and instructional personnel, nor any of the other factors now deemed essential for wholesome aquatic recreation; participation in impromptu, unorganized, competitive games, such as baseball, in an area not yet required for commercial or residential purposes; an excursion, individually or in social groups, with a bicycle as

the means of locomotion; or on infrequent occasions a trip to an adjacent region with the view of acquiring edible specimens of the wild life characteristic of that geographical area. In respect to this last-named form of recreation, the observation should be made, in passing, that the area in which successful pursuit of such sports was practicable in view of the results obtained was tending to be increasingly remote from the community itself, inasmuch as no governmental agency had yet instituted the policy of replenishing the wild life in the more easily accessible waterways and wooded areas. An additional aspect of rural recreational experience, not mentioned above, was the practice of attempting to acquire momentary physical and mental diversion by following on foot a rigidly patterned route in the region immediately adjoining the community. This practice, while undoubtedly beneficial to the physique of the participants, was of questionable value as regarded the development of their social instincts, their mental capabilities, or their manual skills. Together with the other above-mentioned uninstitutionalized means for the employment of leisure time, it illustrates the degree to which the individual choice of action was restricted in the circumstances described, with a resultant detrimental effect upon the realization of potentialities for self-fulfilment.

3. There is a certain period of life, say from eight to fifteen or sixteen years of age, when the mind, like the body, is not yet firm enough for laborious or close operations. If applied to such, it falls an early victim to premature exertion; exhibiting, indeed, at first, in these young and tender subjects, the flattering appearance of their being men while they are yet children, but ending in reducing them to be children when they should be men. The memory is then most susceptible and tenacious of impressions; and the learning of language being chiefly a work of memory, it seems precisely fitted to the powers of this period, which is long enough, too, for acquiring the most useful languages, ancient and modern.

Circumlocution and Euphemism

There is one more important aspect of this matter of using diction to conceal truth, and that is the function of circumlocution and euphemism. A circumlocution is an expression which takes one on a pleasant detour around a disagreeable idea; a euphemism is a device, usually consisting of a single word, by which the objectionable idea is given a more pleasant appearance as we pass it. Both are based on the interesting psychological principle that an idea can be made less unattractive if it is spoken of in words possessing as pleasant a connotation as possible.

The most obvious examples of such whitewashing devices come to mind immediately: the host of expressions which soften the idea of death (*to pass away, to enter into rest, to expire, to be deceased*—and the less sentimental, more facetious ones, *to kick the bucket, to turn in one's checks, to give up the ghost*); the equally great variety of expressions typified by *rest room;* those which attempt to gloss over the unpleasant truths relating to disease (*mental illness, rest home, malignancy, lung affliction*); and those which attempt to cover up other unlovely phases of life (*halitosis* for *bad breath, expectorate* for *spit, plant food* for *manure,** *county home* for *poor house, intemperance* for *drunkenness, infidelity* for *adultery, visually handicapped* for *blind, indigent person* for *pauper, public assistance* for *dole*).

The use of euphemisms is particularly common in referring to occupations, where they serve either to conceal a definite unpleasantness or to improve social status. There are now relatively few *foremen, bookkeepers, office girls, rat-catchers, undertakers,*

* The earlier euphemism for *manure* was *fertilizer*. However, the unpleasant connotations of *manure* eventually caught up with it, too, and when certain manufacturers wished to promote their product for use indoors, with potted plants, they had to find a new, deodorized name for it. *Plant food* was the inspired result.

pawnbrokers, shoemakers, press-agents, hired girls, or *janitors;* they have become, respectively, *plant superintendents* (or, collectively, *supervisory personnel*), *accountants, secretaries* (or *receptionists*), *exterminators, morticians* (or *funeral directors*), *proprietors of loan offices, shoe-rebuilders, public relations counsels, domestics,* and *custodians.* An example of double promotion (or *upgrading!*) by use of euphemisms is found in the case of *salesman.* The word having acquired a rather vulgar connotation, businessmen began to speak instead of *sales* (or *customers'*) *representatives.* But the word *salesman* was not thereupon retired, for it then was used to designate the former *milkman* (*milk salesman*), *door-to-door canvasser* (*brush salesman*), and even *gas station attendant* (*service salesman*). Earlier in this chapter, when discussing the inefficiency of business jargon, we referred to "time- and motion-study experts." The term is a euphemism developed to fit a crying need. Some years ago the *efficiency experts* who were introduced into manufacturing plants to increase production by getting more work out of the employees became, among those employees, the object of ridicule if not of actual indignation. The term *efficiency expert* thus acquired an irretrievably bad connotation. And so the new terms, *time-study* and *motion-study,* were created. Perhaps in time they too will acquire the negative connotations of the older term.

Business euphemisms and circumlocutions are by no means limited to names for occupations. *Termination of employment* is a common euphemism for the *firing* or *laying-off* of ordinary workmen. On the white-collar level it is perhaps more frequent to *request one's resignation* (or to point out that *opportunities for advancement are limited*). A similar desire to take maximum advantage of the connotations of words is found in merchandising ("selling"). The *budget* (or *economy*) *shops* of department stores are places for the disposal of cheap goods; the installment plan is *deferred payment;* artificial ("fake") material is *simulated;* a floorwalker is an *aisle manager,* a clerk a *sales person;* a place at which to register complaints, an *adjustment* (or *service*) *desk.* Advertisements, of course, are filled with such attempts to escape the negative connotations of certain familiar words.*

Exercise 11.

1. What is meant by the phrase *restricted clientele* found in the advertisements of some hotels and resorts?
2. Why is the word *institute* used so often to designate establishments devoted neither to education nor to research, as in Good Housekeeping Institute and American Iron and Steel Institute?
3. Why is the word *family* frequently used in the advertisements of great corporations, when referring to their employees or to the subsidiary companies of which the corporation is made up?
4. What is the meaning of *information* in the names of such agencies as the Office of War Information and the British Ministry of Information?
5. During World War II, German "information" broadcasts used such phrases as the following: "defensive success," "successful disengagement," "elastic defense," "fluid defense," "mobile defense," "retrocessive maneuver," "unencircling maneuver," "shortening of the front," "withdrawal to the enemy's surprise." What did they mean?
6. Make a list of the modern euphemistic synonyms for the old-fashioned *saloon.*

* See the lively pages on euphemisms in Mencken's *The American Language,* 4th edition, pp. 284–294, and *Supplement One* thereto, pp. 565–595.

EXERCISE 12. Comment on the language used in these passages, and rewrite the passages in the plainest English possible:

1. Because of production cutbacks caused by the termination of government contracts, the management is required to announce that the services of some personnel in this department will be dispensed with beginning September 1.
2. In reviewing our accounts for the past few months we find to our regret that we have not received a remittance from you for a statement payable last April 1, although we have sent you several letters reminding you of that fact. Perhaps these letters have failed to reach your personal attention. If this is the case, we trust you will make remittance immediately. In the absence of word from you, on November 1 we will be forced reluctantly to place the matter in the hands of our attorney.
3. To my great personal regret, I find it necessary to inform you that the conduct of your son Wilmer has once again failed to measure up to the standards set up here at Dotheboys Academy for the common good of all. You will recall that earlier in the term he was counselled several times in this regard. All of us here at Dotheboys had hoped that Wilmer would find it possible to adjust himself to group living. Last Saturday night, however, he was involved in an incident which I am afraid cannot be overlooked, including as it did his having partaken of an intoxicating beverage, which as you know is in disobeyance of the rules maintained for the guidance of our students. Accordingly, therefore, we have asked Wilmer to withdraw from the academy.

Clichés

Thus far in this chapter we have seen that we, as readers, can reasonably demand that those who write for us express themselves as simply and directly as the subject-matter warrants. Those who fail to do so lay themselves open to charges of windiness, cloudy thinking, egotism, or deliberate deceitfulness. We have also seen that there is a common denominator among users of jargon: they are nearly all imitators. Unable or unwilling to clothe their thoughts in their own words, and thus to give individual distinction and force to what they have to say, they blindly adopt the phraseology that others use, regardless of its effectiveness or its aptness. The businessman must write and speak like other businessmen; the sociologist or lawyer or teacher must express himself in the language in which his colleagues speak and write, and never give a thought to the possible unloveliness or unnecessary complexity of that language.

The stock expressions we have cited in the preceding pages were preliminary samples of the vast treasury of clichés, to which we must now pay more specific attention. When a printer has occasion to use a certain word very often in the course of setting up type, he may save time and effort by making a single type-block bearing the whole word, which he then inserts each time the word is called for, instead of setting up the word from individual letters. When a writer, likewise, wishes to express a familiar idea, he saves himself time and effort by inserting a block-phrase that has been widely used for that purpose. This is a cliché: a ready-cast expression that saves one the trouble of inventing a fresh new way of saying something.

Superficially it might seem that the cliché is an admirable device; for have we not said that it saves time and effort, and therefore promotes efficiency? But good writing is not merely efficient: it is effective. And clichés are never effective, for the simple reason that they never impress the reader, who knows them all too well. Effective writing must be fresh and original. It must impress readers with the sincerity of the author. It must convince them that he is in earnest by showing that he is writing for a special occasion and addressing himself to them in particular. Form letters are usually ineffective because they fail to meet these requirements of individuality and freshness; and clichés are nothing but form letters in miniature. The writer who uses clichés betrays to his readers that he doesn't care whether or not they are really impressed by what he says. He is writing mechanically; his phrases smell of mimeograph ink.

Nor is fondness for the cliché a sign simply of insincerity. It may be that a writer's affection for threadbare words is a clue to the quality of his thinking. In the first place, fresh new ideas by their very nature require fresh new language—they cannot be expressed in any other way. Ready-made language can be fitted only to ready-made thoughts. Again, since there is a demonstrable relationship between general intelligence and effective use of language, it is likely that a writer who fails to recognize stale terms when he uses them also fails to recognize stale ideas. Therefore, readers who can quickly detect hackneyed phraseology are forearmed against sloppy thinking. If, for instance, a man begins a letter-to-the-editor or a luncheon-club address in this manner: "The talk about the abolition of the smoke nuisance reminds me of what Mark Twain once said about the weather: everybody talks about it but nobody does anything about it"—the audience is entitled to wonder whether this could possibly be the preface to anything worth listening to. Is the writer or speaker not sufficiently intelligent to realize that the story about Mark Twain and the weather was a chestnut forty-five years ago? Similarly with the speaker who must somehow drag in Mark Twain's remark about the false report of his death—and with the one who insists upon involving the hapless Topsy in his description of how a city or a business or a club, instead of developing according to a plan, just grew.

The wilful or ignorant use of hackneyed phrases, then, can expose a writer to suspicion of being intellectually as well as verbally imitative. One does not have to be a perpetual coiner of flamboyantly "original" phrases that might be welcomed in the "Picturesque Speech" department of the *Reader's Digest;* indeed, one can err almost as far in that direction as in the other. But readers can demand that he write in a manner which will unobtrusively provide traction for their minds rather than allow them to slide and skid on a slippery surface paved with well-worn phrases.

It would be pedantic, not to say useless, to insist that good writers never, never use clichés; let him who has never sinned cast the first stone. But good writers, if they use clichés at all, use them with the utmost caution. In informal discourse, furthermore, clichés are almost indispensable. When we are relaxed with our friends, we do not want to be bothered to find new or at least unhackneyed ways of saying things; we rely upon our ready supply of clichés, and if we do not overdraw our account, no one thinks the worse of us. So long as we succeed in communicating to our friends the small, commonplace ideas we have in mind, no harm is done.

When does an expression become cliché? There can be no definite answer, because what is trite to one person may still be fresh to another. But there is a great body of expressions which are universally understood to be so threadbare as to be useless except in the most casual discourse. A good practical test is this: If, when you are listening to a speaker, you can accurately anticipate what he is going to say next, he is pretty certainly using clichés; otherwise he would be constantly surprising you. "Such a precautionary measure would stand us —" ("in good stead," you think—correctly, as it turns out) "—in our time —" ("of need," you think, and you win). "We are gathered here today to mourn" ("the untimely death") "of our beloved leader. Words are inadequate" ("to express the grief that is in our hearts"). Similarly when you read; if one word almost inevitably invites another, if you can read half of the words and know pretty certainly what the other half are, you are reading clichés. "We watched the flames" ("licking") "at the side of the building. A pall" ("of smoke") "hung thick over the neighborhood. Suddenly we heard a dull" ("thud") "which was followed by an ominous" ("silence").

The degree to which a reader is aware of clichés depends directly upon the scope and sensitivity of his previous reading. If he has read widely, in both good books and bad, and has carefully observed authors' styles, he has probably become quite alert for trite language. Clichés to him are old but exceedingly tiresome friends. But if a reader's experience of books and magazines has been limited, obviously he will not recognize so many overripe expressions; in his eyes most clichés still have the dew on them.

A great number (but by no means all) of the familiar clichés are figures of speech. Now a figure of speech is useful only so long as it illuminates an idea, enabling the reader to visualize an abstract concept in concrete terms. If the reader has become so accustomed to it that it no longer stimulates his imagination, it is useless. And that is what has happened to many such images, clever and vivid at first but now almost lifeless. Many are similes (a comparison directly stated): *busy as a bee, like greased lightning, bright as a pin, slow as molasses in January, tight as a drum* . . . you can add hundreds and thousands of examples to the list. Many more are metaphors (a comparison implied): *in one ear and out the other, the apple of one's eye, a diamond in the rough, bite the hand that feeds you, keep the pot boiling, the arms of Morpheus, fly off the handle, calm after the storm, hit the nail on the head, have the inside track, a chip off the old block, put out one's shingle, in the doghouse, music to my ears . . .*

Another large category of clichés includes those which insist upon associating a particular descriptive adjective (epithet) with a given noun. Such stereotyped word associations include *palatial mansion, deathly pale, humble origin, grim determination, last-ditch stand, doting parents, almighty dollar, sylph-like figure, open-handed generosity.* Is there any real reason why an origin should always be *humble,* or generosity be characterized as *open-handed?* None at all, except that people have adopted such phrases as convenient ways to evade their obligation to make their own language.

Other common types of the cliché are verb- and noun-phrases. Outworn verb-phrases include *to look with jaundiced eye, to give no quarter, to run afoul of the law, to heave a sigh of relief, to pass with averted eye.* Noun-phrases of dubious freshness include *the bonds of friendship, the depths of despair, the pangs of remorse, the shadow of a doubt, the innocence of a child, a cry of anguish, a round of applause, the sweat of the brow, the life of Riley.*

Nowhere is the cliché more to be avoided than in descriptive and narrative writing, the whole success of which depends upon the freshness and exactness with which the writer communicates his impressions to the reader. A virtually fool-proof mark of the inexperienced writer is his willingness to see his settings and characters through the eyes of someone else—to wit, the man who has used his clichés before him. "He walked with catlike tread" . . . "they were drenched by mountainous waves" . . . "the child was bubbling over with mirth" . . . "there was a blinding flash" . . . "he made a convulsive grab for the rope" . . . "they heard a rustle of leaves" . . . "the flowers nodded in the gentle breeze" . . . "the shadows were lengthening" . . . "he looked at her with a glassy stare." The only delight we can find in such writing is that of seeing old familiar faces. Surely we are allowed to participate in no new experience; we cannot see things from any new angle, or receive a fresh interpretation of their meaning. A "creative" writer who depends upon clichés is really not creating anything. His stock-in-trade is not genuine experience, and without genuine experience no writer can succeed. All he has to offer is words—*mere* words, empty shells incapable of meaning.

A great many of our clichés, obviously, are derived from books that have had the greatest influence upon the common speech. *To kill the fatted calf, his name is legion, covers a multitude of sins, the spirit is willing but the flesh is weak, the blind leading the blind, the parting of the way*—all have their beginning in the Bible, even though in most cases their original Biblical connotations have been forgotten. Many sermons are tissues of such clichés, and their dullness is due to the fact that these phrases, originally so full of flavor and meaning, have lost their charm through unremitting use. Few people react to them as deeply as did those to whom the English Bible was a new and wonderful book, the phrases shining like coins from the mint. And that is true, unfortunately, of many of the finest things that have ever been said in the world. The opening sentences of the Declaration of Independence, Lincoln's Gettysburg Address, certain portions of Gray's "Elegy"—some of the most moving poems and political documents have become hackneyed through constant use.

"Newspaperese"

The jargon peculiar to newspapers is a combination of the cliché, dead wood, and the weak passive or impersonal construction. The great objection to it, as to all jargon, is that it is machine-made. It is written according to formula, and material written to formula inevitably loses much of its color and interest. Here is a short sampling of newspaper clichés, together with their simpler equivalents:

The death toll rose to ten today in the wake of the disastrous fire . . . (*or:* Death today claimed four more victims . . .)	Four more people died as a result of the fire . . .
The mercury soared to a record high for the year . . .	Today was the hottest day of the year

At an early hour this morning the identity of the victim had not yet been established . . .	Early this morning the body was still unidentified . . .
State Police, aided by local law enforcement officers, today were combing the area adjacent to Center City in search of clues that might lead to the solution of the mystery of the murder-kidnaping . . .	State and local police were looking for clues to the man who kidnapped and murdered . . .
Traffic was snarled (*or* paralyzed, *or* at a standstill, *or* moved at a snail's pace) as snow blanketed the metropolitan area . . .	The snowfall slowed traffic. . . .
Three persons suffered injuries when the automobile in which they were riding figured in a collison with a large truck . . .	Three people were hurt when their car hit a big truck. . . .
Preparations for the convention neared completion . . .	Everything was just about ready . . .
As he completed his investigation, the coroner said it was his opinion that death was instantaneous . . .	The coroner said he thought the man had been killed instantly

In addition, there are many single words, especially epithets and verbs, which are seemingly indispensable to newspaper reporting. Any better-than-ordinary fire or auto accident is *spectacular;* an accident that is more peculiar than disastrous is *freak;* when public men approve of something they *hail* it, when they disapprove of it they *attack* it, and when they want something they *urge* it; when two factions have a disagreement they *clash;* when anything is announced it is *made public;* and when men accuse others of wrongdoing they *allege* (*assert,* another newspaper warhorse, has a slightly less negative connotation).

The weak passive is used in newspaper writing for the same reason for which it is used in governmental correspondence: to achieve the impersonal note, and thus, in many instances, to disclaim direct responsibility for statements that are based on hearsay. When newspapers send a reporter for an eye-witness story of a disaster or a court trial, or when they quote a press release or statements made during an interview, they can assert dogmatically that this and that are true. But a great deal of news cannot be treated in so open and confident a fashion—news based on private information picked up by reporters or on rumors circulating in the city hall or the stock exchange. Although the papers wish to relay this news, they cannot do so on their own authority; the man who gave the reporter his information refuses to be quoted, and the public will be suspicious of anything plainly labelled "rumor." The solution, then, is to use weak passive or impersonal constructions which do not require an agent: "It was revealed (*or* learned *or* reported)" (*not:* the City Commissioner told our reporter but warned him not to use his name); "indications increased" or "a survey today showed" (*not:* our reporter asked several people, and their replies, when put together, suggested). Another device of passing on news without revealing its source (or, it may be, without revealing that it has no source outside the mind of an inventive reporter) is the use of those mysterious oracles, the *officials who asked that their names be withheld, spokesmen, informed quarters, observers,* and *sources usually considered reliable.* In Chapter Six we shall have much to say of the art of reading newspapers. We are interested here only in showing the relation of newspaper language to jargon. Judged from the viewpoint of clear, accurate communication, "newspaperese" has as little to recommend it as does any other kind of roundabout, machine-made language.

Exercise 13. Fill in the blanks:

1. More in than in
   In the spring a young man's fancy
   God's in His heaven,

Veiled in
A strong man
A little lady
He views the situation with
He emerged from the ordeal sadder but
When the news of the defeat came, our spirits
But when the report proved false, our spirits
He is in the of condition
Listen to her tale of
People who live in glass houses
A snake in the
It burned like blazes
I'm a little under today
It must be true; I got it straight from the
I don't remember your name but
Sorry, I can't direct you; I'm a myself

2. Clear as
Pretty as
Flat as
Smart as
Fast as
Old as
Sly as
A voice like a

EXERCISE 14. Bartlett's *Familiar Quotations* is a vast treasury of oft-repeated expressions, a great many of which have become cliché.

1. From Bartlett, or better yet, from a reading of the play itself, make a list of the phrases in *Hamlet* which have become cliché.
2. See the great list of clichés lurking in Cervantes' *Don Quixote,* collected in Bartlett (1937 edition), pp. 1033–43.

EXERCISE 15. Some clichés are enduring; they pass from generation to generation without seeming quite to wear out. Others, the products of contemporary events and fashions, are short-lived. "Back to normalcy!" was the great cliché of the early 1920's, just as "Two cars in every garage, a chicken in every pot" was the cliché of the Hoover era. "Prosperity is just around the corner" was heard from every mouth in the early 1930's; and then came phrases from Mr. Roosevelt himself—"We have nothing to fear but fear itself" and the rest. After his Charlottesville speech in 1940, Mr. Roosevelt's characterization of Mussolini's attack upon France as "a stab in the back" became the standard cliché on the subject. In another realm of American life, clichés spring from popular songs, the comic strips, movies, and the radio. They have their brief life and then disappear as suddenly as they appeared. At the moment this book is being written, "on the beam" and "the sixty-four dollar question" are clichés "of the first water." By the time you read these words, those clichés may have become dead as a ——. Slang clichés and catch-phrases are the froth on the sea of language.

1. What are the clichés most frequently heard at the moment you are reading this book? Where did they originate? What chance have they of becoming established?
2. For those who are interested in recent social history, it would be fun to browse in the several volumes of Mark Sullivan's *Our Times* and in Frederick Lewis Allen's *Only Yesterday* and *Since Yesterday* to discover what were the favorite catch-phrases and clichés in the years between 1900 and 1939.
3. The humorist S. J. Perelman makes great use of current clichés, especially those with a quasi-literary flavor. See his skits in *The New Yorker* and his book, *Crazy Like a Fox.*

EXERCISE 16. Here is a news item, written in standard journalese. Translate it into simple, direct, unhackneyed English.

> Police today were conducting an intensive search for a sailor in connection with the brutal slaying of Rose M——, a night

club entertainer, whose battered body was found crumpled in a vacant lot in a remote section of Brooklyn early this morning. The sailor, in whose company the murdered girl was seen at 7 p.m. yesterday is wanted for questioning in connection with her whereabouts last night. "We know his name," Police Captain S—— declared to newspapermen this afternoon, "and we have reason to believe he had left the girl before she met her death. However, we wish to trace the movements of the pair."

Meanwhile, investigators from the detective bureau were questioning scores of persons acquainted with the slain girl, most of them residents of the neighborhood in which she and her sister, who is employed as a waitress, maintained a small two-room flat. It was reported that they have located a woman who saw Miss M—— engaged in conversation with a tall man on a streetcorner near her home at midnight. However, it was said that the witness was able to furnish police with only a vague description of the man.

Miss M——'s body was discovered at 4 a.m. by Arthur P——, a milk deliveryman who was making his rounds. Crossing the vacant lot as a short-cut between two houses, he noticed a bloody handkerchief caught on some tall weeds, and upon investigation found the fully clothed body of the victim lying face downward. He ran to the nearest house and summoned police who responded in two squad cars. After a preliminary survey, the first police on the scene enlisted the aid of the detective bureau.

Police Surgeon A—— announced after an examination of the body that death had been caused by a crushed skull. Marks on the victim's head indicated that she had been struck several hard blows by a blunt instrument.

Police were at a loss to advance a motive for the crime. The girl had not been criminally assaulted, and her purse was found a few feet away from the body, its contents intact.

CHAPTER THREE

Logic

OF ALL THE HABITS we acquire in the course of our early years, none is more deeply ingrained in us, or does us more harm in the long run, than that of believing everything we see in print. For some reason the appearance of an alleged fact or an opinion in cold type gives it a high authority which one is almost superstitiously reluctant to question. In grade school and high school and now in college, in the casual reading of newspapers and magazines and books by war correspondents and biographers and popularizers of science, we become accustomed to accepting as gospel truth whatever is put down in black and white. Perhaps our reverence is due to the fact that we regard anyone who succeeds in getting into print as an authority *per se*. Our logic seems to be that a man who can "crash" the glamorous world of journalism and publishing, *must* know what he is talking about, and can be depended upon to give us truth, the whole truth, and nothing but the truth.

To many college freshmen it comes as a shock, therefore, to discover that their faith has been grievously misplaced. They can take in their stride the demonstration that most daily newspapers are repositories of misinformation and half-truths, for they have often heard rumors to that effect, even though they forget to be critical when they are actually reading the evening paper. But they are often startled when they are told that the magazines upon which they base their knowledge of what is going on in the world—*Time* and *Life* and the *Reader's Digest*—cannot be depended upon always to tell the truth. And their disillusionment is complete when they are given evidence that the very books they draw from the library and even, on occasion, the textbooks they use in their college work contain errors—poor reasoning, unsupported opinion, misinterpreted information, special pleading, and the like.

As we said in the foreword, this book would be of little use if it served merely to substitute an attitude of habitual disbelief for one of uncritical belief. It is probably just as easy to believe nothing as it is to believe everything. It is harder, but in the long run infinitely more satisfying, to be able to separate the true from the false—to be able to detect opinions masquerading as facts, as well as half-truths and distortions of the truth. The practised reader, while he always remains alert for these evidences of careless or deliberately abused logic, discovers that plenty of truth remains in the world; there is no dearth of things for him to believe, or to believe in. But he finds an astringent pleasure in his cultivated awareness of deception; the quick detection of error and the equally quick recognition of truth become not only an inexhaustibly rewarding game but also an abiding evidence that he is not so easily deceived as his neighbor. In a word, the practice which the ensuing pages will afford you in the art of telling truth from falsehood can result in a powerful and justifiable bolstering of your confidence in yourself. It can make you consciously more mature—more adult—in your mental processes.

Objectivity and Subjectivity

We begin by remembering that all our experience, all our knowledge of the world, is made up of two sorts, objective and subjective. Objective data are data which everyone will agree upon: Columbus made a voyage to America in 1492, giraffes are found in Africa, this book has certain dimensions. Subjective data is data which depends upon one's personal feelings or opinions: General Eisenhower is the greatest military man that World War II produced, Roquefort cheese is repellent, Anne's new hairdo is much less attractive than her old one.

For the first group, one can adduce "proof" that will be acceptable to all reasonable persons. We have not only Columbus' own journal of his voyage to America in a year that is designated by common agreement as 1492 A.D., but also much independent supporting evidence; although four and a half centuries have passed, we can be very sure that Columbus did make that voyage, just as the historical documents say he did. We know that giraffes are found in Africa because many trustworthy explorers have brought them back from there. We know that this book has certain dimensions because a hundred people can measure it with an accurately calibrated ruler (a universally agreed-upon standard of measurement) and give the same answer.

But there can be no such agreement concerning the second group of assertions. Many people may agree with us that General Eisenhower was the greatest military leader in World War II, but many others will violently disagree; in the nature of things there can be no agreement, because, in the first place, we have not defined what we mean by "greatest," and, in the second place, even if we could arrive at a universally acceptable set of standards for "greatness," by no means everyone would agree that Eisenhower most adequately fulfilled those requirements. Roquefort cheese may be repellent to some of us, but to others it may be irresistibly delicious; it is a matter, as we say, of "personal taste." Anne's new hairdo may be less attractive to half of our number, but to the other half, and probably to Anne herself, it is a great improvement over the old one. Who can say which party is right? Such matters can never be decided one way or the other.

Just as there is no sharp line of demarcation between denotation and connotation, so there is no plain division between the realm of the objective and the realm of the subjective. What is the color of the walls of a classroom? Some may call it buff, some cream, some eggshell, some "an off shade of white," some yellowish; there is no community of opinion because our common names for colors are based upon more or less personal standards. Yet a pigments expert or an optical physicist could say authoritatively that the walls are painted one specific color, and one color alone. That is because experts have agreed upon a system of color-names which is based upon scientific measurements; using a colorimeter, they can easily reach a conclusion which no one who accepts their standards will dispute. In other words, where there is no commonly accepted measure of truth, there can be no objective fact; everything that is judged by the individual, on the basis of his own personal standard, is subjective. But what are subjective data in one aspect, as for example the measurement of a table by eye alone, are turned into objective data when verified by measurement by agreed-upon standards and procedures.

The degree to which we must be aware of the distinction between objectivity and subjectivity depends upon the reason why we are reading at any given moment. If we are reading a newspaper, we want *facts* about the day's happenings; if we are reading a textbook on economics, we want *facts,* or at least well worked-out and logically supported theories (themselves supported by facts), of economic phenomena; if we are listening to a radio commentator's report on international developments, we want the *facts* of what has actually taken place.

Whenever we seek *information,* therefore, we are concerned to get facts, not fancies dressed up as facts. But when we do not need verifiable data, as almost any time when we are seeking relaxation and pleasure, we can read subjective writing with our guards down. Nearly all of the best literature in the world is subjective: it is the report, in one form or another, of private, personal experience—of the inner feelings and moods of a highly sensitive man or woman, of the way in which the external world impinges upon that person's senses and spirit. A personal essay, a biographical portrait, a love lyric, an appreciation of the art of Shakespeare, a bit of nature-writing, a poetic meditation—each is intensely subjective. The objective facts contained in such pieces, we can easily obtain from encyclopedias; but the impressions and reactions reported in them are unique to that writer. And that, indeed, constitutes one of the chief values of literature: the opportunity we are thus afforded to view life and people through the spirit of someone else, someone peculiarly gifted both in experience and in the ability to recapture and communicate that experience to us.

When we are dealing with writing that makes no pretense of objectivity, writing in which the author frankly acknowledges that he is spinning material out of his own substance, there is no question of authority. On matters that go on inside his own self, every man is best qualified to speak. We never question the truth *so far as the writer alone is concerned* of any statement made by Charles Lamb, let us say, or Max Beerbohm, or Henry Thoreau, or E. B. White, or anyone else who reports on himself. There is no means of checking up on him, anyway.

The Question of Authority

But when we turn back to matters of objective fact, the case is quite different. Here we are obliged constantly to decide whether or not to believe what we hear or read. Who is writing or speaking? Does he know what he is talking about? Are his opinions based upon study and observation and experience, or have they been formed hastily and carelessly? Is he in a position to know more about the subject than you do? Is he shrewder, more sensitive, more analytical than the majority of people, so that his personal judgments carry more weight than most? Why is he saying what he does: because he sincerely believes it, or because he has some ulterior motive? Does he want you to vote a certain way or buy a certain product? Does he belong to a certain group or party that wants to recruit new members? These are a few of the questions that should hover forever in your head when you read, for they will help you pierce to the basic truth or falseness of any piece of writing.

Take first the matter of an "expert's" qualification. Not long ago, Albert Einstein was interviewed for the *Atlantic Monthly* on the subject of the atomic bomb and the political problems it raised for the whole world. As a great mathematician, whose work prepared the way for the science of nuclear physics, Einstein could speak with some authority on the scientific aspects of the subject. But, as many were quick to point out, Einstein's recommendations for international political measures to control atomic energy had no more weight than would those of any layman, because Einstein is not a political scientist or statesman and has no special knowledge of the problems which confront the leaders of nations. Nevertheless it is probable that many readers, revering Einstein as a scientist, accepted his political ideas without serious question.*

It is a mistake, therefore, to assume that only men who are qualified to speak with authority on a certain subject have access to the printing press. Actually, the greater part of what we hear

* It should be pointed out, however, that the political scientists and statesmen seem little better equipped to deal with the tremendous issus raised by the atomic bomb than is the intelligent layman. We do not mean to imply that Einstein's counsel should be disregarded simply because he is not an expert in the conduct of international affairs; we mean only that his prestige as a scientist does not give his political views any more validity than those of any thoughtful layman.

and read on a given topic comes from persons who have no special right to make pronouncements on it but who, for one reason or another, assume the privilege just the same. Members of the House of Representatives and the Senate are constantly sounding off on every topic of current discussion in Washington. Sometimes they must be listened to with attention and respect, because they may have made a special study of their subject and may actually know much more about it than most people. But on the other hand they may know nothing at all about the issue they are pronouncing upon, apart from what they read in the newspapers or in pressure-group publicity handouts, or hear by word of mouth from their colleagues. Part of our responsibility as citizens is to follow the activities of Congressmen and governmental officials, so that we may know whose utterances should be disregarded, as based upon nothing but casual opinion, or prejudice, or political strategy.

This habit of cultivating discrimination applies to all of our reading. "Says who?" is an invaluable watchword. Who tells us about a new scientific discovery? If it is an ordinary newspaper reporter, covering a meeting of scientists, not understanding a tithe of what he hears and yet obliged to return to his office with an "interesting" story, what he writes is scarcely worth reading except for amusement; certainly it can never be taken seriously as a piece of scientific information. But if it is a man like W. L. Laurence of the *New York Times,* who specializes in science, reads the scientific journals and knows the leading scientists, his report should be read at least with respect. And if it is a professional scientist who has been personally involved in the scientific experimentation of which he writes, we should give him our full attention. He knows what he is talking about. In particular, we should be skeptical of reports in popular magazines and newspapers of "new advances in medical science." Responsible medical men seldom will commit themselves on such matters, except cautiously and in the relative privacy of professional journals.

In every field of information there are charlatans as well as honest, reliable writers. It always pays to find out which writers belong to which category. Obviously the most reliable authorities on any subject are those who specialize in it and therefore know the most about it: professional historians, literary scholars, pathologists, geneticists, physical chemists, economists, musicologists. Human capability being a variable quantity, there are many shades of competence even among the experts, Historian A being more dependable than Historian B, and so forth; but in general we may look to the specialists for the most authoritative information and expert interpretation of data.

Unfortunately, however, many of these experts have neither the ability nor the inclination to write for the layman. To cull the most essential information from their scholarly treatises and put it into a form that is agreeable to the layman, there exists the so-called "popularizer," whose indispensable qualification is that he can write simply and interestingly about complex matters. There are good popularizers and bad popularizers, and it is often useful to know which are which, because reading an article by the bad kind is a waste of time. Good popularizers have sufficient knowledge of the subject about which they are writing and sufficient scholarly sense to be able to report accurately to their audience. They may simplify their material—indeed, they have to do so; but in simplifying they guard against distortion or misinformation. Bad popularizers, on the other hand, fail to understand their subject in the first place, but they nevertheless proceed to give their readers a badly twisted account of it, filled with misstatements, exaggerations, and fancies.

"Does the man know what he is talking about?" is, then, a question that must remain uppermost in our minds as we read anything that purports to give information or to offer an opinion.

Again and again we must conclude that the writer knows no more about his subject than do we, who also read the newspapers, and that therefore his data and opinions may be ignored without loss.

"What is his motive in saying what he does?" is a second, equally important question. In many cases the motive is easily apparent: the writer of a popularized book on science, for example, wants to make some money. But what of those numerous articles and books on politics, economics, religion, social affairs, education? Although the superficial reader may seldom be aware of it, nearly all of them are written from a particular viewpoint. Few of them are impartial or disinterested; the great majority are biased, if only because the subjects with which they deal are controversial.

Take for example the columnists who discuss national affairs. They all develop their discussions from a hard kernel of indisputable fact: the President has actually made this statement, Congress has actually taken that stand on a current issue. But their interpretations of these facts differ tremendously, for two reasons. One is that every so-called "commentator" has a bias for or against certain persons, parties, and principles. Westbrook Pegler, Walter Lippmann, Samuel Grafton, Frank R. Kent, Arthur Krock, Max Lerner, I. F. Stone, David Lawrence, Mrs. Roosevelt, and George Sokolsky represent different shades of opinion, and when we read their columns we must keep those biases always in mind: remember that each of them construes an event or situation in terms of what he personally judges to be right and wrong. Their reporting is largely, indeed almost completely, subjective, even though, except in the case of Mr. Lippmann's articles, the qualifying "I think" or "I believe" or "it seems to me" is nearly always missing.

Some columnists have a high sense of public responsibility; they write with no other thought than to inform their readers of the significance of events *as they see it.* They are aware, of course, of their prejudices, but such prejudices are the result of honest study and analysis. Every man, after all, must take his stand somewhere. But other columnists are frankly sensation-mongers. Their only aim is to gain attention, and they achieve it by digging up scandal (an occupation which, it is true, sometimes serves a useful end), by reporting rumors (which they often fail to identify as such), and by making wild but confident "predictions" (which can seldom stand the scrutiny of hindsight). At their best, political commentators are the most intelligent means by which the public can be informed of what the government is doing and should do; at their worst, they spread vicious misinformation and groundless rumor, and encourage people to political action based upon irrational bias rather than upon intelligent grasp of issues.*

Just as it is necessary to know what allegiance a so-called "Washington political observer" holds before we can evaluate what he says, so is it necessary in every discussion of controversial matters to discover the bias of the writer, particularly, if possible, his connection with a party or organization. When we know that Eric Johnston was president of the United States Chamber of Commerce, an organization with definitely conservative leanings, we read his book on Russia with constant awareness that he sees Russia with the eyes of an American capitalist. When we know that Henry Wallace has long been identified with liberal politics, we read his book on full employment knowing that he speaks from a viewpoint that will not be shared by many conservative readers, lay or expert. Undoubtedly there is much of value to be learned from such books; but we must keep in mind that everything is modified by the writer's particular philosophy, and that what we have here is but one side of

* See page 294, Exercise 9.

a complex problem. The writer is weighting the discussion as he wishes it weighted. He is not disinterested.

So much for fact, and fact as it is being constantly colored by personal opinion. In the process of interpreting objective or subjective data to serve specific ends, writers often abuse the laws of evidence and reason. They generalize from too little data, they evade the main issue, they reason from a faulty premise, and perform a host of other tricks that fool the unwary. In the following pages we shall examine some of the most common means by which readers may be deluded.

EXERCISE 1.

1. Here are three selections which combine subjective and objective materials in various proportions. Analyze each one. In the case of every bit of objective data, decide how the writer's statement can be verified to the satisfaction of all reasonable people; in the case of subjective data, decide to what degree each item is purely a matter of private opinion or impression or is, on the other hand, an opinion or impression likely to be shared by many people though not capable of objective proof.

   (a) The canal boat is of very simple construction, requiring but little ship timber, and, as we were told, costs about two hundred dollars. They are managed by two men. In ascending the stream they use poles fourteen or fifteen feet long, shod with iron, walking about one third the length of the boat from the forward end. Going down, they commonly keep in the middle of the stream, using an oar at each end; or if the wind is favorable they raise their broad sail, and have only to steer. They commonly carry down bricks or wood,—fifteen or sixteen thousand bricks, and as many cords of wood, at a time,—and bring back stores for the country, consuming two or three days each way between Concord and Charlestown.

(b) My heart is like a singing bird
  Whose nest is in a watered shoot;
My heart is like an apple-tree
  Whose boughs are bent with thick-set fruit:
My heart is like a rainbow shell
  That paddles in a halcyon sea;
My heart is gladder than all these,
  Because my love is come to me.

(c) On the left of the spectator lay the ruined wall, broken in many places, and in some, overhanging the narrow beach below in rude and heavy masses. Huge knots of sea-weed hung upon the jagged and pointed stones, trembling in every breath of wind; and the green ivy clung mournfully round the dark and ruined battlements. Behind it rose the ancient castle, its towers roofless, and its massive walls crumbling away, but telling us proudly of its own might and strength, as when, seven hundred years ago, it rang with a clash of arms, or resounded with the noise of feasting and revelry. On either side, the banks of the Medway, covered with cornfields and pastures, with here and there a windmill, or a distant church, stretched away as far as the eye could see, presenting a rich and varied landscape, rendered more beautiful by the changing shadows which passed swiftly across it, as the thin and half-formed clouds skimmed away in the light of the morning sun.

2. Examine in the same way the selections quoted in Chapter One, especially the advertisements; or analyze a group of advertisements found in current magazines.

EXERCISE 2. From the current *Reader's Digest,* select five or six articles which seem to you to call for specialized knowledge of a certain topic—aviation, science, diplomacy, etc. Then, using reliable reference works, such as *Who's Who in America, Ameri-*

can Men of Science, and *Living Authors,* try to determine how well qualified was the author of each article.

Try the same experiment with the current issue of *Harper's.*

EXERCISE 3.

1. The following persons are well known as "popularizers" in various fields. Try to find out from an expert in each field—the most learned professor you know, for example—how each popularizer is regarded by the experts, and why.

   Frances Winwar (literary biography), Hendrik Willem Van Loon (history and art), John Gunther (contemporary history and world affairs), Stuart Chase (economics), Paul DeKruif (bacteriology and medicine), E. E. Slosson (general science), Lewis Browne (comparative religions), Walter B. Pitkin (applied psychology), Julian Huxley (biology).
2. Look up excerpts from the reviews of representative books by these authors in the *Book Review Digest.* Note the frequent differences of opinion concerning a given book. How can you account for them? Which reviewers seem most trustworthy and authoritative? Why?

EXERCISE 4. How much attention should be paid to the pronouncements of the following writers on the stated subjects? Why?

1. Thomas Henry Huxley (great English biologist and popularizer of science, died 1895) on electrical waves.
2. Congressman X (Massachusetts Republican) on the necessity for a high tariff.
3. The world's champion heavyweight boxer on who should be elected President of the United States.
4. The chief chemist of a plastics company on the development of new synthetic materials.
5. A report of No. 4 written by a feature writer for the Sunday supplements.

6. The most popular movie starlet of the year on the best foundation garment to buy.
7. A columnist syndicated in the Hearst papers on Russia's foreign policy.
8. An educational psychologist on how to teach children not to lie.
9. A Catholic archbishop on the social implications of birth control.
10. Carl Sandburg on Abraham Lincoln.

EXERCISE 5. In the above discussion (page 110) a number of popular American political commentators were named. What can be said of the bias of each one? Are some more independent than others? Give a detailed report on the "line" taken by each columnist syndicated in the local newspapers.

Deductive Logic

There are two kinds of reasoning: the deductive and the inductive.

Perhaps the easiest way to remember the distinction between the two is to set it down in memory that *de*duction is employed in every *de*tective story ever written. It is the means by which one reasons from a general truth to a particular conclusion. When, in "The Case of the Norwood Builder," Sherlock Holmes welcomed John Hector McFarlane to his Baker Street rooms, he said, "I assure you that, beyond the obvious facts that you are a bachelor, a solicitor, a Freemason, and an asthmatic, I know nothing whatever about you."

"Familiar as I was with my friend's method," writes Dr. Watson, "it was not difficult for me to follow his deductions, and to observe the untidiness of attire, the sheaf of legal papers, the watch-charm, and the breathing which had prompted them."*

Watson, following Holmes, had reasoned in this manner:

1.	(Major premise)	Men who dress untidily are bachelors.
	(Minor premise)	This man is dressed untidily.
	(Conclusion)	This man is a bachelor.
2.	(Major premise)	Men who carry legal papers about with them are lawyers.
	(Minor premise)	This man is carrying legal papers with him.
	(Conclusion)	This man is a lawyer.

And similarly with the other two deductions.

What Watson did was to construct, for each item of observation, a syllogism, which is a series of three statements: a major premise (a statement which is, or is assumed to be, universally true), a minor premise (a statement of a particular fact which is an instance of the major premise), and a conclusion, which must follow inevitably if the two premises are correct.

Algebraically,

(Major premise)	A is equal to B
(Minor premise)	C is equal to A
(Conclusion, since quantities equal to the same quantity are equal to each other)	C is equal to B

It is also true that, algebraically speaking,

A is equal to B	(All collies have soft coats)
C is equal to B	(This dog has a soft coat)
C is equal to A	(This dog is a collie).

But this is the so-called "fallacy of the undistributed middle," which disregards the possibility that the middle term ("soft coats") also applies to a group other than that mentioned in the

* Sherlock Holmes materials are used in this chapter by special permission of the executors of the late Sir Arthur Conan Doyle.

major premise ("collies") and hence that "this dog" may belong to that other group. In testing a syllogism, therefore, you should remember that the middle term (the one which is common to both premises but is lacking in the conclusion) is A (as in the first series above) and not B. Or to put it in terms of sentence structure (a useful device for testing syllogisms): if the syllogism is correctly phrased and constructed, the subject of the conclusion (C) is the subject of the minor premise (C), and the predicate of the conclusion (B) is the predicate of the major premise (B)—as in the first series.

If every statement which we heard or read in the course of an ordinary day were made into a syllogism and then examined for errors, we should all be wiser men and women. There are two great loopholes for the entry of error into the syllogism: the premises themselves, and the logic by which the premises lead to the conclusion.

The major premise, as we have seen, is a statement of a general truth. But, you must ask in every single case in which you are examining the logic of an assertion, is the major premise *true?* By this time, it is hoped, you will have become seriously disturbed by our seeming approval of the logic by which Holmes and Watson deduced the marital state, occupation, fraternal connections, and health of Mr. McFarlane. "Men who dress untidily are bachelors": but is this true? Does untidiness always accompany lack of a wife? And even if so, are there no other untidy men but bachelors? In any case, the generalization simply is untrue. "Men who carry legal papers about with them are lawyers"—but are lawyers the only men who could conceivably be seen carrying legal papers? "Men who wear Freemason's emblems on their watchchains are Freemasons": here we are on sounder ground; although we cannot say beyond possibility of question that every man who wears such an emblem is a Freemason, the overwhelming probability is that he is. "Men who breathe heavily after climbing a flight of stairs are asthmatic"—but cannot mere corpulence, for example, produce similar symptoms? In at least three out of four cases, Holmes was basing his deductions upon perilously unsound major premises. His spectacular success in this sort of logical exercise, for which he has become so famous, was due more to luck than to good management.

The first thing to do, therefore, in examining every exercise of deductive (general-to-particular) reasoning is to scrutinize the major premise. If it is a statement that can be verified by observation (as all of the ones above conceivably could), or by controlled experimentation, can it stand such a test? "The intelligence level of Negroes is lower than that of whites"; "business depressions occur every twenty-one years"; "blue-eyedness is a dominant characteristic, brown-eyedness is a recessive characteristic"; "all bluebirds have red breasts"; "you can always identify a Model T Ford by its hand-throttle"; "guinea pigs reproduce at a faster rate than any other animal suitable for laboratory purposes"; "every nation which borrowed money from the United States during, or as a consequence of, World War I, eventually defaulted." In every case, means can be found of proving or disproving these major premises to everyone's satisfaction. That is, they are capable of objective verification.

There are two types of major premises: those which maintain that a given fact is always true under the conditions stated—there being no possibility of exceptions; and those which admit the possibility of exceptions but maintain that the stated fact is true most of the time, or under most conditions. The critical reader must therefore examine every premise to see whether it admits or denies the possibility of exceptions. Clever persuaders often omit such words as *always, never, only, every, all,* because without them, statements sound less sweeping, less uncompromisingly strict, and are therefore easier to accept. But if we insist upon inserting one or another of those words into an apparently sound premise, it very often collapses—its falsity, which had been cleverly hidden, is now dramatically revealed. And if there can be exceptions to the generalization made in the major premise, then the conclusion does not inevitably follow. This was the flaw in the facile "deductions" of Sherlock Holmes, one of which we now restate:

(Major premise)	Men who carry legal papers about with them *can only* be lawyers.
(Minor premise)	This man is carrying legal papers.
(Conclusion)	This man *can only* be a lawyer.

An acceptable syllogism in this case would be:

(Major premise)	Men who carry legal papers about with them are *probably* lawyers.
(Minor premise)	This man is carrying legal papers.
(Conclusion)	This man is *probably* a lawyer.

Major premises which provide for exceptions are perfectly valid, so long as that possibility is also admitted in the conclusion. The conclusion can be positive and sweeping only to the degree to which the major premise is. We shall have more to say of this matter when we discuss the inductive reasoning by which such premises are established.

In addition to the major premises which are capable of objective proof, there is also the class of basic assumptions which, by their very nature, must always remain no more than assumptions. Obviously there are many ideas in this world which we cannot hope ever to prove: ideas which we must be content to take on faith, or else to reject. Every tenet of religion, for example, is a basic assumption incapable of objective demonstration. Countless volumes have been written attempting to "prove logically" this or that article of religious doctrine, but every so-called "proof" rests upon some basic assumption behind which it is impossible to go. Every argument ever conducted on questions of ethics, esthetics, philosophy—any field of human interest except the exact and (to a lesser degree) the social sciences—is based ultimately upon such unprovable assumptions. "For the sake of argument let's assume . . ." is the essential, though often unexpressed, prelude to the beginning of any argument on such matters; without an arbitrarily agreed-upon common ground upon which to stand, the disputants can get nowhere. "God is immanent in the universe"; "there is a life after death"; "democracy is the form of government under which the individual man has the greatest freedom and opportunity"; "common sense is the best guide to conduct"; "wars are unmitigated evils"; "the most important element in artistic creation is sincerity on the part of the artist"; "no society can endure when home ties and family life disintegrate." These statements may be true, or they may not. They are perfectly legitimate major premises, however, *if* they are used with the clear understanding that they are assumed and not proved. The conclusion to which they lead must similarly be understood to be not a proof but only a logical development of ideas based upon an unprovable assumption.

The major premise must be phrased with the utmost exactness and clarity. "The intelligence level of Negroes," for example: what, precisely, does that mean? The over-all average I.Q. of southern Negroes tested between 1920 and 1945? The I.Q. of Negroes now in the colleges and universities of six midwestern states? And what about "that of whites"? The major premise is phrased too vaguely, too loosely, for the syllogism to be soundly developed; it needs to be an exact statement that can be backed up by statistical evidence. Again, precisely what is a "business depression"? What statistical criteria are to be adopted—what is the difference between a depression, a panic, and a slump?

Similarly with major premises which contain unprovable assumptions. What is meant by "the greatest freedom and opportunity" which "democracy" (what is *it?*) affords to the individual? What is "sincerity on the part of the artist" and how are we to measure it? Every such phrase cries out for definition. If it is left undefined, for each party to the argument to interpret according to his own wishes, the argument is worthless, because the parties will not be talking the same language. You will recall that we pointed out the same thing in connection with "glittering generalities" in Chapter One.

The chief requirements for the minor premise are that it be true and that it represent a particular instance of the general case stated in the major premise. "This man is carrying legal papers": a perfectly acceptable premise, first because our eyes, which can be trusted in this case at least, tell us that he *is* carrying legal papers, and secondly because this particular man who is carrying legal papers is plainly a member of a larger category of (all) men who carry legal papers. The major premise thus applies to him.

If these conditions hold, we are then ready for the conclusion, which simply says that what is true of the general class mentioned in the major premise is also, *necessarily,* true of the specific case mentioned in the minor premise. However, one must constantly be on guard against the *non sequitur*—a conclusion which does not logically derive from the premises. Some *non sequiturs* are so apparent as to be merely absurd: "She is a fine dental technician, and so she plays a fairly good hand at bridge." But often, sometimes because they are more slyly phrased, sometimes because they have been repeated so often that they have achieved a kind of specious authority, we encounter such statements as this: "Franklin Roosevelt could not prevent divorces within his own family; therefore he was totally unfitted to lead the nation." In every case, a suspected *non sequitur* can be exposed by the attempt to build upon the conclusion a rigid syllogism which will state the admitted facts in the order A is B, C is A. That C cannot be B, as the conclusion asserts, will become evident from the failure to achieve two sound premises, the second of which is a valid instance of the first and both of which, taken together, lead to the conclusion.

In our everyday reading we seldom encounter statements ready-made into syllogisms. Instead, the logical process is usually implied, with a confident "therefore" (never to be taken on faith) marking the transition from the premises to the conclusion. In order to construct syllogisms we must, therefore, erect our own major and minor premises.* In order to do so, so that we shall be able to construct a conclusion from the subject of the minor premise and the predicate of the major, we often must change the wording of the original statement. There is no harm in doing this, *provided always that we do not change in any way the thought of the author*. The words we select for our statements, if different from his own, must be perfectly equivalent to them in meaning.

Exercise 6. Each of the following statements is an enthymeme (a syllogism in rough form, lacking one premise). Restate each one in the form of a rigid syllogism, and where there is a faulty major or minor premise, or a *non sequitur*, identify it. (Do not include rhetorical flourishes in your syllogism—such gratuitous comments as "everyone agrees", etc. They have no part in logic; as will be pointed out later [pages 142–143], they are often inserted to conceal the lack of logic.) (Sometimes more than one syllogism may be needed.)

* Anyone who wishes to have a syllogism must have a major and a minor premise.
We wish to have a syllogism.
Therefore: We must have a major and a minor premise.

1. When Holmes and Watson drove up to a London house they found the railings in front of the house lined by a crowd. "By George!" exclaimed Holmes. "It's attempted murder at the least. Nothing less will hold the London message-boy. There's a deed of violence indicated in that fellow's round shoulders and outstretched neck."
2. Holmes "deduced" that the owner of a pair of pince-nez glasses was "a person of refinement and well-dressed," because the glasses "are, as you perceive, handsomely mounted in solid gold, and it is inconceivable that anyone who wore such glasses could be slatternly in other respects."
3. Don't be silly. There have always been wars; why do you think they can be done away with now?
4. The French have no kick coming if they are left out of major international discussions, because their defeat in 1940 was a serious blow to the Allied cause and undoubtedly prolonged the war.
5. You wouldn't drink pure alcohol, would you? Then why drink any liquor at all—it's alcohol just the same, even if it is diluted.
6. It was testified at the hearing that in the ten minutes before the crash occurred, the bus had covered four miles in the city, along a route including six traffic lights, and had made five stops to discharge passengers. Therefore, the prosecutor contended, the crash had been caused by the persistent reckless driving of the operator.
7. You deserve only the best—therefore insist on Sweet-Swig Mouthwash!
8. The atomic bomb is an inhuman weapon of war. It should therefore be outlawed by international agreement.
9. If you attempt to regulate the contents of magazines to protect public morals, you are abridging the freedom of the press, which is a fundamental right guaranteed by our constitution.
10. We should not have socialized medicine, because the possibility of making money is the most powerful incentive doctors have, and this would be removed if we placed them all under government control.

Inductive Logic

We turn now to the second of the two great methods of reasoning: the inductive, or particular-to-general, type. This is the means by which all major premises of the verifiable type are established. Any "truth" which can be proved at all can be proved by inductive reasoning.

The process, although it has many hazards, is essentially simple. One examines all possible evidence which bears on a particular moot point (the "hypothesis")—the intellectual superiority of whites over Negroes, the recessiveness of brown-eyedness, the cyclic repetition of business depressions, the reproductive rate of guinea pigs in comparison with that of other animals—and reaches a conclusion which either establishes or disproves the point. This is the procedure followed by all who work with objective data: the exact scientists—biologists, physicists, chemists, mathematicians, and the like—who try to find the principles and "laws" by which the physical universe operates, and the social scientists—sociologists, economists, political scientists, etc.—who try to find patterns and tendencies in human conduct and institutions. Because of the very different character of the materials with which these two groups work, the generalizations which they reach are of different quality. The exact scientists can verify their hypotheses either by direct laboratory experiment (manipulating their bacteria and compounds and light rays as they wish) or by rigidly controlled observation. They can, in other words, virtually create the conditions under which they examine and measure their evidence. Thus their conclusions can be much more positive than can those of the social scientists, who cannot ordinarily create ideal laboratory conditions involving human beings but must, instead, rely upon records of human behavior, past and present.

In any case, all inductive reasoning leads to generalization.

The great question, then, is: How dependable is each generalization?

A little while ago we remarked that if a syllogism is to be logically sound, its major premise must openly account for the possibility of exceptions either by denying it or by admitting it. Many premises, ostensibly unassailable, prove untenable when we insert in them such words as *all, never, only, every,* and *always.* They simply are not universally true. And unless a premise is universally true, no conclusion *inevitably* follows from it.

If we apply that bit of advice consistently to the countless sweeping "truths" which we meet every day, we discover before long that actually there are comparatively few generalizations which always hold true. Most of the ones which are incontestably true are found in the realm of exact science. Men are mammals, trees have roots, steel buildings conduct static electricity, magnesium burns with an intense white flame, human beings have a glandular system, light travels at a speed of 186,300 miles a second, and carbon monoxide gas, if inhaled in a specified quantity, is fatal. In all recorded history, with its billions of individual men, each offering the possibility of an exception, there has been no instance of a man not conforming to the criteria which scientists have set up for a mammal. Similarly, of all the millions and billions of trees men have actually seen, not one has been without roots. Although theoretically there is always the possibility of an exception, the odds against it are so astronomically large that we are well justified in saying that *all* men are mammals and that *every* tree must have roots. There have been somewhat fewer steel buildings to observe and draw conclusions from, but the number is still great enough for us to be able to make a sound generalization as to their electrical conductivity.

The confidence with which we may assert that (in the absence of a single known exception) a given statement is *always* true, stands, therefore, in direct proportion to the number of instances observed. Thus any statement which a biologist makes concerning the life cycle and habits of a certain rare deep-sea fish must be tentative. While all the examples of this fish that have been studied have behaved in the same way, the scientist has not been able to study enough examples to be fairly certain that there are no exceptions.

In examining any generalization, then, the first thing to do is to look for the word which asserts that the alleged "truth" is unexceptionably true. If it is there, we should question it: Are there *really* no exceptions? If it is not there, but is implied, we should question it still: are there *really* no exceptions?

We have already spoken of the other type of generalization, equally valid if correctly stated, which freely admits the possibility of exceptions, perhaps of many exceptions; all it claims is that a certain phenomenon occurs in a majority of cases—that "in general" or "viewing society as a whole" or "as a group" something is true, or that "the trend is toward" something else. This kind of generalization is especially frequent in discussions of human behavior, which is notoriously less predictable than the behavior of molecules or amoebae. Scientists use it just as freely as they do the sweeping kind which admits no exceptions. But when such a qualified generalization stands as the major premise of a syllogism, the conclusion must be carefully framed to preserve the idea of probability rather than certainty. If the major premise admits the possibility of exceptions, the conclusion also must do so.

(Major premise)	Studies show that adults have a harder time memorizing material than do children.
(Minor premise)	Mr. Smith must memorize some formulas for his night school class.
(Conclusion)	Mr. Smith will have a harder time memorizing this material than if he were a child.

This is incorrectly stated, because, although the general import of the premise is true beyond question, the phraseology does not provide for the occasional exception. The conclusion therefore does not provide for the possibility, however small, that Mr. Smith may be unusual in respect to memorizing ability. A correct statement would be:

(Major premise)	Studies show that *most* adults have a harder time memorizing material than do children.
(Minor premise)	Mr. Smith must memorize some formulas for his night school class.
(Conclusion)	Mr. Smith *probably* will have a harder time memorizing material than if he were a child.

In assessing the validity of syllogisms based on such generalizations, therefore, we must ask if the writer took the possibility of exception into account. It is really not necessary, in ordinary writing, to be so careful to qualify a premise; in practice, especially when discussing questions of individual or mass human behavior, the writer tacitly allows for exceptions: "men who come to college after army service (taken as a group) are better students than the rest"; "the crime rate (in most cities) is highest in the slums"; "the efficiency of stenographers is improved (in nine cases out of ten) if they work in air-conditioned offices"; "the children of divorced parents (as a rule) have two strikes against them in life." But the danger here is that the uncritical reader will not provide for the possibility of exceptions, if it is not specifically mentioned, and will therefore follow the reasoning through to an unwarranted conclusion. "Psychologists show that boys' minds mature more slowly than girls'. Bob and Mary are both sixteen. Therefore Mary's mind is more mature than Bob's."

But even if the generalization is hedged with what seem to be sufficiently cautious qualifications, its truth is still to be demonstrated. Often a reader is thrown off guard by the writer's willingness to concede the possibility of exceptions, which suggests that he is a careful, sober, scientifically-minded person, unwilling to sacrifice truth for the purposes of his argument. Granting that such cautiousness is a good sign, we must still ask for evidence for the generalization. To be sound, it must be based upon three conditions: (1) the number of instances examined must be sufficiently large to permit a confident generalization; (2) these instances must be as typical as possible, not selected or weighted in any way; (3) the results of the investigation must show a definite numerical preponderance on one side or another. It must not be forgotten that there are many situations in which the cases may be pretty evenly distributed on both sides of the dividing line. Statistics which show that women, who constitute one-third of all the licensed automobile drivers of a certain state, are involved in one-third of all the fatal accidents in that state, prove nothing except that women can compete on equal terms with men. But if on the other hand it were shown that women were involved in more than one-half of the fatal accidents, a fairly acceptable generalization could be drawn concerning the ability of women, in at least one state, to handle cars.

Suppose we take the question of the superiority of veterans over non-veterans as college students. A college professor may say that "veterans are better students than non-veterans." What he means is that in his necessarily limited experience, and to his probably biased mind, veterans have proved better "teaching material" (however he may define the term) than non-veterans. Such a judgment must be regarded solely as an expression of personal opinion, being subjective and based on far too few instances. The dean of the college—which, let us say, is one specializing in engineering—may then issue a statistical report which shows that for the year just ended, the veterans' average grade score (on a 4.0 basis) was 2.756, while the non-veterans' average was 2.447. There were 967 veterans and 477 non-veterans in college that year. Such a report is of more value than the professor's, but its value is still limited, because while it is based on objective statistics, the cases are few in comparison with the total number of veterans in colleges throughout the country. Furthermore, the difference between the two point-scores is not great enough to be significant; and the college is of a specialized sort in which the veterans' army-learned skills would be of some value. The dean says, in effect, "In our college the veterans were somewhat better than the non-veterans." But now suppose that an ambitious research worker assembles reports from some fifty institutions of every description, from liberal arts colleges to schools of engineering, and geographically scattered from Maine to California. He emerges with a report showing that in these fifty institutions, with a total of 76,980 veterans and 27,805 non-veterans, the veterans' average in point-scores for the year was some 35% higher than that of the non-veterans. Now, at last, we have adequate justification for the generalization. It is based upon a sufficient number of examples, widely scattered, and the margin of superiority is clear. If the research worker were to analyze the records of fifty more institutions, it is probable that his new results would closely approximate the first ones.

The operation of the most responsible of the public opinion polls, whose stock-in-trade is the making of trustworthy generalizations, illustrates this principle of statistical caution. They go to elaborate lengths to interview a number of persons sufficient, they feel, to permit generalization, and to distribute their interviews among various sections of the country and among various income-groups and occupations so that they will have a reasonably true cross section of that amorphous entity known as "the American public." A generalization on the state of national feeling regarding America's participation in the United Nations Organization would be worthless if it were based upon interviews with, let us say, fifty Iowa farmers, fifty students at the College of the City of New York, fifty Atlanta housewives, and fifty Los Angeles bus drivers—and no one else.

General statements containing or implying such phrases as *tends to, majority, most, as a group,* etc., should, therefore, be examined no less critically than those which contain or imply the categorical *every, only, always,* etc. There is as much danger in the generalization that says "Most Germans are incurably militaristic" as there is in the one that says "All Germans are incurably militaristic." To assert that something is true in the majority of cases requires as much carefully gathered and examined evidence as to say that it is always true.

Exercise 7. Comment on the inductive reasoning reflected in each of the following examples:

1. A Gentile college student roomed with a Jewish classmate for three years. "The Jews are O.K.," he says. "My roommate was a straight shooter, intelligent, modest, a real friend." His father, a salesman, worked under a Jewish sales manager for the same length of time. "The Jews ought to be run out of America," he says. "My boss was arbitrary, overbearing, conceited, and ignorant."—Which judgment, the son's or the father's, is more nearly true?
2. I don't like to be snobbish, but give me the rich children to teach any day. I've been teaching for five years, and consistently the children from well-to-do homes have been more intelligent and better-trained than those from poor homes.
3. I'll never deal with him again; he sells inferior merchandise. Last week he sold me a can of peaches that were spoiled.
4. If you doubt that the labor movement in America is corrupt, read Westbrook Pegler's exposures of some of the racketeering unions. Every union in the country ought to be broken up.
5. On two separate occasions today I was jostled in the streetcar

by Negroes. You can't tell me the colored aren't getting too big for their boots. They behave that way to whites all the time.

6. If you want to lose your faith in democracy, go into the Senate Chamber some day and watch the lawmakers reading the newspapers, paring their nails, chewing tobacco, and sleeping while one of their number makes a speech.

EXERCISE 8. Judge the validity of the following conclusions:

1. In surveys conducted in ten leading American cities, it was found that more women use Gl'amour Soap for their skins than any other brand! It must be good!
2. If you seek evidence of the total bestiality of the German people, remember Belsen and Dachau.
3. In one sorority house, 75% of the girls admitted that they indulged in heavy petting. This generation of American youth is hopelessly immoral.
4. The success of the course, which was established purely as experiment, may be gauged from the fact that Professor N—— has received over fifty letters of approval and not a single one of protest.
5. Yes, he may have been born in this country, but he's a Jap just the same. Whenever I see him, I think back to Pearl Harbor. I wouldn't trust him for *anything*.

EXERCISE 9. The following statements are the results of inductive reasoning. Criticize them first on the basis of phraseology—that is, are all terms accurately defined? Then specify the kind of evidence you would require if you were to be convinced of the truth of each statement.

1. A declining birthrate inevitably accompanies the industrialization of a country.
2. A college education is an indispensable prerequisite to success in the business world.
3. Difficulties in training men for technical jobs in the armed serv-

ices during World War II revealed how inadequate had been the public schools' teaching of science and mathematics.

4. The New Deal economic measures succeeded in effecting a more equitable distribution of the national wealth.
5. The I.Q.'s of school children can be noticeably raised over a period of years if their home environment and their health are improved.
6. Prices of a commodity drop if the supply increases but rise if the demand increases.
7. In the past century the life expectancy of both men and women has steadily increased.

Other Abuses of Logic

Thus far we have noted the following kinds of loose thinking:

1. The major premise (generalization) which declares that a given "fact" is *always* true when such is not the case.

2. The major premise (generalization) which declares that a given "fact" is *usually* true—decidedly more true than its contrary—when such is not the case.

3. The minor premise which is not covered by the generalization of the major premise.

4. The *non sequitur*—a false conclusion based upon individually sound premises.

We need now to add to this list a number of other often-met abuses of logical thinking. Here are the most common of them:

5. The argument *ad hominem*. This is the fallacy which diverts attention from the true issue by appealing directly to one's personal feelings. A student who is about to receive a failing grade in a college course says to his instructor, "Put yourself in my place. How would *you* like to flunk this course?" The argument, while admittedly touching, is unreasonable. The

point at issue is solely whether or not the student had done passing work in the course. The instructor can reply with justice that while he probably would not like to flunk, he would have taken better care to make a passing grade.

6. The argument *ad populum*. We have already encountered this extremely common fallacy under the terms "name calling" and "glittering generality." It consists of appealing to one's emotions and prejudices rather than to his reason. "The strike obviously was engineered by communistic and Bolshevik elements in the union." "By the merger the industrial dynasty founded a century ago by the robber baron C—— tightened its vise-like grip upon the cotton industry."

7. The argument *ad verecundiam*. ("Transfer" is a more easily remembered name.) In this device, the writer or speaker, instead of following a course of logical persuasion, attempts to clothe his pet policy or principle in borrowed raiment which will lend it a strength and dignity it could not possess by itself. Like the use of name-calling and the glittering generality, it depends upon one's willingness to associate one idea with another, even though the two are not logically connected.

A common example of it is the habit which political orators have of working into their speeches quotations from Scripture or from the secular "sacred writings" (the Declaration of Independence, the preamble to the Constitution, the Gettysburg address). Such quotations are depended upon to arouse favorable emotions in the breasts of the auditors, emotions which are then transferred to the orator's pet policy. Much of William Jennings Bryan's success as a public figure was due to the way in which he transformed an ordinary political campaign into a quasi-religious crusade by his "Cross of Gold" speech: "You shall not press down upon the brow of labor this crown of thorns; you shall not crucify mankind upon a cross of gold!" Actually, although the underlying idea, that the national monetary policy at the end of the nineteenth century worked to the serious disadvantage of the "common man," was entirely valid, the metaphor in which it was expressed was not. There is no connection between economics and the passion and crucifixion of Jesus. But the metaphor succeeded admirably in rallying to Bryan's ranks millions of Americans to whom Biblical quotation and allusion had the most powerful of connotations. It is noteworthy that as the influence of the Bible upon men's emotional habits declines, knowing politicians make less use of Biblical references; but such standard emotion-rousers as mention of Valley Forge, the Founding Fathers, and Abraham Lincoln are still found sprinkled through much propaganda. Whether they have any logical connection with the issues discussed is, to the speaker and (he hopes) to his audience, irrelevant; what they do is shed their own emotional effulgence upon ideas and pleas which might not otherwise be so acceptable.

The advertiser employs the transfer device just as commonly. Perhaps the most familiar instance of it is the use of the picture of a beautiful girl, not merely to attract attention to the advertisement but also to place the reader in a receptive frame of mind. Whether the girl has anything to do with the subject of the advertisement does not matter—so long as the reader is pleasantly affected. At certain periods when patriotic sentiment runs high, as during a war, commercial advertisers use the emotional symbols of patriotism for their own ends. Not only do they use the national colors and pictures of, or references to, the fighting men; their text often is designed to arouse fervent patriotic emotions which can then be transferred to a particular product. During World War II the following advertisement, dominated by a large drawing of the eagle on the United States seal, appeared in eastern newspapers:

PRIDE IN THE AMERICAN WAY

The way of life that is American, that expounds democracy, is a proud way of life. It is a manner of living so fine, so high in ideals and purpose that it stands over and above all others. The Grabosky Family, makers of Royalist cigars, are proud to be members of The American Family, proud to present a cigar so fine in quality that it stands above all others. Over 50 years of superb cigar-making experience lie behind Royalist . . . a proud name in a proud America!*

The device of borrowing prestige from one institution, such as religion or nation, to adorn something else, perhaps less admirable, is also used increasingly in the case of science and medicine. The American people have come to feel for the laboratory scientist and the physician an awe once reserved for bishops and statesmen. The alleged approval of such men thus carries great weight when it is a question of selling something, or (which is the same thing) inducing someone to believe something. Phrases such as "leading medical authorities say . . ." or "independent laboratory tests show . . ." are designed simply to transfer the prestige of science, which presumably is incapable of either error or corruption, to a toothpaste or a cereal. Seldom if ever are the precise "medical authorities" or "independent laboratories" named. But the mere phrases have vast weight with the uncritical. Similarly too the honorific "Dr." or "professor" implies that the person quoted speaks with all the authority of which learned men are capable—when as a matter of fact "doctorates" can be bought from mail-order colleges. Whenever, therefore, an attempt is made to convince by appeal to the prestige that surrounds the learned, the reader should demand full credentials. Just *what* medical authorities say this? Can they be trusted? *What* independent laboratories made the test—and what, actu-

* Note that the brand name of the cigar is not conspicuously in harmony with the sentiments expressed in the advertisement itself; yet it probably sells the cigars. Why?

ally, did the tests reveal? Who is this man that speaks as a qualified educator or psychologist or economist? Regardless of the fact that he is called "doctor," does he know what he is talking about?

8. Begging the question. Here the statement which is ostensibly offered as a proposition to be proved, actually assumes the proposition as already proved. "This ordinance will certainly reduce juvenile delinquency, because it provides for steps which will prevent crimes on the part of teen-agers." In other words, A is good because A is good. "The reason why Sally is so mischievous is that she has just a little of the devil in her." "I would trust him with any of my personal affairs because he is certainly a reliable lawyer."

Every instance of name-calling or of the glittering generality is an example of question-begging. When a writer or speaker brands someone a "dangerous radical" or acclaims a policy as "the only way to escape national disaster" he is using words the truth of which he never questions—nor expects his audience to question. Yet all such words and phrases, weighted as they are with emotion and charged with controversy, stand very much in need of proof. Any piece of persuasion that uses them is false, because the issue actually has been pre-judged.

9. The *post hoc ergo propter hoc* fallacy. In Sinclair Lewis's *Arrowsmith,* the bubonic plague in a West Indian island subsided after the inhabitants had been inoculated with a certain hitherto unproved vaccine. Many people immediately proclaimed the new treatment as the positive cure for the plague; but Arrowsmith, a careful scientist, knew that the reason why the plague subsided might equally well have been that it had already reached its peak at the time the inoculations began. In other words, he refused to assume that because B (the subsidence of the plague) happened *after* A (the immunization), B therefore happened *because* of A. That is the literal meaning of *post*

hoc ergo propter hoc: "after this, therefore because of this." It is a most common error to assume that because something occurred after something else, it must necessarily have been caused by that antecedent circumstance. "No wonder you have a cold today. You didn't change your wet clothes when you came home yesterday." "We gave the administration a free hand in regulating our national economy. Now look what we have on our hands: a first-class depression." "It rained hard the night after the battle, thus proving the old notion that the firing of the guns precipitates rain." The simple answer to all such assertions is, "Weren't there any other possible causes?"

10. False analogy. This fallacy consists of presenting a situation which is acknowledged to be true, and then, on the basis of it, commenting on another situation which is said to be similar. It is usually employed in an attempt to simplify and make more vivid a complex issue. Newspaper political cartoons are often nothing more than pictorial analogies. Often, of course, such analogies serve admirably to point up, dramatically and colorfully, the crux of a problem. The analogy of a governmental agency in the role of the legendary Dutch boy, trying desperately to stop a leak in the dike ("national economy") while the waves of the sea ("inflation") are already spilling over the top of the dike, is plainly very useful. But the ever-present danger is that the analogy will assume a vital resemblance between the two objects of comparison, where none really exists. "Don't change horses in the middle of a stream" is a familiar cry in political campaigns when, pleading a national emergency, the partisans of the incumbent in office declare he cannot be superseded without grave danger to the country. There is, of course, a superficial similarity between the two situations: changing horses in the middle of a swift stream is dangerous, and so too may be changing public officials at certain junctures in national affairs. But riding horseback is not much like being president of the United

States, and while there may be only one or two reasons why one should or should not change horses, there may be very many reasons, none of them having anything to do with horseback riding, why one man should be elected president and another not. Equally dangerous is any attempt to prove a point which is based on the fancy that the nations of the world are like schoolchildren, and that when one nation does not have its way it goes into a corner and sulks; or that two opponents, labor and capital, for example, may be likened to two prize-fighters squaring off in the ring, with some governmental official or agency as referee. Such analogies are, we repeat, useful in dramatizing a situation; but it is always perilous to maintain that because two situations are "alike" in one or two respects, what is true of one is necessarily true of the other.

11. Oversimplification. False analogy may well be considered a particular type of oversimplification—than which there is no more common error. With our natural human indolence, to say nothing of our intellectual limitations, we are always eager to view questions in their simplest terms and to make our decision upon the basis of only a few of the many aspects which the problem involves. Few, if any, of the decisions which we are called upon to make are so simple that we can say with confidence that one choice is completely right and the other is completely wrong. The problem of the so-called minority groups in America, for instance, is not simply one of abstract justice, as many would like to think it; it involves deeply complex questions of economics, sociology, and politics. Nor can one say with easy assurance: "The British should give India her independence." Morally there is no question that they should; judging the issue as a simple one of right or wrong, most people would agree that any nation deserves to be free. Viewed against the background of history, furthermore, India's claims seem even more solidly justified; there are many unlovely chapters in the history of British imperial

rule of India, chapters involving merchants' greed and civil servants' stupidity and soldiers' wanton brutality. But as in so many situations—and this is as true in connection with the relations between individual persons as it is with the relations between countries—a judgment based on an ethical ideal collides head-on with practical realities. Anyone who is at all familiar with the Indian situation knows that the question of British rule in India is tied up not only with the economics of empire but also with the infinitely delicate problem of the Indian religions—which in turn vitally affects the Indian social system. The abrupt and complete withdrawal of British rule from India would result in unthinkable chaos. The triumph of "right" would precipitate countless new "wrongs." And that is the dilemma in which the British find themselves. Undoubtedly they honestly want to assure justice for India. It is only the naïve man, blind to the realities of the Indian situation, who can reduce the issue to the simple one of right or wrong.

Countless false generalizations concerning parties, races, religions, and nations—to say nothing of individuals—are the result of the deep-seated human desire to reduce a complex idea to its simplest terms. Democrats tend naturally to think of all Republicans as progress-obstructing conservatives, when in fact many Republicans may be more "liberal" than many Democrats. Many Protestants regard Catholics as bigoted and superstitious, even though the views they regard as "bigoted" and the practices they regard as "superstitious" may have their roots deep in the philosophical grounds of the Catholic religion. Similarly many Catholics regard Protestants as infidels or atheists, although there may be as much philosophical justification for Protestant doctrine as there is for Catholic. It is easier to condemn than to understand. But every man and woman has a pressing moral, as well as intellectual, obligation to examine the basis of every judgment he or she makes: "Am I examining every aspect of the issue that needs to be examined—do I understand the pros and cons of the problem sufficiently to be able to make a fair decision—or am I taking the easiest way out?"

12. This innate intellectual laziness of human beings invites one further, crowning device of deception: the distortion or the actual suppression of the truth. If men will not actively demand the truth, why should persuaders provide them with it, when doing so would hurt their chances of success? And so it is usual in all forms of persuasion to prevent considerations which would damage the cause from reaching the minds of those who are to be persuaded.

One such device—there are many—is card stacking (also called "smoke screen"*), which is used by a group, a political party for instance, to divert attention from certain issues which it does not care to have discussed. Card stacking consists of laying heavy and insistent emphasis upon certain selected topics, discussion of which can probably do the party no harm. The party then hopes that the public, its attention centered on these topics, will not bother about the less attractive side of the party's record or program. A state administration, running for re-election, may devote all its propaganda to boasting about the reduction in state taxes which it has effected in an "economy program"—and it will assiduously fail to mention the way in which state services have deteriorated as a result of the "slashed budget." This same practice is evident in virtually every advertisement one reads. The attractive points of a product are dwelt upon unceasingly; the less attractive ones, never. An automobile may be streamlined and easy-riding, it may have fast pickup in traffic, it may have a one-piece body—these facts will be proclaimed from every

* Although their purposes are the same, card stacking and the smoke screen have slightly different techniques. The first is usually prepared in advance; the second is impromptu, being devised to meet exigencies as they occur in the course of an argument.

newspaper, magazine, and billboard; but that the car eats up gasoline and oil, has a poorly made engine block, and costs $200 more than other cars in the same price-class—these facts are religiously suppressed. But, as you will no doubt agree, they are worth knowing about.

Another, closely related, means by which attention is drawn from the whole truth is one dear to every practical politician: the red herring. The red herring is an irrelevant issue which is drawn across the path of an argument when one side or the other is becoming embarrassed and wishes to change the subject. In a campaign for the mayoralty of a large city, for example, Party A (which is in office) may find itself in serious trouble because Party B has successfully given evidence of its waste of public funds. Four days before the election, therefore, Party A suddenly "discovers" that Party B's candidate has been seen in night clubs with a lady who is not his wife. Party A hopes that the injection into the contest of another, more appealing, topic of discussion will allow the public to forget the serious accusations that have been levelled against it. Whether or not Party A is able to prove that the B candidate's private frailties (if they do exist) disqualify him from holding public office, the red herring will have served its purpose if it ends the embarrassing talk about Party A's own shortcomings.

A third such device is that of wrenching from context. A sentence or a phrase can easily mean one thing when it is quoted alone, and a quite different thing if it is read against the background of the whole discussion to which it belongs. An extreme example is the case of a sentence from a newspaper review of a new movie: "For about five minutes 'Fruits of Desire' is a top-notch show, brilliantly acted and magnificently photographed. After that it degenerates into a dismal spectacle of Hollywood hokum." It would not be surprising to see the subsequent advertisements of the movie flaunting this headline: " 'A top-notch show, brilliantly acted and magnificently photographed . . . a spectacle'—Smith, *Daily News*." The familiar "avoid foreign entanglements" advice in Washington's farewell address, when read in full context, means something very different from what it means when quoted separately. And probably no public figure whose statements are quoted in the newspapers or on the radio has ever escaped the chagrin that comes from seeing prominence given to one or two paragraphs of his latest speech which, thus isolated, completely distort his total argument. Such quotations must always be read with the greatest caution. The only way to be sure that they fairly represent the author's viewpoint is to read the complete text of his speech as printed in, for instance, the *New York Times*.

In this chapter we may seem on many occasions to have wandered rather far from our principal theme, the use of language as such; but surely it has become obvious, by now, how intimately and inextricably language and logic are associated. A word remains to be said as to how the essential weakness of many ideas can be concealed from the unwary by plausible language.

The more confident the manner of the writer or speaker is, the more necessary it is to inquire what makes him so confident. His forthright assertion that "every right-thinking man will agree . . ." or "there can be no question that . . ." or "it has been proved time and again that . . ." may be completely unjustified; certainly it should not be accepted on his mere say-so. Dogmatism—which is what this fault really amounts to—has no place in genuinely intelligent discussion. The dogmatic writer or speaker is using devices of style to hypnotize possible doubters. "This man knows what he's talking about!" . . . Does he?

Rhetorical questions also serve to hypnotize the uncritical.

"Has this party not served the state faithfully for twelve critical years? Has it not increased the state's industrial capacity? Has it not completed a highway system that is the envy of the nation? Has it not set up a fine social security system to protect the unfortunate and helpless? Can the people of this state therefore *afford* not to return this party for another four years?" Rhetorical questions always take the answer for granted: disagreement is not provided for. But it should be. The expected answers are not necessarily the right ones. And in any event, the questions have been carefully chosen for the purpose. The opposition might with equal propriety ask another set relating to the past twelve years of state government—and get very different answers.

The use of proverbs, axioms, and other "folk truths" also has its gently narcotic effect upon the critical intelligence. Because we have lived so long with such generalizations, few of which we have ever bothered to examine, and because they came to us from sources whose authority and wisdom we revere—Scripture or parents or teacher—we accept them on sight. "All is fair in love and war"—"to the victor belong the spoils"—"the gods help them that help themselves"—"a soft answer turneth away wrath" —these are observations which undoubtedly contain much truth, springing as they do from the long experience of the race. But they can never be used to "prove" anything. A man defending a certain governmental policy of expediency says succinctly that "the end justifies the means"; but does it *in this case?* Might not the means result in more harm than failure to achieve the end? Merely because we have grown up accustomed to believing such a thing, are we obliged therefore to accept it as justification for a deed which, if we were to come right down to it, could not be justified on any logical or moral grounds? Familiar gems of popular wisdom, then, have only limited usefulness in intelligent discussion. They may never be taken on faith.

EXERCISE 10. Identify the specific fallacy or fallacies involved in each case.

1. We must, in our own hearts, destroy intolerance. Protestants and Catholics, Jews and Gentiles, colored and white, first generation Americans and Mayflower descendants, we are all Americans. There can be no divided allegiance. He who is not with us is against us. There is no middle way. There is no place for the merchant of hate in America. "Fox holes" in desert and jungle and rafts adrift in open seas make for deep religious convictions. Sacrifice and sweat on the home front should soften men's hearts. Peace and religion are essential to American life. They are our assurances for the future.

   Peace with liberty was the hope, the ambition and the prayer of those who founded this Republic. Its achievement is still the great issue and the object for which the present conflict is being waged. The conditions under which it can be achieved are no different today than they were in the bitter winter of Valley Forge. These conditions were set forth simply and truthfully by the Apostle Paul when he said, "Where the spirit of the Lord is there is liberty."
2. I like Hemingway's "The Killers" because I always have liked stories such as this, and I particularly like Hemingway.
3. Maybe I *was* too hasty in hitting him, but let me ask you this: what would *you* have done if he had said that to you?
4. The radio has been chiefly responsible for the great increase of interest in serious music in the past twenty years.
5. You're SURE when you say Metropolitan Opera . . . Sure that the "Met" offers the finest opera in the world . . . presented with true artistic perfection since its opening with Gounod's "Faust" on October 22, 1883.

You're SURE when you say Royal Worcester . . . Sure of lovely porcelain unsurpassed for beauty . . . prized by collectors as the finest examples of eighteen-century English pottery-making.

You're SURE when you say Seagram's . . . Sure of superb whiskies unsurpassed for true pre-war quality . . . prized as the finest examples of exquisite taste and mellow smoothness!

6. Shakespeare seems to have left Stratford-on-Avon soon after the birth of his first children, who remained behind with their mother. This lends great weight to the idea that his frequent representations of domestic troubles upon the stage had their origin in the events of his own personal life.
7. "That God is, the Bible affirms. Whatever the Bible affirms is true, because it is from God, and declares it is impossible for God to lie. Therefore the existence of God is surely proved."
8. You can argue for universal military training all you want, but how would you like *your* son to be forced to spend a year in the army?
9. It is not you who are bombed out, shivering, homeless, and hungry in the depth of winter; it is not you who look trustingly to unscathed, comfortable Americans for aid in surviving until spring! Then help the suffering citizens of the European nations which bent under the Nazi yoke! Give generously to the Relief Fund!
10. Figures can't lie. In nine cases out of ten, men with throat irritations who switched to Smootho cigarettes reported that within two weeks their irritations either disappeared or were definitely improved. What more dramatic proof is needed that Smoothos are kinder to the delicate membranes of the throat?
11. The Commonwealth will prove, gentlemen of the jury, that this criminal sitting before you, this ruthless enemy of society, shot —— —— in cold blood, with malice aforethought.
12. "It is noteworthy that all these men . . . are professors of physics, which means that they know what they are talking about and that their explanations are accurate."

EXERCISE 11. Make a collection of current newspaper cartoons as examples of possibly false or misleading analogies. What is the basis of the implied resemblance between the two situations? What does the cartoonist imply by selecting that particular analogy? How far can the analogy be logically extended?

EXERCISE 12. Make a collection of "letters to the editor" in the local newspapers and analyze them intensively for examples of the various types of fallacies discussed in this chapter.

EXERCISE 13. Comment on the oversimplified thinking reflected in parts 4, 8, 9, and 10 of Exercise 6 (page 123).

EXERCISE 14. This is a group of miscellaneous quotations to be examined for all sorts of fallacies as well as for abuses of connotative language.

1. "To those who are denied the opportunity of a college education, International Correspondence Schools offers a satisfying substitute. I know. I studied an I.C.S. course myself."

2. Comment on the following letter, printed in *Time,* December 3, 1945, and on the reply, published three weeks later:

   Sirs:

   There seems to be a lot of criticism of the behavior of our Army of Occupation. Some of our free-born citizens are showing shocked surprise that the American soldier is not acting like the true, red-blooded, 100% American the blueprints originally called for. Well, gentlemen, brace yourselves; I am coming out swinging.

   Just what do you critics expect from a generation that has been brought up on comic books, flabby popular music, motion pictures that are hag-ridden by the Hays office and the Legion of so-called Decency, and the unending flood of nauseating pap that drools from our shiny little radios? Who is responsible for the fact that our young men now helling about Europe and lousing up the reputation of the U. S. have their heads stuffed with nonsense?

You are, gentlemen, and you might as well face it. Our young people don't think because they haven't been taught to think. . . . Have you done anything to remedy this?

You can't take his comic book or his radio away from him now because he's used to them and he might cry, but you can work for, fight for a decent, liberal educational system, for better pay for teachers so that better teachers will come to nourish the minds of the next generation. You can stop patronizing the stupidest 90% of Hollywood's products until they stop making them and are forced to use talent, intelligence and new ideas. You can demand that your radio station devote more time to adult entertainment. You can club together and go out after the hide, ears and tail of the Prohibition Party, the Watch and Ward Society and all other Nosey Parker institutions for the small, unoccupied mind. In a nutshell, you can throw your weight around for a more mature, tolerant, beautiful America into which to lead the next dewy-eyed batch of moppets. . . .

I have five young children, healthy, handsome, confident that they live in the best and most beautiful part of the finest country in the world. I will hate to see their faces when they discover they are citizens of a third-class country with first-class equipment.

Leroy Blodgett

Sirs:

Did you print that letter about the States being a third-class country to start a riot, or did you think you had to show us that there are 4-Fs like Leroy Blodgett?

This man, Leroy Blodgett, is supposed to be old enough to have five children, but does not have sense enough to hold his tongue, or ink, when he hears a report of misbehavior of our Army of Occupation. We all know the kind of personality who tries to build himself up, by seizing every opportunity to run down the people who are doing a big job. . . .

I came home with the conviction that an American is about the finest thing you can find in a dirty European street, and I'm hanging on to that conviction in spite of the bird-brained Blodgetts who live in a third-class country of their imaginations.

J. O. Harvey

3. Comment on the following letter, printed in the *New York Times,* January 13, 1946, in reply to one by Bing Crosby in which he deplored a popular jazz adaptation of a Chopin polonaise:

"The orchestra played 'Till the End of Time' on my wedding day and it is my favorite song. I first heard the song in the Pacific and later saw it in the Army 'Hit Kit.' I have always liked Crosby, but I certainly know he pulled a 'boner' when he criticized this beautiful love song.—Ex-G.I."

4. "My friend took the lady's ungloved hand, and examined it with as close an attention and as little sentiment as a scientist would show to a specimen.

" 'You will excuse me, I am sure. It is my business,' said he, as he dropped it. 'I nearly fell into the error of supposing that you were typewriting. Of course, it is obvious that it is music. You observe the spatulate finger-ends, Watson, which is common to both professions? There is a spirituality about the face, however' —she gently turned it towards the light—'which the typewriter does not generate. This lady is a musician.'

" 'Yes, Mr. Holmes, I teach music.' "

5. JANUARY 14

SIX QUESTIONS EVERY SERIOUS-MINDED TIMKEN MAN AND WOMAN SHOULD ASK THEMSELVES BEFORE MAKING ONE OF THE MOST IMPORTANT DECISIONS OF THEIR LIVES.

Should a strike be called January 14? If it is, you will have an important decision to make: whether to go out or not, and you must make that vital decision yourself. No one can honestly make it for you.

But before you decide ask yourself these questions:

1. With Whom Should I Place My Destiny?
2. Who in the long run can do most for me, my family and my community?
3. Who aside from my Company can better assure me regular employment?
4. How will this strike affect the regular inflow of orders and the final steadiness of my job?
5. Am I honestly convinced that the strike is justified—that no other means can be found to settle the issue involved without my losing a lot of money and jeopardizing my Company's ability to go on employing me?
6. Who but my Company protects me and my family with hospitalization; and me with insurance against accident, sickness and death?

These are some of the questions you and you alone must answer, before you make one of the most important decisions of your life.

6. The following appeared in a widely syndicated newspaper column written by a man whose specialty is applying psychology to the emotional problems of his readers.

CASE J-206: Dr. Galen Starr Ross, aged 54, is the president of Capitol College at Columbus.

"We are trying to set an example to the larger universities," he informed me recently when I visited in his office.

"In our curriculum and faculty we emphasize that this nation is a republic, and that the 'free enterprise' system is not only typically American, but has given us the highest standard of living enjoyed by any people, anywhere on the face of the earth.

"Too many college professors have taken a somewhat sneering view of American enterprise, and are preaching the age-old system of Socialism where the central government dictates to its citizens in the outlying provinces.

"America was founded by God-fearing men and women who did not want a controlled economy by a central dictatorship. They had seen such dictatorships all around them in Europe when they fled to America as a land of liberty and freedom of initiative."

For 25 years I have been associated with our leading universities in the East and Midwest, where I have likewise witnessed this pernicious infiltration of Socialism into our curriculum.

"Government control" is now the fashionable viewpoint and motif of many college professors of economics and sociology.

But "government control" is an alien, un-American doctrine. It is what Nero demonstrated. It was Napoleon's policy. It was Hitler's thesis.

I have publicly debated with a prominent professor of the University of Chicago, who is a rabble rouser, advocating Socialism and sneering at American business.

He is typical of a large number of college professors who stand before gullible teen-agers, for students enter colleges at 17.

He has done enough soap-box orating to be glib and clever, at least before the untutored teen-agers. They think he is clever as he brashly indicts big business and wants the state to own and operate our country.

It is right and proper that Socialism and Communism be taught to college students, IF they likewise obtain a clear exposition of our republican type of government and the free enterprise system in the same orientation course.

But the danger is that so many students major under a man like this University of Chicago professor, who gives them but one side, so they graduate without ever having a clear picture of the American system.

Our system was summarized succinctly by Woodrow Wilson when he said it should offer "a free field and no favor."

It believes that Uncle Sam should be a referee or umpire, but not a competitor with his citizens.

Wherever possible, Uncle Sam should stay out of business and mining and railroading and other ventures in which private citizens try to earn their livings and derive the money to pay Uncle Sam the taxes which he demands.

This republic is the most unique type of government in the world today, and under our free enterprise system, it even furnished the tanks and guns and planes and trucks with which Communistic Russia helped win the war.*

* Reprinted by permission of Dr. George W. Crane.

CHAPTER FOUR

Sentences and Paragraphs

THUS FAR we have seen how it is possible to "read between the lines" by analyzing the implications of a writer's choice of words and by examining his habits of thought. We turn now to still another means by which we can discover more than appears on the surface of any example of communication: the analysis of form.

The sentence is a basic unit of communication. Individual words have relatively little meaning until they are arranged into a sentence. Nouns stand for objects, verbs for actions, and so on, but they do not stand for a complete idea until they are fitted into a certain sequence and their interrelationship made clear by the use of prepositions, conjunctions, and other parts of speech. Babies begin by uttering single words. Often, it is true, they succeed in communicating important ideas to their parents, but that is only because the parents are able to infer from single words the sentences which the baby is as yet unable to put together. Later the child begins to utter simple sentences; and when he does, we know that he has reached the stage where he understands elementary relationships between ideas. As he progresses toward adulthood, his sentences become more and more complex: a sign that he is gradually extending his command of ideas to include more complicated relationships. And to his college instructor, his ability to write good sentences is a more valuable measure of his ability to think than is a whole battery of intelligence tests. The college freshman who writes in short, simple, elementary-school sentences, shying away from subordinate clauses and other such complications, will seldom prove to have great intelligence. On the other hand, the freshman who knows how to use the devices of grammar and rhetoric to clarify and sharpen his meaning, and for whom such things as subordination hold no terrors, cannot fail to impress his teacher with his ability to recognize thought-relationships and to discriminate between the essential and the auxiliary parts of what he has to say.

Thus the length and structure of sentences, as well as the length and structure of paragraphs (the next largest unit of composition), can serve as valuable clues to the mental ability of the writer or speaker. They can also throw light upon his sincerity of purpose and upon his skill in judging the capabilities and expectations of his audience. And in this chapter we shall take some space to examine also the closely connected subject of sentence- and paragraph-rhythm. In the end we shall have put another string to the bow by which we can pierce to the heart of meaning.

(At this point, if you have any doubt at all as to what is meant by "subordination," look up the subject in your handbook of composition and study it thoroughly. The following discussion assumes a sound elementary knowledge of the principles of subordination and sentence-construction from the writer's viewpoint.)

Sentence Length

First of all, how long a sentence is most desirable for the purposes of normal expository communication? Obviously we can rule out both the extremely short, which does not allow the writer to show the logical interrelationships of his ideas, and the extremely long, which confuses the reader. The former type has no room for the necessary subordination; the latter, by having too much room for subordination, tempts the writer to put too much into a single thought-unit. Evidently, then, we must seek a happy medium.

Of course there never can be a universal standard of sentence length. For one thing, sentence-length depends upon the complexity of the idea to be expressed. A simple, unqualified, blunt statement requires a very short sentence; a statement of a more subtle idea, hedged about with modifications and restrictions, usually requires a longer sentence.

Furthermore, fashions in sentence-length change. Whenever we read in older books—Dickens, for example, or Scott, or Shakespeare, or Boswell, or Milton—we are struck by their authors' frequent use of what seem to us to be very long sentences. Milton's poems contain sentences running to thirty or more lines of verse. In some epochs the best writers of English prose produced sentences several hundred words in length. And they are good sentences, too; though their thought is complex, and they can scarcely be skimmed through, they are themselves works of art; they have an unmistakable architectural beauty, graceful and at the same time massive.

But in our time the tendency has been steadily in the direction of shorter sentences. The reasons are plain. About a hundred years ago, the great masses of people in England and America for the first time had the chance to learn to read. Since as a rule they went to school only for a few years, their reading ability was limited; everything that they read had to be in simple English, the vocabulary limited to familiar, everyday words, and the sentences brief and simple. And since these readers constituted an immense new market for reading matter, especially for newspapers, the publishers took great pains to have their writers adapt their styles to the limited abilities of the new audience. The trend toward simplicity was not confined by any means to the large-circulation newspapers and popular magazines; it spread to many fields of writing. Even people whose education permitted them to read the more complicated styles came to prefer the simpler forms. Thus, in the course of time, the magazines and books intended for the higher-level audiences also were written in shorter sentences.

Another reason for this trend toward the shorter sentence was the influence of the "age of speed." In the last century, as everyone knows, the pace of living has been tremendously accelerated. Dickens' contemporary readers, for example, were a leisurely lot; they did not object to reading at the moderate speed required by his comparatively long sentences. But since that time, the man who reads while he runs has become virtually the symbol of our culture; and the long sentence cannot be read and comprehended except by those who are not running or about to run. Newspapers and magazines and all books which are designed to sell must be tailored to the needs of people who fit their reading into the odd moments of their day, between business and social duties, telephone calls, movies, and radio programs. Thus the shorter sentence is virtually required by two basic peculiarities of our modern civilization—the existence of a vast reading public incapable of grasping the complexities of longer sentences, and, in the face of so many other claims upon our time, the absence of leisure to do so.

We now return to the question of how long a "normal" modern sentence is. By "normal" we mean a sentence typical of writing addressed to a wide audience, an audience of average education, intelligence, and impatience—the audience to whom *Newsweek,* a motion picture magazine, a best-selling novel, the advertisements in the *Saturday Evening Post,* and a daily newspaper are addressed. If we made a statistical analysis of a number of samples of such writing, we should find that the average sentence runs to between twenty and thirty words. This means, in effect, that the average sentence is longer and more complex than that of a fourth grader ("George Washington was born in 1732. His father was a wealthy plantation owner. The story about the cherry tree is not true . . .") but that it is shorter and less complex than that of a writer addressing himself to an audience of superior education and intelligence ("The difference, so far then, between sleeping and waking seems to be that in the latter we have a greater range of conscious recollections, a larger discourse of reason, and associate ideas in longer trains and more as they are connected one with another in the order of nature; whereas in the former, any two impressions, that meet or are alike, join company, and then are parted again, without notice, like the froth from the wave").

When we find a writer using sentences whose *average* length is about "normal" (the length of the individual sentences may vary widely, of course), there is nothing especially significant to deduce concerning him or his motives. He is simply following the customary practice. But when present-day writers deviate constantly from the norm, it may be possible to infer something from their writing beyond the information which the words themselves convey.

In the first place, we have already noted that the extremely brief, uncomplicated sentence is characteristic of the child. It is also characteristic of the mind which remains immature beyond the years of physical immaturity. Suppose, for example, a grown woman wrote in a personal letter:

Henry came to see us today. He brought his new bride with him. We were glad to see them. We hadn't seen Henry for at least a year. Of course we had been wondering what sort of girl he was going to marry. She is rather tall. She has light hair and looks much younger than he is. She seemed a little shy. I suppose that will wear off in time. She probably sensed she was being looked over. They stayed only an hour. Henry seems very much wrapped up in her.

—There writes someone who must handle her thoughts one at a time, in separate and distinct units, without any regard for their relationship one to another or for their relative importance. A mature mind would have instinctively seen that the information to be conveyed could be grouped conveniently about two or three main ideas, to which the remaining details should be attached as explanatory pendants:

Henry and his new bride spent an hour with us today. We were glad to see them, because we had not seen Henry for at least a year and of course we had been wondering what sort of girl he was going to marry. She is a light-haired girl, rather tall and seemingly much younger than he is. We thought she was a little shy, but she probably sensed that she was being looked over; I suppose her shyness will wear off in time. Henry seems very much wrapped up in her.

Secondly, because there is no room in a very short sentence for anything but the main thought, it follows that an idea set forth in such a sentence will receive a degree of emphasis impossible if it is surrounded by qualifying details. Every writer or speaker who wishes to persuade his audience knows that he will succeed best when the argument is couched in brief, almost staccato sentences.

Our city is on the threshold of a great era. We know this. But in order to fulfill the promise of the future, we must be willing to work —and to spend. We need a larger police force for public protection. We need a modernized fire department. We need an enlarged library. We need to increase the pay-scale of teachers in the public schools. We need to improve our water supply. For all these needs there is but one solution. We must see that the bond issue is approved by the voters at the November election.

By the use of such brief sentences, the successive ideas are hammered into one's consciousness, separately and emphatically. The same material could easily have been incorporated into three sentences of fairly "normal" length; but much of their force would have been lost.

From the point of view of the reader, the great danger in a writer's use of brief, sharp sentences is that it can make the ideas appear much more important than they really are. Anyone can write in short sentences, but not everyone has something to say that deserves the prominence and emphasis of short sentences. In most readers' minds, the short sentence carries an unmistakable connotation of wisdom, because down through the ages it has acted as the setting for all the familiar gems of "truth"—"people who make no noise are dangerous"—"he that spareth his rod hateth his son"—"the reward of a thing well done, is to have done it." And so when a writer wishes to convince his audience of the deep truth of his ideas, he takes care to couch them in the language which they habitually associate with proverbs and axioms and the sayings of philosophers.

Our nation has always taken the middle road. Its motto is, Nothing to excess. On the one hand, it spurns the advice of the Cassandras that change means disaster. On the other hand, it rejects the proposals of those who would create Utopia overnight. Nothing is more profoundly characteristic of Americans than their reverence for the golden mean. And thus progressivism is the true American philosophy. Neither conservative nor radical, it believes in gradual, well-considered, above all *sound* evolution.

In essence, what we have here is simply another manifestation of the "transfer" device—the borrowing of prestige. Here the prestige is obtained, not so much from the words themselves, with whatever affective connotations they may have, as from the manner of the sentences—short, dignified, reminiscent of the style of popular philosophers. But the result is the same. The questionings of the mind tend to be stilled, and the reader is swayed by devices of rhetoric rather than by reason.*

Finally, the short sentence is used for special dramatic effects, such as suspense and excitement. Often such use is perfectly legitimate and honest. What would a crime thriller be like without the terse, clipped sentences that portend a crisis or describe a thrilling episode? Similarly, such writers as Ernest Hemingway employ the short sentence to give the effect of stark reality. The very absence of elaboration, the concentration upon a few bare simple facts, adds a peculiar sense of horror to the narrative. But often the short sentence is used to work up dramatic effects which are not justified by the facts involved.

Little need be said here of longer-than-average sentences. Although such sentences are common in older writing, they are not often encountered in the course of our everyday reading. They are most frequently found in legal writing and in the correspondence, records, and other documents of the government. A sufficient commentary on such sentences is contained in the following excerpt from a recent War Department publication:

> The present movement toward simplification of language and directness of statement in government writing and the elimination of jargon and unnecessary wordiness as well as the use of short, direct statements instead of long sentences which are difficult to understand because the reader is apt to get lost before he arrives, if he ever does, at the meaning intended by the writer, is a valuable attempt to achieve economy and intelligibility, for many pamphlets, instruction sheets, ordinary memoranda and assorted missives circulated through the War Department fail of their primary purpose

* See page 144, Exercise 10 (1).

through befogging their contents by use of pseudo-official phraseology which only the initiated can hope to understand and of which even they cannot be certain without reference either to the key works needed for translating them or to their own garbled and confused memories of dealing, usually without much success and always after a long period of time and travail, with similar kinds of wording in similar situations, so, though don't be too hopeful, for someone with unusual gifts and energy in applying them will manage triumphantly to misunderstand you no matter what you say or how you say it, try saying what you have to say as simply and as briefly as you can, and then after you've said it, stop saying it and don't say it any more.

EXERCISE 1. Since this book is intended for an "average" audience, its sentences should be of "average" length according to present-day standards. To check this, count the words in a sufficient number of sentences to permit a sound generalization and then strike an average. (At the same time, in anticipation of later pages in which the topic of paragraph-length is discussed, find what is the average number of sentences contained in a paragraph in this book.)

EXERCISE 2. The following sentences are taken from essays written between 1800 and 1850. What changes would have to be made if they were to be printed in a contemporary magazine? Try your hand at rewriting each of them in modern prose.

1. O mighty poet! Thy works are not as those of other men, simply and merely great works of art, but are also like the phenomena of nature, like the sun and the sea, the stars and the flowers, like frost and the snow, rain and dew, hail-storm and thunder, which are to be studied with entire submission of our own faculties, and in the perfect faith that in them there can be no too much or too little, nothing useless or inert, but that, the farther we press in our discoveries, the more we shall see proofs of design and

self-supporting arrangement where the careless eye had seen nothing but accident!

2. There was a stewardess, too, actively engaged in producing clean sheets and tablecloths from the very entrails of the sofas, and from unexpected lockers of such artful mechanism that it made one's head ache to see them opened one after another, and rendered it quite a distracting circumstance to follow her proceedings, and to find that every nook and corner and individual piece of furniture was something else besides what it pretended to be, and was a mere trap and deception and place of secret stowage, whose ostensible purpose was its least useful one.

Exercise 3. Comment on the appropriateness of the style to the subject-matter and the probable effect the author desired to achieve:

He lighted a match and held it up to the number on the door. It flickered and went out. He cursed under his breath. Somebody was coming down the pavement. A cop? Wait and see. Took his good old time coming, too. As if this was a balmy night in June instead of gusty March. No, not a cop. Just a fellow smoking a cigarette. Wonder if he saw anybody in the shadow of the doorway. Now back to the number. This must be the place. Devil to pay if it isn't. Another match: cup it with the hands. There—first numbers both two's. Out goes the match. Not many more left. Not much more time, either.

Sentence Arrangement

Once more we refer to materials contained in every handbook of composition. You are told there that the precise order in which you arrange the various elements of your sentences has much to do with the emphasis and clarity with which you will succeed in communicating your ideas. Looking at this same topic from the standpoint of the reader, what do the most usual kinds of sentence-arrangement suggest? What happens in the reader's mind when it encounters sentences of various types?

From first grade onward you have learned that the normal sentence order in English is subject-verb-object (or complement): "The cat caught a mouse"; "The women who went shopping found nothing to suit them"; "The President, while admitting that some of the criticism might have been justified, defended the general policy of the cabinet-member." This sequence is so common that our minds soon adopt it as a habit-pattern; instinctively, when we read or listen, we expect the same order—subject (and modifiers), verb (and modifiers), object or complement (and modifiers). Therefore, when any writer wishes to bring his reader to sudden attention, in order to put over an important point, he may unexpectedly shift the sequence of his sentence in what is called an inversion: "The car sped on. Jack's foot pressed down on the accelerator. Then suddenly the foot lifted and jammed down on the brake pedal instead. Looming dead ahead, its black mass lying inert directly across the concrete highway, was an overturned truck." Here the expected sentence-order, under whose familiar impetus the reader's eye has been traveling swiftly through the narrative, suddenly is broken. The last sentence has the order, complement (modifier), verb, subject.

Such inversions are quite common, especially in writing which seeks to achieve dramatic effect. However, they can easily strike a false note if used indiscriminately or too often. "Glum was Senator Green's face as he read the news"—"dark and deserted lay the amusement park in the grip of winter"—such writing smacks unpleasantly of mere mannerism. It suggests that the writer more than likely is under the spell of *Time,* which has overpopularized the brief, snappy inversion. Whatever the intrinsic virtues of this and the other hallmarks of *Time*-style, imitators seldom use them to real advantage. There is too strong an intimation that such writers depend upon the Luce publications, rather than their own fount of inspiration, for their literary style.

The inversion, used discriminately, has another element in its favor besides unexpectedness. In the sentence about the overturned truck, you will notice that the reader, in addition to being "alerted" by the unaccustomed word-order, is kept in suspense until the very end of the sentence. The subject of the sentence is reserved for last. Now if we were to examine in slow-motion the process by which a sentence impresses itself upon the mind, we should see first of all that between each sentence there is a definite break in the reading function. The mind, signalled by the full-stop punctuation (period, exclamation point, or question mark), pauses for an infinitesimal instant before proceeding with the next sentence, just as there is a short lapse between sentences in the electric signs that spell out news items and advertisements in large cities. As we read, we are of course completely unaware of this pause, but it occurs nevertheless. In it, our mind is momentarily refreshed and made ready to absorb the next idea. Therefore, since the mind is particularly receptive to the idea contained in the first few words of the next sentence, a writer is well advised to place an important idea in that initial position. If this is done, then it seems reasonable to suppose that the portion of the sentence which follows (*i.e.,* the middle) is a less favorable position for important ideas, because the mind is busy with that first thought, and though it takes in these following ideas, it does not give them the same degree of attention. But then the mind reaches the end of the sentence; the punctuation signals another pause; and what happens? The last words of the sentence are not obscured by anything following; the mind has a chance to echo them; they "sink in."

Of the three main positions in a sentence of normal or greater-than-normal length, therefore, the end is the most desirable for the placing of the idea which the writer wishes to impress upon his reader's mind. This is the principle underlying the so-called "periodic sentence"—a sentence which either wholly postpones the most important idea, or else delays its completion, until the very end. The periodic sentence is effective for three reasons: (1) It keeps the reader's mind alert throughout the sentence, waiting for what is to come (if the reader is satisfied that he has received the main idea at the very outset of the sentence, his mind will relax, even doze, for the remainder of the sentence). (2) Having thus stimulated the mind to alertness, the technique will make the main idea, when it does finally appear, the more impressive. (3) It enables the mind, in its brief pause between sentences, to register the final idea more vividly.

In the light of this discussion of how the mind works when reading a sentence, compare these two sentences:

> The girl somehow suggested a Chinese princess, with her jet-black hair, her singularly high cheekbones, her slanting eyes, her hands with their long, tapered fingers.
>
> With her jet-black hair, her singularly high cheekbones, her slanting eyes, her hands with their long, tapered fingers, the girl somehow suggested a Chinese princess.

There is nothing the matter with the first sentence: it covers all the details, systematically and clearly. But if the writer wished above all to impress his reader with the fact that the girl resembled a Chinese princess, he would have done better to keep that fact for the last, leading up to it by a process resembling that of inductive reasoning. In the first sentence, though the Chinese-princess idea is presented to a mind refreshed by its pause between sentences, that general idea is immediately pushed into the background by the details of the girl's appearance, and the item upon which the mind dwells, when it completes its course through the sentence, is the fact that she had long, tapered fingers—which may be the least significant of all the details. These faults are corrected in the second version, which presents a series of details that merge in the mind and then are effectively summarized by the core of the sentence—the noun, verb, and complement.

The following sentences all follow the same scheme:

With all their faults, and they were many, it is safe to say that such WPA projects as the Federal Theatre and the Federal Writers' Project were the most significant cultural developments of the middle 1930's.

Staring into space, absently twirling the silver keychain attached to his belt, he realized for the first time the ambiguity of his position.

If there is no change in his condition by tomorrow noon, and if, as I hope, I can get a reservation, I shall fly back to Chicago.

Those are instances of the *complete* delaying of the principal idea. Another very common means of maintaining reader-interest throughout the sentence is that of beginning the clause containing the main idea and then postponing its completion by inserting modifiers or other interrupting material. "A few minutes after noon the police, who had been awaiting the arrival of reinforcements from several other precincts, rushed the barricaded house." "The nations of the world, because another world war would result in complete and unthinkable annihilation, have no alternative but to unite." There is, however, the danger that such sentences may defeat their purpose if the interruption between subject and predicate is too long. The intervening matter may completely erase the subject of the main clause from mind: "A fresh approach to the problem, free of partisan bias, motivated by a realization of the disaster that would result from neglect or unintelligent handling of the complex factors involved, utilizing the information amassed by the experts who have been studying the question for many months—" (at this point the mind suddenly realizes that it has completely forgotten what all these phrases were supposed to modify, and must go back to the beginning) "is needed." And the end, when it comes, is so brief and, in comparison with the important-sounding phrases that preceded it, so flat, that the mind may feel cheated of its labor.

(It would be a wholesome exercise to criticize in turn that last sentence. It is a periodic sentence; the two *so's* force the mind to look forward to some completing thought, which comes only in the final clause. But is it effective? Or are there too many interruptions; is the development of the idea too piecemeal? Notice that the two elements *when it comes* and *in comparison . . . preceded it,* break up the sentence into unpleasantly small chunks.)

Of course there are many degrees of periodicity in sentence-structure. At the opposite end of the scale is the so-called "loose" sentence, which gives away its secret at the very outset, or else sandwiches it between subordinate ideas. Again we should emphasize that there is nothing grammatically wrong with loose sentences, nor are they avoided by any intelligent writers. It would be desperately monotonous, indeed, to read a passage composed of nothing but periodic sentences, beginning with details and leading up to the main thought at the end, beginning with details and leading up to the main thought . . . and so on, *ad infinitum*. The best writers mix sentences of all degrees of periodicity and looseness in their paragraphs, though never forgetting that the most important ideas naturally deserve the most prominent positions. But they also never forget that clumsy use of the loose sentence can spoil the effect they strive for. "The supreme spot of the performance was Miss Anderson's sleep-walking scene, I think." Here the tacking of "I think" onto what had purported to be a positive, forthright statement erases any pretense of authority which the author wished to make. Presumably the reader was believing him—he seemed sure of himself. And then the cautious "I think"! Or take this sentence: "The coolest, most restful spot on the campus, nestling as it did in the bend of the river, dotted with great old elms, was the area called Seniors' Solace, which boasted also a few worn green benches." Here the logic of the sentence leads steadily forward to "the area called Seniors' Solace"; but then there is a sudden descent into the unimportant, and when the sentence ends, the mind is left contemplating the worn green benches instead of Seniors' Solace. In a word, the inexpert use of loose sentences is very likely to take the edge off any piece of writing.

Which brings us to the matter of climax. If we define a climax as the peak of interest or importance, we can see that any periodic sentence is built with an eye to climax: most important thing last. But there is one particularly effective kind of periodic sentence—the one which carefully arranges several coördinate ideas in order of increasing importance. Every competent user of language employs climax as a rhetorical device to impress his audience with the supreme importance of one idea which he wishes to stress above all others.

Whatever the defects of American universities may be, they disseminate no prejudices; rear no bigots; dig up the buried ashes of no old superstitions; never interpose between the people and their improvement; exclude no man because of his religious opinions; above all, in their whole course of study and instruction, recognize a world, and a broad one too, lying beyond the college walls.

It was good for me to live under sharp discipline; to be down on the realities of existence by living on bare necessaries; to find out how extremely well worth living life seemed to be when one woke up from a night's rest on a soft plank, with the sky for canopy and cocoa and weevilly biscuit the sole prospect for breakfast; and, more especially, to learn to work for the sake of what I got for myself out of it, even if it all went to the bottom and I along with it.

The principle of climax may also be used for the purpose of humor. Since the mind naturally expects a sentence to be kept on an even keel of seriousness, if not to arrange its elements in order of ascending importance, any departure from this habit is bound to attract attention. A sudden descent into the trivial or the incongruous at the end of a sentence, which is what we call an anti-climax, always arrests the reader's mind, and if it is skillfully done it will raise a laugh. We have always cherished a sentence written by a freshman: "Some of the other points of interest in the Finger Lakes region are Keuka Lake, which is shaped like a huge Y, the Robert H. Treman State Park, with a waterfall higher than Niagara, Ithaca, the home of Cornell University, and Phelps, the home of the largest sauerkraut canning factory in the world." One who writes such a sentence in all seriousness is completely lacking in a sense of relative values. On the other hand, the use of the anti-climax may be a sign of wit of a high order—of a mind which instinctively perceives the ridiculous side-by-side with the solemn. Byron's poetry, for example, is filled with anti-climaxes, in which, after sustaining a high, serious tone for perhaps many lines, he deliberately destroys it with a stroke of humor:

> They looked up to the sky, whose floating glow
> Spread like a rosy Ocean, vast and bright;
> They gazed upon the glittering sea below,
> Whence the broad Moon rose circling into sight;
> They heard the waves splash, and the wind so low,
> And saw each other's dark eyes darting light
> Into each other—and, beholding this,
> Their lips drew near, and clung into a kiss;
>
> A long, long kiss, a kiss of Youth, and Love,
> And Beauty, all concentrating like rays
> Into one focus, kindled from above;
> Such kisses as belong to early days,
> Where Heart, and Soul, and Sense, in concert move,
> And the blood's lava, and the pulse a blaze,
> Each kiss a heart-quake,—for a kiss's strength,
> I think, it must be reckoned by its length.

Exercise 4. Here is a group of sentences illustrating the various principles of arrangement discussed in the preceding pages. In each instance, decide what point the author wished to emphasize; whether he was successful in doing so; and if not, how he might have revised the sentence.

1. Little less contradictory was that other branch of the twofold problem now set before Johnson: the speaking forth of *Truth*.
2. Yet, though we believe that the intentions of Cromwell were at first honest, though we believe that he was driven from the noble course which he had marked out for himself by the almost irresistible force of circumstances, though we admired, in common with all men of all parties, the ability and energy of his splendid administration, we are not pleading for arbitrary and lawless power, even in his hands.
3. In the first place, she persisted in disbelieving the whole of the matter; secondly, she was very sure that Mr. Collins had been taken in; thirdly, she trusted that they would never be happy together; and fourthly, that the match might be broken off.
4. When I got into the streets upon this Sunday morning, the air was so clear, the houses were so bright and gay, the signboards were painted in such gaudy colors, the gilded letters were so very golden, the bricks were so very red, the stone was so very white, the blinds and area railings were so very green, the knobs and plates upon the street doors so marvellously bright and twinkling, and all so slight and unsubstantial in appearance, that every thoroughfare in the city looked exactly like a scene in a pantomime.
5. I have often thought of it as one of the most barbarous customs in the world, considering us as a civilized and a Christian country, that we deny the advantages of learning to women.
6. Morning arises stormy and pale,
   No sun, but a wannish glare
   In fold upon fold of hueless cloud;
   And the budded peaks of the wood are bow'd,
   Caught, and cuff'd by the gale:
   I had fancied it would be fair.

7. He was, if we are to give any credit to his own account or to the united testimony of all who knew him, a man of the meanest and feeblest intellect.
8. His brother-in-law, Mr. Hurst, merely looked the gentleman; but his friend Mr. Darcy soon drew the attention of the room by his fine, tall person, handsome features, noble mien, and the report which was in general circulation within five minutes after his entrance, of his having ten thousand a-year.
9. To the blessings which England has derived from the Revolution these people are utterly insensible.

Sentence Rhythm

Now it is a basic truth of language that the human voice, and, in imitation of it, the mind itself when silently reading, always lays most stress upon those elements of a sentence which are most important in meaning. Substantives and verbs receive the most stress, modifying words (adjectives and adverbs) less, connectives (prepositions and conjunctions) least. However, if a modifier or a connective has an unusually important function in the sentence ("I was going to wear my *black* dress, but Jim wanted me to wear my *blue* one"; "I'm going the whole hog. I'm going to order the Beethoven Fifth *and* Eighth Symphonies") it is stressed more than it would be ordinarily.

There are all degrees of stress in prose (as well as in poetry). Any scheme which tries to mark off each prose syllable as being unstressed, lightly stressed, or fully stressed, is a mere approximation. The voice, reading an ordinary passage without attempting any more than ordinary "expression," rises and falls, emphasizes and modulates, in a way far too subtle for precise analysis or notation. Yet we often speak of "bad rhythm" and "good rhythm" in sentences. If we cannot measure such rhythm, except by the roughest of standards, how can we distinguish between the bad and the good?

With all his equipment of technical theory, a writer on music must depend upon his cultivated ear for a final verdict on the quality of the music he hears. And in exactly the same way, a reader who would judge the rhythm of a passage he reads or hears must first teach his ear to be sensitive, and then trust its judgment. There are elaborate treatises on English prose rhythm, but one cannot go to them for much practical advice on the quality of the rhythms typical of the material he reads. All that a sensible counsellor on reading can do is make several very broad observations on an extremely complex and unanalyzable subject.

In the first place, prose lacks something which verse possesses: namely, meter. As we shall point out later, underlying nearly all verse is a regular rhythmic pattern, made up of a constantly recurring combination of accented and unaccented syllables. Judging a given poem on the basis of regularity of meter is a part of the critical process, though it is grossly overemphasized by the novice. In prose, however, there is no such metrical pattern, iambic, trochaic, or any other. Indeed, one of the surest earmarks of bad prose is a tendency to suggest the regular rhythms of verse. English prose rhythms have their own charms, but regularity is not one of them. You will recall that one of the articles of our attack on jargon in Chapter Two was its unmusical quality. We meant simply that a long string of noun-phrases, for example, gives an intolerably monotonous pace to the sentence: "The observation of the construction of the portion of the road between Mifford Center and the county line is incorrect in nature, inasmuch as the road is actually rough in character." Read that aloud (which you should do whenever testing for rhythmic quality) and you will understand what we mean. It is true that there have been, and are, prose writers, such as Sir Thomas Browne, Thomas DeQuincey, and Walter Pater, who attempt to approximate poetic rhythms. Sometimes they produce prose of genuine beauty; but it is nevertheless highly mannered and artificial. If a writer is not a highly sensitive word-musician, he is well advised to avoid any suggestion of regular rhythm in his prose.

Secondly, unless it is written by a very expert craftsman, an overlong sentence is nearly always unrhythmical. The sentence from a War Department publication, quoted on pages 159–160, has little rhythm. If you have studied music, you no doubt know that the twin essences of rhythm are phrasing and accent—the grouping of a few notes (words) into an agreeable accentual pattern, and the shrewd distribution of rests (punctuation). The most important of these rests are the long ones—which correspond to the intervals between sentences, the intermissions during which, as we have already pointed out, the reader has a chance to pause and take stock of what he has just read. Plainly if those all-important full stops are long delayed, the reader will become fatigued and lose the continuity of the thought. In addition, the successive thought-units within the sentence must be given just the right grammatical length, and greater or less pauses must be inserted to set off the units. We freely admit that such a phrase as "just the right grammatical length" is not at all helpful, because we have failed to define our terms—and in the nature of things we cannot do so. Rightness varies from sentence to sentence, idea to idea, writer to writer. Everyone probably would agree, however, that a long sentence written without any stops at all is unrhythmical, and that on the other hand a sentence which is excessively interrupted by punctuation—which means that the thought is chopped into little pieces—is no better. We can suggest what we mean by two examples:

> The problems of reconversion to peacetime production and prosperity to be faced by the man you elect to the office of governor of this state are greater and graver than those faced by any chief executive of this commonwealth in a similar set of circumstances since the days immediately following the War Between the States.

This sentence is perhaps not long enough to be a leading entry in *The New Yorker's* "Non-Stop Sentence Derby"; sentences just as long as this, and as innocent of punctuation, are found all around us in everyday life. Yet the eye cannot comprehend in a single sweep, nor the voice utter in a single breath, a sentence as unbroken as this. There is no rhythm because there is no phrasing.

On the other hand:

> Society, through every fibre, was rent asunder: all things, it was then becoming visible, but could not then be understood, were moving onwards, with an impulse received ages before, yet now first with a decisive rapidity, towards that great chaotic gulf, where, whether in the shape of French Revolutions, Reform Bills, or what shape soever, bloody or bloodless, the descent and engulfment assume, we now see them weltering and boiling.

In this sentence there is far too much phrasing. If you analyze the thought, you will see that the fault lies primarily in the author's insistence upon qualifying phrases and clauses. Putting aside the first independent clause (down to the colon), we see that the remainder of the sentence is based upon the simple predication "all things . . . were moving onwards . . . towards that great chaotic gulf, where . . . we now see them weltering and boiling." All the rest is a sort of spasmodic parenthesis. Not only is the mind led, with justifiable reluctance, through a tortuous labyrinth of subordinate ideas; there are too many jerky stops and starts.

A third requirement for good sentence rhythm is only superficially in conflict with the first. Although we have said that an approach to regular meter in prose is nearly always unpleasant, it is also true that regularity in the larger design of the sentence can often be a most attractive and effective rhetorical device. A sentence that sounds like a trolley car with a flat wheel is disagreeable; but one whose larger elements recognizably match, like the three arches in the façade of a cathedral, gives pleasure. This is the principle that appears in the handbooks of composition under the topics "balance" and "parallelism." The matching of phrase against phrase, clause against clause, lends an unmistakable eloquence to prose. That indeed, is one of the principal glories of the King James Bible:

Behold, the day of the Lord cometh, cruel both with wrath and fierce anger, to lay the land desolate; and he shall destroy the sinners thereof out of it.

For the stars of heaven and the constellations thereof shall not give their light: the sun shall be darkened in his going forth, and the moon shall not cause her light to shine.

And I will punish the world for their evil, and the wicked for their iniquity; and I will cause the arrogancy of the proud to cease, and will lay low the haughtiness of the terrible.

I will make a man more precious than fine gold; even a man than the golden wedge of ophir.

Therefore I will shake the heavens, and the earth shall remove out of her place, in the wrath of the Lord of hosts, and in the day of his fierce anger.*

And, to some extent in reminiscence and imitation of the Bible, English prose all the way down to our own time has tended toward balanced structure for the sake of contrast or antithesis or climax:

What he attempted, he performed; he is never feeble, and he did not wish to be energetic; he is never rapid, and he never stagnates. His sentences have neither studied amplitude, nor affected brevity; his periods, though not diligently rounded, are voluble and easy.

* On the subject of the rhythms of the King James Bible, as well as other aspects of Biblical prose which illuminate points made in the course of this book, see John Livingston Lowes' fine essay, "The Noblest Monument of English Prose," in his *Essays in Appreciation;* now available in a number of college anthologies.

Whoever wishes to attain an English style, familiar but not coarse, and elegant but not ostentatious, must give his days and nights to the volumes of Addison.

Study hard; divert yourself heartily; distinguish carefully between the pleasures of a man of fashion, and the vices of a scoundrel; pursue the former, and abhor the latter, like a man of sense.

It is the addition of strangeness to beauty, that constitutes the romantic character in art; and the desire of beauty being a fixed element in every artistic organization, it is the addition of curiosity to this desire of beauty, that constitutes the romantic temper.

We should add here that in the past two or three decades many important literary experimentalists have renounced the very principles of rhythmic language which we have been emphasizing in these pages. Writers like James Joyce, E. E. Cummings, John Dos Passos, and Archibald MacLeish, to name only a few, have often deliberately abandoned punctuation and the other usual devices by which thought-units are marked off and rhythmic pleasure communicated. One main reason why they have done so is that many of them are deeply interested in representing the "stream of consciousness"—the uncontrolled, vagrant, fragmentary thoughts and moods that course continuously through the human mind. Since in their raw state such thoughts and moods have nothing of the neat packaged quality which sentence- and paragraph-organization suggests, these writers argue that their chaotic nature should be suggested by a chaotic style. Perhaps the most famous example of this manner is the representation of the flow of Mrs. Bloom's thoughts in the last section of Joyce's *Ulysses*—forty-five closely printed pages without a punctuation mark!

Another effect which modern writers wish to achieve by their abandonment of conventional phrasing and familiar rhythmic patterns is an impression of the underlying chaos and patternlessness of modern civilization. Since rhythm suggests orderliness and control, and the contemporary prose writer or poet often wishes above all to impress his reader with the absence of these qualities from our world, he uses a style whose disregard of any principle of regularity is designed to suggest that absence.

A cultivated awareness of rhythm inevitably increases the reader's pleasure in whatever he reads, heightening an emotional experience whose other principal element is the suggestiveness of the words themselves. The first great requirement for rhythm, as has been remarked, is that it be pleasant. The second is that it be appropriate to the context; for a passage of quiet imaginative beauty demands a slow, even (though never monotonous) rhythm, a passage of exciting narrative a rapid rhythm, a passage intended to sway patriotic emotions a measured but vigorous rhythm, and so on. Readers come to associate certain rhythmic effects with certain intentions on the part of the writer or speaker. Rhythm, in other words, has its own connotative value. And just as word-connotations may be employed to affect emotions rather than reason, so too may rhythm-connotations.

Consider first these grave sentences:

It is the pleasure of the creators of Beaver Tweeds to be able to announce that once again, after the long wartime interruption, their fabrics will soon be available to their American clientele.

Not since 1939, when the full weaving and styling facilities of this world-renowned manufactory were placed at the disposal of His Majesty's Government, have Beaver Tweeds been available on either side of the Atlantic.

At this very moment, however, the first fine bolts of Beaver Tweeds are on their way to New York aboard the S.S. *Olentangy Victory*. In a few days they will be distributed to the few carefully selected tailoring establishments which for many years have been the means by which superb suiting has been transformed into superb suits.

The creators of Beaver Tweeds respectfully suggest to their many clients in New York that they consult with their tailors at the earliest possible moment, in order that a sufficient quantity of their chosen tweed be reserved for their personal requirements.

After our study of word-connotations in Chapter One, we need not stop to analyze the implications of the language itself. But what of the rhythm?

> Here is the long-awaited announcement from the creators of Beaver Tweeds! Once again, after long wartime interruption, their fabric will soon be available to their American clientele.
>
> Six long years ago—in 1939—all the weaving and styling facilities of this world-renowned manufactory were placed at the disposal of His Majesty's Government. Not since then has a single bolt of Beaver Tweeds been available in England or America.
>
> But right at this moment the first fine bolts of Beaver Tweeds are on their way to you—aboard the S.S. *Olentangy Victory!* In a few days they will be distributed to a few carefully selected tailoring establishments. Not to many—just a few. The few that have been famous for many years for their skill in transforming superb suiting into superb suits.
>
> Attention, all Beaver Tweed clients in New York! Don't delay —see your tailor as soon as you possibly can. Reserve a quantity of tweed sufficient for your personal requirements. Supply is strictly limited!

The question here is, which advertisement would persuade you to pay a high price for the cloth in question? Obviously (unless you are already aware of the tricks that rhythm can perform) the first. It has the more elegant "sound." It suggests that here is something precious and rare—and if it is expensive, it is worth it. Whether the tweed *is* worth the price is another question altogether, which can never be settled by connotative language. In brief, sentence-rhythm has been deliberately employed to give a false air of lofty dignity to a product.

Dynasty and empire come and are gone. Conquerors ride and ride no more. A gun speaks and a gun is silent, and time, the slow tendril, conceals the green years. What endures, then? Art, and music, and the imperishable convictions of the soul. Melody heard in an April garden will enchant a thousand Aprils. Fragments of song addressed to the heart will die only when time dies. Music abides. It stays and will stay. Enjoy it, now, with the new Capehart or the new Farnsworth.

Here the key to the effect of the advertisement is the balanced structure of more than half of the sentences and the matching tone of the rest. Read this excerpt aloud and you will hear the sentences almost singing. All the devices of the prose-poet-turned-advertising-writer are found here: the balanced clauses, the constant repetition (*ride . . . ride no more, gun . . . gun, April . . . Aprils, die . . . dies, stays . . . will stay*), the highly "poetic" diction (*time, the slow tendril, conceals the green years; the imperishable convictions of the soul*). In fact, only the last sentence identifies the passage as a commercial appeal. Up to that point, one is willing to accept it as an extract from some slightly overwritten book of literary meditations. And that is exactly what the writer desires. The reader is put into a meditative frame of mind; presumably he is made receptive to whatever attractive ideas are in store for him; and then he is presented with the chance to buy a radio or phonograph.

But when the appeal is to the active, fun-loving side of one's nature rather than to one's contemplative faculty, another type of rhythm is needed—probably the most familiar variety in advertising:

Got an eye for beauty? Then you'll like the big, new 1946 Mercury. Here's a car that's smart all over. A car designed with a clean, sturdy, youthful look. Inside, too, you'll find that you get style aplenty. Broad, deep seats, faultlessly tailored with rich fabrics. Appointments that are colorful and luxurious.

There's eager yet thrifty power in that advanced V-type, 8 cylinder engine. There is real in-built, deep, easy-chair lounging comfort. And new hydraulic brakes to make stops sure and silent.

Here the rhythm, short, snappy, lively, suggests that this is a car for people who are young at heart—wanting to go places and do things, and enjoy themselves on the way.

In contemporary advertising, one of the most-used and therefore supposedly one of the most effective devices is the use of the points of suspension (. . .). In imaginative writing of the past generation or two, especially in certain types of verse, the dots were a highly popular rhetorical device to suggest continuation of thought or mood even after the actual words had stopped. The reader was expected to imagine more than he actually found on the printed page.

A shadowy glade,
The murmur of a hidden brook,
Your white hand in mine . . .
Candlelight through the wine glass,
Oblivious of the snow without,
Silence binding us into one . . .
A Beethoven sonata,
The Gauguins at the Metropolitan,
The skyscrapers' sharp upward tilt.
And you . . . always you . . .

And so now, more often than not, any advertisement that wishes to evoke a dreamy, complaisant mood in the reader, one of forgetfulness of the crass considerations of money or need, liberally uses the three dots of enchantment.

It's the night of the big dance . . . the dance of the year. He's asked you, of course . . . and now he's calling for you. His orchid is pinned to your new gown . . . so svelte and flattering . . . the faintest breath of that special fragrance hovers about your adorable young person

. . . Are you ready for the evening . . . perhaps the biggest evening of all? Have you brushed your teeth with the one toothpaste that can do the job right?*

EXERCISE 5. Comment on the rhythm of the following sentence, from a dispatch to the *New York Times:*

> Counsel appointed to assist the royal commissioners in the investigation of the Canadian espionage case announced today that oral and documentary evidence already confirmed the serious nature of the disclosures and that the reasons for proceeding *in camera* became more apparent every day and revealed that eleven men and two women were under detention in connection with the leakage of secret information to a foreign mission.

EXERCISE 6. Analyze in detail the rhythmic devices used in the following excerpt from the *Autobiography* of Edward Gibbon, a writer famous for his rhythmic prose:

> The proportion of a part to the whole is the only standard by which we can measure the length of our existence. At the age of twenty, one year is a tenth, perhaps, of the time which has elapsed within our consciousness and memory; at the age of fifty it is no more than the fortieth, and this relative value continues to decrease till the last sands are shaken by the hand of death. This reasoning may seem metaphysical; but on a trial it will be found satisfactory and just. The warm desires, the long expectations of youth, are founded on the ignorance of themselves and the world; they are gradually damped by time and experience, by disappointment and possession; and after the middle season

* You may detect a note of anti-climax here—and you are right. But the example is not an extreme one; hundreds like it can be collected in a few hours' search of magazines. Read advertisements carefully and you will find that a great many of them are just as silly—or sillier.

the crowd must be content to remain at the foot of the mountain; while the few who have climbed the summit aspire to descend or expect to fall. In old age, the consolation of hope is reserved for the tenderness of parents, who commence a new life in their children; the faith of enthusiasts who sing hallelujahs above the clouds; and the vanity of authors who presume the immortality of their name and writings.

EXERCISE 7. Here are two versions of the same paragraph. From the standpoint of rhythm and effectiveness, which is the better?

1. While the world contents itself with putting to rights the surface of things, the Church aims at regenerating the very depths of the heart. She always begins with the beginning. Not only that, but, at least as far as most of her children are concerned, she never can get beyond the beginning; she is continually busy laying the foundation. She is engaged with what is essential, the essential being a necessary preliminary to the ornamental and the attractive. She is curing men and keeping them clear of mortal sin. She is "treating of justice and chastity, and the judgment to come." Her insistence is on faith, hope, devotion, honesty, and the elements of charity. It has so much to do with precept that she almost leaves it to Heaven to suggest what is of counsel and perfection. Rather than aim at what is desirable, she aims at what is necessary. She is for the many as well as the few. In order that souls may, if called upon, be in a condition to aspire to the heroic, and to attain not only the full proportions but also the rudiments of beauty, she is putting souls in the way of salvation.
2. The world is content with setting right the surface of things; the Church aims at regenerating the very depths of the heart. She ever begins with the beginning; and, as regards the multitude of her children, is never able to get beyond the beginning, but is continually employed in laying the foundation. She is engaged with what is essential, as previous and as introductory to the ornamental and the attractive. She is curing men and

keeping them clear of mortal sin; she is "treating of justice and chastity, and the judgment to come"; she is insisting on faith and hope, and devotion, and honesty, and the elements of charity; and has so much to do with precept, that she almost leaves it to inspirations from Heaven to suggest what is of counsel and perfection. She aims at what is necessary rather than at what is desirable. She is for the many as well as for the few. She is putting souls in the way of salvation, that they may then be in a condition, if they shall be called upon, to aspire to the heroic, and to attain the full proportions, as well as the rudiments, of beauty.

EXERCISE 8. For examples of the way in which, for various purposes, contemporary authors have abandoned the conventional ideas of punctuation and sentence-organization, see the following: James Joyce's *Ulysses;* the "Camera-Eye" sequences in John Dos Passos' *U. S. A.;* T. S. Eliot's "Ash-Wednesday"; Archibald MacLeish's "You, Andrew Marvell" and "Immortal Autumn"; E. E. Cummings' "Impression: IV" and "Chanson Innocent."

EXERCISE 9. Comment on the use of rhythm (as well as of connotation) in each of the following excerpts from advertisements:

1. The clouds have rolled away; the wedding day dawns clear and bright. For he is home—whatever care or crisis now betides throughout their lifetime they will meet always together. . . . If a diamond ring is to reflect such clarion joy as then fills hearts to bursting, obtain it from a trusted jeweler. For color, brilliance of cutting, purity can outrank actual carat weight in beauty and value.

2. Across the river, the lights were beginning to glimmer through the winter mist. From far below, came the faint hum of homeward-bound traffic, punctuated now and then by the hoarse notes of passing ships.

Here, in his own apartment, the world's greatest violinist had just put aside his Stradivarius and turned to his Magnavox radio-phonograph. Now he sat listening as the instrument poured forth an ecstasy of sound. Full-throated it was; crystalline in clarity . . . music that had been immaculately conceived in the hope that it could thus be so perfectly reproduced.

3. They have an inconspicuous seam down the center—that's the only reason under the sun why they're priced so low. Otherwise, they are absolutely top quality blankets. All wool, of course—beautifully finished—in three lovely colors. You'll want to stock up—winter will soon be here! Come down tomorrow, early. We don't have too many of these blankets—and we won't keep them long!

4. Not so long ago
When a man sailed
His voice sailed with him

There was no way
He could talk to folks back home
Or discuss plans with those ahead

Then, in Twenty-nine
Aboard the S.S. *Berengaria*
In mid-Atlantic
A voice spoke into a phone
And another voice in distant England
Answered

That day . . .
As a result of pioneering research
By International Telephone and Telegraph
Laboratories
Ship-to-shore radio-telephone service
Was born

Soon . . . through collaboration between
The British Post Office
And IT&T's associates,
International Marine Radio Company
And Standard Telephones and Cables, Ltd.
Service was inaugurated between England
And leading liners
With remarkable success

Service in other countries quickly followed
So that a ship in the China Sea
Could talk to London . . .
And passengers in Alexandria
Could converse with friends in New York

Today aboard fishing fleets
Remote iceberg patrol cutters
Even lifeboats . . .
The telephone
Carries man's voice across the sea

Exercise 10. Re-read the three revisions of the beginning of the Declaration of Independence printed on pages 65–66, and explain the differences in sentence rhythm in terms of the job each version was designed to do, and of the audience to which each was addressed.

Paragraphs

Since the paragraph, the next largest unit of expression, is, in a way, merely a larger, more complicated sentence, it would be reasonable to assume that many of the observations we have made about the length, organization, and rhythm of sentences could also apply to the paragraph. And such is the case.

The ability to construct good paragraphs is even more important an indication of a writer's intelligence than is his ability to write good sentences. For although constructing a sentence so as to show the proper relationship of ideas requires a mind that can both analyze and synthesize, constructing a paragraph, in which the same procedure must be followed on a larger and more complex scale, takes even more intelligence. And while the majority of college freshmen can write acceptable individual sentences, most instructors would agree that only the superior student, at least at the beginning of his course in English, can write whole paragraphs that "hang together."

One basic thing to remember about the paragraph, as about the sentence, is that it is a *unit*—which means that it is concerned with one topic only, not with a group of topics. The paragraph differs from the sentence in that it tells more about that single topic than a sentence can do. It expands a definition, it offers examples and analogies, it breaks down a main argument into subheads, it presents a chronological narrative; but always it sticks to one main point. In a handbook of composition much stress is laid upon the so-called "topic sentence" of a paragraph—the sentence which contains the essence of what the paragraph is about, and to which every other sentence must be logically connected. Sometimes the topic-sentence is implied rather than expressed; but the other sentences must be bound to it nevertheless.

The second basic thing to remember is that a paragraph must take the reader somewhere, and take him by a fairly direct route. No piece of writing is worth the paper it is written upon if it does not move along, taking the reader into some new region of information or argument. When he finishes it, the reader must feel that he has progressed; "something new has been added" to his store of knowledge and experience. And since writing is made up of paragraphs, each paragraph must contribute, each in its own way, to the total effect of progress. The reader must come out with more than he took in with him. Furthermore, he must be given his new facts systematically, not haphazardly. He must be enabled to follow the writer's line of thought. There may be no bypaths or detours, unless they are plainly marked as such and their presence can be completely justified.

This is the substance of what is said in all the textbooks of writing. What, then, are the rewards in store for the close reader, who remains always alert to the writer's obligation to produce unified, progressive paragraphs?

The most obvious clue which paragraphs can offer is to the orderliness of a writer's mind. If the organization of a paragraph is clear, if the sentences are arranged in a logical pattern with each leading directly into the next, it is reasonable to assume that the writer has his material under control, knows just what he wishes to say about it, and is able to present it so that the reader can follow his thought without trouble. None but the most inexperienced writers are usually conscious of the process by which they organize their material; to any practised writer it is an instinctive, automatic occurrence. When we wrote the next-to-last paragraph, for example, we did not say to ourself, this sentence should go so far, and the next sentence should serve such-and-such a purpose, and the two should be tied together by a connective. . . . Yet, though we hesitate to offer it as a model of what all paragraphs should be, it can illustrate the way in which sound paragraphs are built.

Sentence 1 is the theme; saying that "the second basic thing to remember" has two aspects. This division of the idea into two parts does not violate the principle of unity, because, as the reader will be aware when he has finished the paragraph, the two aspects are very closely related. Unless each demands an exposition which would make the paragraph too unwieldy, both can legitimately be included in a single paragraph.

Sentence 2 momentarily leaves the subject of the paragraph in order to relate the idea being discussed to the larger topic of writing in general. But unity remains: "taking the reader . . ." ties up directly with "take the reader somewhere" in Sentence 1.

Sentence 3 amplifies the idea of Sentence 2.

Sentence 4 now shows the relevance of Sentences 2 and 3 to the specific idea of the paragraph: "since writing is made up of paragraphs."

Sentence 5 concisely summarizes the idea of progression.

Sentence 6 turns the reader's attention to the second aspect spoken of in Sentence 1. "Furthermore" is the signal for a turn of thought.

Sentences 7 and 8 amplify Sentence 6, Sentence 8 by re-stating the idea of Sentence 7 in a negative way.

The whole paragraph has been unified, furthermore, by constant reference to "the reader," who is spoken of in four of the eight sentences. The "point of view," as the textbooks call it, must be kept constant. Frequent and unjustified shifting of the subject leads only to confusion.

We should go a step further and show how the next paragraph is connected with the one we have just analyzed. "This is the substance": a sign that this sentence summarizes what has just been said. "What, then" is a phrase designed, like "furthermore," to guide the reader's mind to the next topic. This brief, two-sentence paragraph is a transitional one; it adds nothing to the reader's knowledge, but it is valuable as a breathing space. It clinches the point previously made and then directs the reader's attention to a new topic which, the writer implies, logically derives from the one just developed. The generous use of such sign-posts, whether they be single words or phrases (*therefore, however, first of all, on the contrary, in conclusion, as we have seen, another example . . .*) or whole little paragraphs, is a mark of the writer who is very careful to keep his reader in close touch with his argument.

We will conclude, therefore, that the two paragraphs just discussed imply that their author has an orderly mind! But what about this paragraph, which is typical of many read every year by a college instructor:

> Why is it that you sit in your dorm room on Saturday nights while the other girls are out on dates? The reason probably is that you don't take enough care to look your best. Science has given every girl the means by which she can become more beautiful. Of course she must have personality, too, but that can be cultivated. She must also take care to be in good health. Sleep eight hours every night, take regular exercise, eat well balanced, nourishing meals. Naturally that doesn't mean that she should neglect her studies. But Saturday night dates are not hard to come by if you will pay a visit to the nearest drug store and equip yourself with a few simple beauty aids, such as the right shades of powder, lipstick, and rouge, and other similar cosmetics. And then learn how to apply them artfully. At the same time you should learn how to cultivate a pleasant speaking voice.

The same influences which have reduced the length of sentences in the past century have also reduced the length of paragraphs. The number of sentences within the paragraph has not been greatly reduced, but as the sentences themselves have shrunk, so has the paragraph. The "normal" modern paragraph contains between three and eight sentences. The shortest are those in newspapers and advertisements—the sort of reading that must be read easily if it is to be read at all. The editorial matter of magazines designed for great popular circulation is divided into quite brief paragraphs; but serious books, as well as magazines intended for a more or less restricted group, have longer paragraphs.

And since the paragraph, like the sentence, is designed to show the relationships between ideas, it follows that the shorter the paragraph is, the less complicated the subject-matter has to be.

Just as short sentences can only state an idea, barely, directly, without qualifications, so short paragraphs can show only the most elementary relationships between two or three ideas.

Short paragraphs have their advantage, then, in that they present ideas in their simplest forms and relationships, without any attempt to explore their implications. But, as is true also of the sentence, this connotation of simplicity may be, and often is, grossly abused. Short paragraphs may persuade the reader that the ideas they present are as uncomplicated as they sound. In other words, short paragraphs are a rhetorical device that aid and abet the fallacy of oversimplification.

And just as short sentences have a connotation also of solemnity and overwhelming importance, so do short paragraphs. Newspaper "philosophers," advertising writers, and others who wish to invest their writing with an impressive air of dignity and authority, often go so far as to use single-sentence paragraphs. This is doubly convenient for their purposes, because in addition to increasing the effectiveness of their paragraphs, such a device releases them from the necessity of developing their idea logically. Short sentences and paragraphs cannot possibly bear a coherent development of ideas; all they can do is present a series of thoughts, and whatever relationship may exist between these separate thoughts is largely implied. The great public, however, will accept such writing without question, because any doubts they may have about the reasonableness of the man's position are stilled by the seeming authoritativeness of his language, which often, as in the following example, has the rhythmic connotation of litany:

> Last Sunday, in a small church in upstate New York, the minister said:
>
> "The men who fought this war don't glory in it. They hate war."
>
> That's what we say. That's what we think we mean.
>
> But it isn't true. We are more war-minded than we know.

I asked myself:

"Do I hate war?"

And I had to answer:

"I don't."

I had to go on from there.

I may secretly love war.

Self-examination shocked me. I suddenly was aware of something I hadn't known about myself. I had always taken for granted I hated war.

Now I don't know.

War is ugliness.

War is death.

War is destruction.

War is heartbreak and sorrow.

* * *

The men who fight wars, when they fight them, hate war.

They hate its blood and carnage.

They hate its grime and filth.

They hate its demands on their bodies.

They hate its regimentation.

They hate its separations.

They hate its standing in line for chow, wearing its uniforms, taking its orders.

But when wars are over, day after day, that's easier to forget.

You don't forget the other side of war.

You don't forget that in war you found the only Christian brotherhood you ever knew.

You don't forget learning in war that a man could love the other fellow more than himself, if only for a minute, an hour, a day.

You don't forget that in war you saw men who loved life give their lives for you.

I didn't know that kind of living before I went to war.

I haven't known it since.

I miss it.

* * *

The absence of it, the brutal contradiction of it, in peace makes it the harder to forget.

We have returned to a world at peace. It is a world of dog-eat-dog. Probably it has always been like this. Probably it hasn't changed much. Probably we haven't, either. Because we've taken up our places in this world. We are living by its rules.

But not particularly liking it. We can't forget that once we knew —and were—men who lived and died by other rules.

Living on that plane for an hour, I am dissatisfied with anything less. William James says the world, in peace, must find the moral equivalent for war. Lacking that, peace is inadequate. Lacking that, peace produces nostalgia for war.

If, in the long run, we're going to do anything about it, our task is at once simple and staggering. We've got to forge a world of peace out of the same steel we forge a world at war. We've got to find William James' moral equivalent. It's insane that war should bring out our best qualities and peace our worst. And yet it's true.*

It is hardly necessary to say anything of the over-long paragraph because it is seldom encountered except in legal and governmental writing, whose shortcomings we have already examined. It is the sign of the man who seems unwilling to give his reader a break, in both the standard and slang senses of the term. And it may also suggest that the writer lacks a very important mental faculty—that of being able to separate his ideas into convenient but always coherent clusters. The writer who writes on and on, without noticing when he has completed a logical subdivision of his exposition or argument, is as much to be pitied as the one whose thoughts, as reflected in his writing, are excessively compartmented.

Exercise 11. What does each of the following paragraphs reveal of the mind of the author?

* Reprinted by special permission of the Scripps-Howard Newspaper Alliance.

1. The exact route which the new highway will take will depend on several factors. The topography of the region will largely dictate how straight it will be; for although it is desirable to have as few curves and hills as possible, the most direct route may involve too many fills and cuts. The cost of land condemnation may make the most desirable route the most expensive, especially if the proposed road would cut through valuable farmland or residential properties. In some cases there will be opposition in communities to having the road run directly through them, since it would increase the traffic with its attendant noise and dangers to pedestrians. Other communities will welcome the road because they think it will increase the business of hotels, restaurants, and stores. The financing of the highway will be done according to the state of the treasury at the time construction is about to begin. If current revenue is sufficient, it will be paid for out of such funds. Bond issues are often floated to finance large road construction projects.

2. As a student he was eager to learn, and his recitations in class, though somewhat irrelevant to the matter under discussion at the moment, were so full of wit and odd miscellaneous information that teachers welcomed his presence. Rather taller than most boys his age, he had a thick mop of brown hair which had a tendency to become uncombed under the stress of ideas, and his brown eyes and wide humorous mouth had the power of putting people under his spell before he was with them for ten minutes. He had not yet got over the adolescent tendency toward awkwardness, and his hands, a little larger than the common run of hands, often sought refuge in his pockets. It was the fashion in his day to wear trousers above the ankles, but the fact that his trousers dangled not far below his calf may have been due more to the rapid, uncheckable upward expansion of his frame than to any conscious desire to be in style. What annoyed his teachers most was his invariable habit of gazing out of the window just when they were making the most important point in their day's lecture. Quite plainly his mind was a thousand miles away; yet when it came to a showdown he always turned

out to have been listening—and retaining. He was too exasperating on occasion to be a model student, but no teacher ever regretted having had the chance to teach him.

3. The inductive method has been practised ever since the beginning of the world by every human being. It is constantly practised by the most ignorant clown, by the most thoughtless schoolboy, by the very child at the breast. That method leads the clown to the conclusion that if he sows barley he shall not reap wheat. By that method the schoolboy learns that a cloudy day is the best for catching trout. The very infant, we imagine, is led by induction to expect milk from his mother or nurse, and none from his father.

The Rhythm of Verse

This is not a book on the "appreciation" of literature. We do not intend, therefore, to say much about the means by which the poet achieves the effects peculiar to poetry: you can read about that in a number of excellent books, such as Earl Daniels' *The Art of Reading Poetry,* Bliss Perry's *A Study of Poetry,* James Harry Smith's *The Reading of Poetry,* and Charles W. Cooper's *Preface to Poetry.* But since we have just been saying a number of things that bear directly on the rhythm of verse, it would be wasteful not to go one step farther and show how you can apply the principles just outlined to your reading of verse.

To begin with, when we were talking about the rhythm of prose we remarked that prose has no recurrent beat—no regular system of accent, or meter. And that is one vital difference between prose and verse—a much more real one than the commonly heard rule that "anything that is printed with straight right-hand margins is prose, and anything with irregular right margins is verse." Unlike prose, all true verse has an underlying regularity of accent.

Now it is a demonstrable fact that rhythm has a very special significance to human beings. Every moment of our lives, though we may seldom stop to consider it, we are involved in a whole complex of rhythmic cycles—the succession of day and night and of the seasons, the beat of the heart, the unending cycle of birth, maturity, decay, death, and renewal found throughout nature. And we seem furthermore to have some innate receptivity to created rhythm. One of the most basic human impulses, even of the savage, is to express oneself in some rhythmic manner; and when one is thus expressing himself in the hearing of others, whether it be by beating a tomtom or by reciting a sonnet, the influence of the rhythm spreads. The heightened emotion of one man becomes, by contagion, the heightened emotion of a whole group. An extreme instance of this is the manner in which, in revivalistic meetings, rhythmic sermonizing, followed by singing and chanting, and physical gestures, culminates in an often uncontrollable mass paroxysm of emotional fervor.

In a highly refined and subtle form, this is what happens when we read poetry, or hear it read. The regular recurrence of accent provides a rhythmic, and therefore at least potentially emotional, context. The reader's mind and his imagination are made more receptive to the emotional suggestions of the words themselves. And thus the total emotional experience of poetry derives from two main sources—the connotative effect of the words and the arrangement of those words in a definitely rhythmic pattern.

But incalculable damage has been done by unenlightened teachers who have insisted that pupils "scan" poetry—that is, mark off the accented and the unaccented syllables into uniform groups which are called "feet." In so doing, they have implied that verse is nothing but a monotonous series of iambs or trochees or whatever: da-*dum,* da-*dum,* da-*dum,* da-*dum;* or *dum*-da, *dum*-da, *dum*-da; or da-da-*dum,* da-da-*dum,* da-da-*dum*. . . . While it is perfectly true that such a regular beat *underlies* verse, that is not the most important thing.

When we were discussing the rhythm of sentences, we remarked that the various words and phrases which make up any sentence receive all degrees of stress: some, like the articles, are passed over so lightly and hurriedly that we often almost fail to hear them, while others, such as the subject and verb of the clause, receive much emphasis. The amount of emphasis depends to a great extent upon the logical importance of each word in context. If you will now read aloud the preceding sentences, with normal "expression," you will hear how subtly your accentuation is modified, from word to word, by the sense itself.

Keeping the all-important fact of "sentence rhythm" in mind, let us now look at a few lines from Coleridge's poem, "Frost at Midnight":

> The frost performs its secret ministry,
> Unhelped by any wind. The owlet's cry
> Came loud—and hark, again! loud as before.
> The inmates of my cottage, all at rest,
> Have left me to that solitude, which suits
> Abstruser musings: save that at my side
> My cradled infant slumbers peacefully.

If we read this passage according to the strict requirements of the meter alone, it would sound—as nearly as we can reproduce sound on the printed page—something like this:

> The FROST perFORMS its SEcret MINisTRY (*pause*)
> unHELPed by ANy WIND the OWLet's CRY (*pause*)
> came LOUD and HARK aGAIN loud AS beFORE (*pause*)
> the INmates OF my COTtage ALL at REST (*pause*)
> have LEFT me TO that SOLiTUDE which SUITS (*pause*)
> abSTRUSer MUSings SAVE that AT my SIDE (*pause*)
> my CRAdled INfant SLUMbers PEACEfully. . . .

Anyone who is not completely insensitive to the beauties of sound would agree that that is a dastardly thing to do to any bit of verse. By paying strict and completely unimaginative attention to the "notation" suggested by the metrical pattern, we have destroyed the sense of the passage. All we have is an intolerably monotonous tick-tock, tick-tock, tick-tock. . . .

We now assume for the moment that the passage is written as prose:

> The frost performs its secret ministry, unhelped by any wind. The owlet's cry came loud—and hark, again! loud as before. The inmates of my cottage, all at rest, have left me to that solitude, which suits abstruser musings: save that at my side my cradled infant slumbers peacefully.

Since we are not forewarned, by the arrangement of the words into lines of what we automatically recognize as "verse," that the passage is written in almost completely regular iambic meter, five accents to a line, we are under no compulsion to stress the beat. Instead, we read it as we would read any prose, with due regard for the sense. Although no two persons will read the same passage in exactly the same way—and fully recognizing the inadequacy of using only two degrees of stress—this is approximately the way in which it would sound, with a single virgule indicating a half-rest, and a double one, a full stop.

> The FROST perFORMS its SEcret MINistry/ unHELPed by any WIND// The OWLet's CRY CAME loud/ and HARK/ aGAIN// LOUD as beFORE// The INmates of my COTtage/ all at rest/ have LEFT me to that SOLitude which suits aSTRUSer MUSings// save that at my side/ my cradled INfant SLUMbers PEACEfully//

If you compare this version with that produced by uncompromising fidelity to the meter, you will see that normally the metrical accents fall upon the syllables which are also accented by the sense. This is as it should be; the result otherwise would be monstrously artificial. But you will also see that in the strictly metrical reading, many syllables are stressed which are left unstressed in the "sense" reading. The unimportant is given a false degree of emphasis. And you will see, finally, that the first version provided for pauses only at the end of each line, and that these pauses often are not called for by the sentence-construction; indeed, they often break the normal flow of the sentence. In the "sense" version, however, the pauses are inserted where the sentence construction requires, regardless of their position in the line. Strict metrical reading, that is, disregards punctuation; reading for sense takes the punctuation into full account.

Obviously the second version is better than the first; it is intelligible, and furthermore, because the metrical accents and the sense accents largely coincide, it preserves the essential rhythm. But it is impossible to represent typographically a much better reading—the ideal reading. We can only describe what it is like.

The *complete* rhythm of poetry, as distinguished from the rigidly mechanical recurrence of stressed and unstressed syllables, is an extremely subtle blending of the two sorts of rhythm we have been discussing. The metrical pattern hovers always in the background; but above it, and along with it, moves the larger, infinitely more varied rhythm of the sentence as a whole. If you listen to the opening bars of the Brahms C Minor Symphony, you will hear a musical analogue of this conjunction of two rhythms. The drums (the regular meter) beat a precise, unchanging accompaniment in the background as the strings (the sense-current) weave a constantly varying fabric of sound. The two movements, taken separately, are unimpressive; but when they are combined, the one "setting off" the other, they give a rich, stately effect.*

This is the most important thing to remember about the rhythm of verse. *Basic* regularity of stress, of course, is essential;

* Another musical analogue is found in the third movement of the Tschaikowsky Sixth ('Pathétique") Symphony.

but it is tolerable only when combined with the varied stresses and pauses dictated by the logic of the sentence. If we overemphasize the meter, we obscure the sense and the overtones of the sense; if we overemphasize the normal intonations, we obscure the pleasurable regularity. Only when the two are fused into a single harmonious pattern are the possibilities of rhythmic language fully realized.

EXERCISE 12. One of the passages printed below is an excerpt from a poem famous for its lovely cadences, which combine a regular meter (iambic pentameter) with the rhythms of natural speech. The other passage is a rewritten, much inferior, version of the same passage. Which is the original? How can you tell?

1. ... For I have learned
To look on nature, not as in the hour
Of thoughtless youth; but oftentimes hearing
The music of humanity, sad, still,
Nor grating nor harsh, though of ample power
To subdue and chasten. And I have felt
A presence that disturbs me with the joy
Of elevated thoughts; a sublime sense
Of something interfused far more deeply,
Whose dwelling is the light of setting suns,
And the ocean round and the living air,
And the blue sky, and in man's mind:
A spirit and a motion, that impels
All thinking things, every object of every thought,
And rolls through all things.

2. ... For I have learned
To look on nature, not as in the hour
Of thoughtless youth; but hearing oftentimes
The still, sad music of humanity,
Nor harsh nor grating, though of ample power

To chasten and subdue. And I have felt
A presence that disturbs me with the joy
Of elevated thoughts; a sense sublime
Of something far more deeply interfused,
Whose dwelling is the light of setting suns,
And the round ocean and the living air,
And the blue sky, and in the mind of man;
A motion and a spirit, that impels
All thinking things, all objects of all thought,
And rolls through all things.

EXERCISE 13. Here are three more pairs of passages. Decide in each case which of the two alternative passages is more pleasing to the ear and which is more successful in matching the rhythm to the mood.

1. (a) The sea is calm tonight,
The tide is full, the moon lies fair
Upon the straits;—on the French coast, the light
Gleams, and is gone; the cliffs of England stand,
Glimmering and vast, out in the tranquil bay.
Come to the window, sweet is the night-air!
Only, from the long line of spray
Where the sea meets the moon-blanched land,
Listen! you hear the grating roar
Of pebbles which the waves draw back, and fling,
At their return, up the high strand,
Begin, and cease, and then again begin,
With tremulous cadence slow, and bring
The eternal note of sadness in.

(b) Calm tonight, how calm the sea is!
Full's the tide, and fair the moon lies
On the straits; the lights of France first
Gleam, then go; the English cliffs stand
Glimm'ring, vast, o'er the tranquil bay.
Come, look out! how sweet the night air!

Only, from the line of spray,
Where the sea meets moonlit land,
Listen! hear the grating roar—
Pebbles, which the waves draw back,
Flinging then upon the strand—
Start, and stop, and start again,
Bringing, with slow and tremulous cadence,
Th' eternal note of sadness in.

2. (a) I came upon a traveller from an antique land
Who said: Two vast, trunkless legs of stone
Stand in the desert. Nearby, on the sand,
Half sunken, lies a shattered visage, whose frown,
And wrinkled lip, and sneer of cold command,
Tell that its sculptor those passions well read
Which yet survive, stamped on those lifeless things,
The hand that mocked them, and the heart that fed;
And these words appear on the pedestal:
"Ozymandias is my name, king of kings;
Ye Mighty, look on my works, and despair!"
Nothing else remains. Around the decay
Of that colossal wreck, bare and boundless
Stretch far away the level and lone sands.

(b) I met a traveller from an antique land
Who said: Two vast and trunkless legs of stone
Stand in the desert. Near them, on the sand,
Half sunk, a shattered visage lies, whose frown,
And wrinkled lip, and sneer of cold command,
Tell that its sculptor well those passions read
Which yet survive, stamped on these lifeless things,
The hand that mocked them, and the heart that fed;
And on the pedestal these words appear:
"My name is Ozymandias, king of kings;
Look on my works, ye Mighty, and despair!"
Nothing beside remains. Round the decay
Of that colossal wreck, boundless and bare
The lone and level sands stretch far away.

3. (a) Shall I, wasting in despair,
Die because a woman's fair?
  Or make pale my cheeks with care
'Cause another's rosy are?
Be she fairer than the day,
Or the flowery meads in May,
    If she think not well of me,
    What care I how fair she be?

(b) Shall I waste all my life in cold despair,
And die because a woman is so fair?
Shall I make pale my rosy cheek with care,
Since I have learned another's rosy are?
And what if she is fairer than the day,
Or even than the flowery meads in May;
If true it is she thinks not well of me,
Alas, what boots it me how fair she be?

CHAPTER FIVE

Tone

WE ARE NOW READY to apply the lessons of the preceding four chapters to the subject of *tone*. We could not do so before, because tone results from the interaction of almost everything that we have been talking about up to this point. Tone is the over-all emotional and intellectual effect of a passage of writing. To it, connotation, diction, and rhythm all contribute.

We have already seen that an important function of language is the creation of an attitude on the part of the reader toward the subject being discussed. It is the tone which the writer adopts that determines precisely what that attitude will be. We have seen, too, that the attitude which a writer has toward what he is discussing is not necessarily the attitude which he wishes his readers to have. An advertising man, for example, or the hired writer of speeches for political candidates, may be completely indifferent to his subject, or he may have very different views from those which he is expected to encourage. But since it is his job to make his reader feel a certain way toward his subject, he deliberately writes in a certain vein which will evoke that feeling. From the reader's standpoint it is highly desirable that such strategy be understood and taken into account before a decision is made and acted upon. That is one reason why you should know what tone is, and how it is created.

But a more important reason is that an understanding of tone and its contributory elements can vastly enrich your pleasure in reading imaginative literature. If you know how tone is created, you can apply that knowledge to whatever you are reading and thus discover what sort of attitude your author has toward the subject. It may be that, once you have analyzed his attitude, you will be reluctant to share it as he desires you to do. That is all right; that is the sacred privilege of the genuinely critical reader. Or it may be that a similar consideration of the tone of a piece of imaginative writing will intensify your experience by clarifying the author's precise attitude and thus revealing subtle meanings of whose existence you had been unaware. In any event, you have everything to gain and nothing to lose by always remembering that tone is meant to influence *you*.

We hope that the foregoing paragraphs sound familiar to you. They should, because they say nothing more than was said in the very beginning of this book. And much that follows should also sound familiar, because as we discuss various specific ways by which the tone of a piece of writing is determined, we shall be drawing constantly upon the ideas presented in earlier chapters. In the following pages there is little that is really "new"; instead, it is a logical extension, development, and application of what we have said in connection with connotation, diction, and rhythm. And the degree of ease with which you understand what we are about to say will be a good indication of how much you have learned to date.

Words, we said in Chapter One, have the power not only to inform, to present an intellectual concept to the reader, but also to touch the reader's emotions, to color his response to whatever is being said. That, in brief, is what we mean by connotation. And we have also remarked that words and phrases are not water-tight compartments; their emotional suggestiveness spills over into the language that surrounds them. The emotional coloration of a single word can be suffused through a whole paragraph, so that the connotations of other words are subtly tinted to match. And it is this suffusion and interaction of many words, each with its own peculiar affective qualities, which in great part sets the tone of any piece of writing.

We shall take for granted by this time that you are adequately aware of this power of words in general. What we wish to do now is to show the influence upon tone of two or three special sorts of language—metaphors, symbols, and allusions.

Metaphors

First, about metaphors. (We use the word here in its inclusive sense of all figures of speech.) You will have no trouble understanding how metaphors operate if you have mastered the two sections of this book which deal with analogy and connotation. The function of a metaphor is to suggest an analogy. If a writer wishes to make something clearer and more vivid, he draws into his discussion, if only by a single word or two, a concrete image which brings to mind the same quality as the situation or object or person or abstract idea which needs illustration. For example, in describing the crowd in Times Square at various hours of the day and night, a feature writer may wish to impress his readers with several dominant characteristics of the crowd—its largeness, its appearance of oneness (people lose their individual identities and are swallowed up in the mass), its motion, and the fact that its size fluctuates at various hours. Now the writer *could* come right out and use those words—"largeness," "oneness," "motion," "fluctuation." But they are abstract words; they fail to make the reader "see." And so the writer may fall back on a well-worn cliché which, even if it lacks freshness, at least conveys the idea: he will speak of "the tides of humanity." As every reader is aware, the tides of the sea have the same characteristics which the writer finds in the Times Square crowd. And so the writer makes his point by an implied analogy between the sea and the crowd. The strength of the analogy, or metaphor, lies in the readiness and vividness with which the reader recognizes the one or more qualities which make the two objects "alike"—their bonds of similarity.

Metaphor therefore is used by writers primarily as a means of intellectual clarification. It makes abstract ideas concrete, complex ideas simple, unfamiliar ideas more comprehensible. But it has an additional effect—one which may be, in the long run, more important than the first. The thing to remember is that metaphors evoke mental images; and mental images, we have said, often have powerful emotional qualities. Thus metaphors themselves have connotations. And thus the selection of metaphors has a great deal to do with the total emotional context—the tone—of any passage of writing.

In our discussion of the cliché (Chapter Two) we saw one way in which a writer's use of metaphor may give us a clue to his thought processes and his sincerity. If he depends upon hackneyed figures of speech to convey his meaning, the probability is that he is seeing with the eyes of others. By cultivating your awareness of trite language, you are arming yourself against the horde of writers who seek to influence you with second-hand ideas, as well as with second-hand language.

But a writer's metaphors may also tell you other things about him and his own attitude, as well as the attitude he wishes you to have. First, we must remember that one of the chief concerns of every writer is to maintain the same tone throughout his unit of composition, whether he be writing a sonnet or a soap ad. Ordinarily, tone cannot be effective unless it is maintained unbroken. And since metaphorical language is one of the elements of tone, it must harmonize with the writer's design and with the subject and atmosphere which he is portraying. Take for example this bit of descriptive writing, from a newspaper report of a concert by the Pittsburgh Symphony Orchestra:

> Having opened the program with Moussorgsky's "A Night on Bald Mountain," a work which has been preserved for posterity by the brilliance of Rimsky-Korsakoff's orchestration, the orchestra launched into the main musical bill-of-fare for the evening, Brahms' second symphony. One could hardly have wished for more, for this Brahms masterpiece stands as a monument of musical architecture to the German master. From the opening, with its haunting principal theme, to the close, Mr. Reiner guided the big orchestra through the maze of sturdy contrapuntal fabric which is Johannes Brahms, with the skill of a harbor pilot steering a boat safely into port through familiar but treacherous waters.

Now the tone of the whole article (not reprinted here) is serious. The writer apparently wishes to present an accurate report of a concert, which is a delicate and complex imaginative experience. But does his choice of language and metaphor support this serious intent? Is it, indeed, at all consistent with the subject discussed? Scarcely. "Launched" has the connotation of impetuous, headlong, forceful, even somewhat disorderly action; one of its dictionary definitions is "to shove off." Can a symphony orchestra be said to "launch" into anything—unless, of course (which is plainly not the case here), the writer wants to ridicule its performance? Is "bill-of-fare," with its connotation of restaurant food, appropriate in a report of an event in the concert hall? "Monument of musical architecture," although it cannot stand too much logical scrutiny and is, in any event, cliché, at least is more consonant with the tone of the whole article. But above all, what about the metaphor by which the conductor is likened to a pilot and the Brahms symphony to an ocean liner, while the difficulties of the work are represented first as a maze and then as the treacherous waters of a harbor? The continuity of tone is rudely disrupted as, against our expectation and our desire, we are forced to envision a grizzled pilot on the bridge of the *Queen Elizabeth* as she slowly makes her way among the tugboats and barges of New York harbor. . . . What has happened to the Brahms symphony? The writer, it is quite plain, completely lacks a sense of fitness. As a result, his report, because it has no steady point of view, no coherent tone, fails to communicate his experience to his readers.

The skilled writer—the one who fully understands what he wishes to accomplish and knows how to go about accomplishing it—always takes care that his metaphors make the same sort of impression upon the reader as the passage would if stripped of its metaphors. The function of the metaphor is primarily to reënforce the tone which has already been established by the writer's choice of language in general. If the writer hopes to establish rapport with his reader on the basis of man-to-man talk, his metaphors will be drawn from common, everyday experience, just as his diction is designed to reflect the normal speech of the reader to whom he is addressing himself. But if he wishes to elevate his reader's feelings, his metaphors will themselves have that elevated quality. Unless each individual metaphor harmonizes with the tone of the whole, the reader will be distracted by the extraneous and irrelevant elements which are unexpectedly forced into his experience.

Whenever you encounter metaphorical language which seems to be inappropriate to the total tone of the passage, you may conclude (as we have in the case of our music critic) that the writer simply does not have a clear idea of his purpose or of the way to achieve it. But there is another alternative: may the writer not be deliberately using incongruous metaphor for some purpose? For one thing, the finest poets and prose writers often use an unexpected and superficially inappropriate metaphor for the sake of contrast. The tone of the play of *Hamlet* is largely derived from the abundance of metaphors referring to disease, corruption, and decay; there is much talk of purgatives, the putrefaction of flesh, and the unpleasant qualities of ulcers and blisters. Such metaphors effectively symbolize one theme of the play, which is the moral degeneration of the people in the court at Elsinore. But in the midst of these figures suddenly occurs a passage (act IV, scene 5) in which the talk is of roses, pansies, columbines, daisies, and violets, whose sweet fragrance is in strange contrast to the noisome odors which have been so much talked of ("My offence is rank; it smells to heaven"). The effect of such seeming incongruity is not to destroy the dominant emotional tone; rather, the flower references intensify it by throwing the corruption-infection theme into higher relief. The physical ugliness which symbolizes moral evil is made to seem even uglier by its juxtaposition with symbols of innocent beauty.

In one of his dispatches from the Spanish Civil War, Ernest Hemingway said of the German planes that were aiding the Loyalists: "If their orders are to strafe the road on their way home, you will get it. Otherwise, when they are finished with their jobs on their particular objective, they go off like bank clerks, flying home." And he continued: "Up toward Tortosa things looked quite deadly already from the way the planes were acting. But down here on the delta the artillery were still only warming up, like baseball pitchers lobbing them over in the bull pen."* Now the "bonds of similarity" between German planes and bank clerks (both are anxious to get home after the day's work) and between the warming-up respectively of heavy guns and of baseball pitchers (leisureliness, no great attention to control) make Hemingway's metaphors effective so far as the clarification of ideas is concerned. But are not bank clerks and baseball pitchers incongruous in the grim context of war? They are: and that is why Hemingway used them. German planes, even in

* Quoted by permission of *The New Republic*.

1938, when this dispatch was written, epitomized ruthlessness—but there is scarcely a less harmful man alive than a bank clerk! By setting the two side by side, Hemingway sought to make the reader more acutely conscious of the sinister meaning of the German planes in contrast to the peaceful inoffensiveness of a homing bank clerk. And the mention of the baseball pitchers in connection with artillery underscores the vast, tragic difference between the motives of gunners and those of pitchers. Hemingway, in a word, developed his readers' attitude toward war by his use of contrasting metaphors from peacetime.

Thus a careful consideration of the appropriateness of metaphor can throw much light on a writer's attitude toward his subject and the attitude that he expects us to have. In a similar manner we can find clues in the consistency, or lack of consistency, of the metaphors in a passage. As we pointed out long ago, the extended or repeated use of concrete language evokes in the reader's mind a series of pictures. And just as the retina of the physical eye retains an after-image, so does the eye of the imagination. When we read at normal speed, the picture that occurs in our mind is not instantly blotted out as soon as we have left the word that has called it forth. Instead, it lingers for an instant; and if another image is suggested before the first one has faded, the result will be a sort of double exposure. Unless the two images are of the same type, so that the second has a natural similarity to the first, they will clash, and the total effect will be one of confusion. That is what happened when our music critic spoke of a launching, a bill-of-fare, a monument of musical architecture, and an ocean liner—all in the space of a sentence or two.

Not long ago a congressman said:

> In other words the eighteen billion dollar industry could be sold to the public at one hundred percent write-up, more or less, or from thirty-three to forty-one billion dollars. Of course, I do not contend

that the public would be milked quite that dry. The bankers would have to sweeten these deals with enough sugar to attract public interest. But if they cut the gravy evenly, they would reap millions.

Here we have a glorious riot of palatal and visual imagery in such close succession that the total effect is surrealistic. First we see a cow (the public) being milked. On top of that picture appear hands (the bankers') doling out sugar (with teaspoons?). And in the climactic sentence we have a picture of the bankers cutting the gravy (only a member of Congress could explain how that is done) and then quickly proceeding to reap a harvest! What has happened is that in the congressman's mind such words as *milked, sweeten, gravy,* and *reap* have lost their metaphorical force—perhaps through overuse. They therefore fail to suggest to him the concrete images which are formed in the consciousness of many of his hearers.

Some writers have the gift of using a single metaphor to support and illuminate a whole long passage of their discussion. If they do it well, we are justified in thinking that they have unusually agile minds, which can follow a single analogy into many ramifications, all of them germane to the argument. But extended metaphors are dangerous devices in the hands of the less skilled. The essence of the successful metaphor is its natural appropriateness to the situation, and often immature writers are tempted to overwork a comparison. A freshman writer of a thousand-word "autobiography," for instance, sometimes begins by likening his life, down to the age of seventeen or eighteen, to the building of a house, and he insists on using the metaphor in every paragraph. ("The ground was broken . . . the architects were my parents . . . slowly but surely the foundations were laid . . . when I began school, it may be said that the first floor was finished and ready for occupancy . . ." etc.) While the initial idea may have been sound, the attempt to show that the stages of childhood and youth are analogous at every point to the stages of building a house results only in absurdity. And even in more serious writing, for a wide audience, an extended metaphor may have the same result, if we examine it closely enough. Some writers, who are more clever than honest, begin with a perfectly acceptable implied analogy. They thus win the faith of their readers, who are likely to accept without serious question every ensuing application of that analogy, whether it is logical or not.

For practice in examining an extended metaphor, read the following passage. Is the analogy sound at every point? Or does the writer sometimes strain his metaphor to make it apply to everything he is saying?

> I find the great thing in this world is not so much where we stand, as in what direction we are moving: to reach the port of heaven, we must sail sometimes with the wind and sometimes against it,—but we must sail, and not drift, nor lie at anchor. There is one very sad thing in old friendships, to every mind that is really moving onward. It is this: that one cannot help using his early friends as the seaman uses the log, to mark his progress. Every now and then we throw an old schoolmate over the stern with a string of thought tied to him, and look—I am afraid with a kind of luxurious and sanctimonious compassion—to see the rate at which the string reels off, while he lies there bobbing up and down, poor fellow! and we are dashing along with the white foam and bright sparkle at our bows;—the ruffled bosom of prosperity and progress, with a sprig of diamonds stuck in it! But this is only the sentimental side of the matter; for grow we must, if we outgrow all that we love.
>
> Don't misunderstand that metaphor of heaving the log, I beg you. It is merely a smart way of saying that we cannot avoid measuring our rate of movement by those with whom we have long been in the habit of comparing ourselves; and when they once become stationary, we can get our reckoning from them with painful accuracy. We see just what we were when they were our peers, and can strike the balance between that and whatever we may feel ourselves to be now. No doubt we may sometimes be mistaken. If we

change our last simile to that very old and familiar one of a fleet leaving the harbor and sailing in company for some distant region, we can get what we want out of it. There is one of our companions;—her streamers were torn into rags before she had got into the open sea, then by and by her sails blew out of the ropes one after another, the waves swept her deck, and as night came on we left her a seeming wreck, as we flew under our pyramid of canvas. But lo! at dawn she is still in sight,—it may be in advance of us. Some deep ocean-current has been moving her on, strong, but silent,—yes, stronger than these noisy winds that puff our sails until they are swollen as the cheeks of jubilant cherubim. And when at last the black steam-tug with the skeleton arms, which comes out of the mist sooner or later and takes us all in tow, grapples her and goes off panting and groaning with her, it is to that harbor where all wrecks are refitted, and where, alas! we, towering in our pride, may never come.

Exercise 1. Here are a number of definitions of slang by eminent writers, past and present. How do the connotations of the metaphor used by each writer define his own attitude?

1. Slang is language that takes off its coat, spits on its hands, and gets to work.
2. Slang is a dressing-room in which language, having an evil deed to prepare, puts on a disguise.
3. Slang is the speech of him who robs the literary garbage-carts on their way to the dumps.
4. The language of the street is always strong. . . . Cut these words and they would bleed; they are vascular and alive; they walk and run.
5. Slang is the wholesome fermentation or eructation of those processes eternally active in language, by which the froth and specks are thrown up, mostly to pass away, though occasionally to settle and permanently crystallize.

Exercise 2. Here is a miscellaneous selection of metaphors from prose and poetry. Examine each quotation for these points:

(1) The vividness and freshness with which the metaphor illuminates the idea; (2) the appropriateness of the metaphor to the subject discussed; (3) the clues which the metaphor offers to the attitude of the writer.

1. I've been meeting minds so earnest and helpless that it takes them half an hour to get from one idea to its immediately adjacent next neighbor, and that with infinite creaking and groaning. And when they've got to the next idea, they lie down on it with their whole weight and can get no farther, like a cow on a doormat, so that you can get neither in nor out with them.*

2. A child said *What is the grass?* fetching it to me with full hands;
   How could I answer the child? I do not know what it is any
      more than he.
   I guess it must be the flag of my disposition, out of hopeful green
      stuff woven.
   Or I guess it is the handkerchief of the Lord,
   A scented gift and remembrancer designedly dropt,
   Bearing the owner's name someway in the corners, that we may
      see and remark, and say *Whose?*

3. Puritanism, believing itself quick with the seed of religious liberty, laid, without knowing it, the egg of democracy.

4. Come, night; come, Romeo; come, thou day in night;
   For thou wilt lie upon the wings of night,
   Whiter than new snow on a raven's back.
   Come, gentle night, come, loving, black-brow'd night,
   Give me my Romeo; and, when he shall die,
   Take him and cut him out in little stars,
   And he will make the face of heaven so fine
   That all the world will be in love with night
   And pay no worship to the garish sun.

5. I get all the country I want in the Park, which is within five

* From *The Letters of William James;* by permission of Little, Brown & Company and The Atlantic Monthly Press, publishers.

minutes of me, and the song of the thrush is more pathetic there, like a quotation of poetry in a dreary page of prose.

6. Whene'er I come where ladies are,
   How sad soever I was before,
Though like a ship frost-bound and far
   Withheld in ice from the ocean's roar,
Third-wintered in that dreadful dock,
   With stiffened cordage, sails decayed,
And crew that care for calm and shock
   Alike, too dull to be dismayed,
Yet, if I come where ladies are,
   How sad soever I was before,
Then is my sadness banished far,
   And I am like that ship no more;
Or like that ship if the ice-field splits,
   Burst by the sudden polar spring,
And all thank God with their warming wits,
   And kiss each other and dance and sing,
And hoist fresh sails, that make the breeze
   Blow them along the liquid sea,
Out of the North, where life did freeze,
   Into the haven where they would be.

7. Teachers and pupils seemed animals of different species, useful and well-disposed towards each other, like a cow and a milk-maid; periodic contributions could pass between them, but not conversation.

8. Shyness is the protective fluid within which our personalities are able to develop into natural shapes. Without this fluid the character becomes merely standardized or imitative: it is within the tender velvet sheath of shyness that the full flower of idiosyncrasy is nurtured: it is from this sheath alone that it can eventually unfold itself, colored and undamaged.*

* From *Small Talk,* by Harold Nicolson; by permission of Harcourt, Brace & Co., publishers.

9. Besides, this Duncan
Hath borne his faculties so meek, hath been
So clear in his great office, that his virtues
Will plead like angels, trumpet-tongu'd, against
The deep damnation of his taking-off;
And pity, like a naked new-born babe
Striding the blast, or heaven's cherubin hors'd
Upon the sightless couriers of the air,
Shall blow the horrid deed in every eye,
That tears shall drown the wind.

10. That joke is like the last drop of greasy water wrung out of an afternoon dish-clout—it came with difficulty and might as well have stayed behind.

Exercise 3. In the light of what has been said about consistency of metaphor, what is the effect of each of the following passages?

1. The pressure in the boiler is up to the bursting point. The lobbyists and the profiteers are licking their chops. It is going to take firm and decisive action—it is going to take team work and support on every hand—if we are to hold this country on an even keel.

2. I have a mistress, for perfections rare
In every eye, but in my thoughts most fair,
Like tapers on the altar shine her eyes;
Her breath is the perfume of sacrifice;
And wheresoe'er my fancy would begin,
Still her perfection lets religion in.
We sit and talk, and kiss away the hours
As chastely as the morning dews kiss flowers;
I touch her, like my beads, with devout care,
And come unto my courtship as my prayer.

3. A feeling of comical sadness is likely to come over the mind of any middle-aged man who sets himself to recollecting the names

of different authors that have been famous, and the number of contemporary immortalities whose end he has seen since coming to manhood. Many a light, hailed by too careless observers as a fixed star, has proved to be only a short-lived lantern at the tail of a newspaper kite. That literary heaven which our youth saw dotted thick with rival glories, we find now to have been a stage-sky merely, artificially enkindled from behind; and the cynical daylight which is sure to follow all theatrical enthusiasms shows us ragged holes where once were luminaries, sheer vacancy instead of lustre. Our earthly reputations, says a great poet, are the color of grass, and the same sun that makes the green bleaches it out again. But next morning is not the time to criticize the scene-painter's firmament, nor is it quite fair to examine coldly a part of some general illusion in the absence of that sympathetic enthusiasm, that self-surrender of the fancy, which made it what it was. It would not be safe for all neglected authors to comfort themselves in Wordsworth's fashion, inferring genius in an inverse proportion to public favor, and a high and solitary merit from the world's indifference. On the contrary, it would be more just to argue from popularity to a certain amount of real value, though it may not be of that permanent quality which insures enduring fame. The contemporary world and Wordsworth were both half right. He undoubtedly owned and worked the richest vein of his period; but he offered to his contemporaries a heap of gold-bearing quartz where the baser mineral made the greater show, and the purchaser must do his own crushing and smelting, with no guaranty but the bare word of the miner. It was not enough that certain bolder adventurers should now and then show a nugget in proof of the success of their venture. The gold of the poet must be refined, moulded, stamped with the image and superscription of his time, but with a beauty of design and finish that are of no time. The work must surpass the material. Wordsworth was wholly void of that shaping imagination which is the highest criterion of a poet.

Symbols

Down to this point, we have been concerned primarily with metaphors whose significance in context depends upon the situation which they are called upon to clarify. A metaphor involving a rose, for example, may serve one or more of a number of purposes. It may be designed to emphasize the idea of color: "Her cheek like the rose is, but fresher, I ween." It may emphasize the idea of odor:

> What's in a name? That which we call a rose
> By any other name would smell as sweet.

Or it may emphasize the idea of softness:

> There is sweet music here that softer falls
> Than petals from blown roses on the grass.

The special quality of the rose which is recalled by the comparison depends upon what quality is being emphasized by the context.

But now consider these other passages in which the rose is mentioned:

> When this, our rose, is faded,
> And these, our days, are done,
> In lands profoundly shaded
> From tempest and from sun;
> Ah, once more come together,
> Shall we forgive the past,
> And safe from worldly weather
> Possess our souls at last? *

---

* Reprinted by permission of Dodd, Mead & Co., Inc.

Loveliest of lovely things are they,
On earth, that soonest pass away.
The rose that lives its little hour
Is prized beyond the sculptured flower.

The fairest things have fleetest end,
  Their scent survives their close:
But the rose's scent is bitterness
  To him that loved the rose.

This world that we're a-livin' in
  Is mighty hard to beat;
You get a thorn with every rose,
  But ain't the roses sweet!

Gather ye rosebuds while ye may,
  Old Time is still a-flying,
And this same flower that smiles today
  Tomorrow will be dying.

In these instances the rose is not used for the sake of specific comparison. Instead, it "stands for" or symbolizes something: namely, transcendent physical beauty (with a frequent suggestion of impermanence). Our response to the mention of the rose is determined not so much by the emotional content as by our well-established habit of thinking of the rose as a symbol of beauty.

Symbols, therefore, are metaphors whose associative meaning is permanently fixed. They are important in communication, above all in imaginative prose and poetry, because writers often allow them actually to bear the full meaning of a passage rather than to act as accessories and commentaries, as is the case with other metaphors. Symbolism, skillfully used, is far more effective than bald literal statement. This is true for two reasons. The first is that symbols, like other kinds of metaphor, evoke an emotional reaction by way of sensuous imagery; the second is that, because most symbols have figured in literature for centuries, they are surrounded by an aura of literary association which evokes in the well-read man a host of reminiscences of passages in older literature, with all that they themselves connote. The use of a river as a symbol of the eternal flux of life, of the absence of anything really permanent and substantial in our human existence, goes all the way back to Plato and Heraclitus, and countless writers of prose and poetry have used it since. One who reads Matthew Arnold's "The Future" finds in Arnold's extended use of the symbol, echoes of a hundred other men who have set down the same poignantly melancholy reflections on earthly vanities.

It is impossible to read imaginative literature with genuine understanding unless we keep constantly on the alert for these pregnant symbols, which "mean" much more than they seem to say on the surface. In a simple word or two, they sum up the most important ideas in life. Here are a few common ones:

gold — The constant symbol of wealth, of material (as opposed to spiritual) possessions. (How does gold as a symbol differ from silver?—Read Browning's "Andrea del Sarto" and see how the poet uses gold to symbolize the painter's tragedy.)

star — Remoteness, purity, permanence. (What is the meaning implied in Shelley's line, "The desire of the moth for the star"?)

> Bright star, would I were steadfast as thou art!
> Not in lone splendor hung aloft the night,
> And watching, with eternal lids apart,

Like Nature's patient, sleepless eremite,
The moving waters at their priestlike task
Of pure ablution round earth's human shores,
Or gazing on the new soft-fallen mask
Of snow upon the mountains and the moors:
No—yet still steadfast, still unchangeable,
Pillow'd upon my fair love's ripening breast,
To feel forever its soft fall and swell,
Awake forever in a sweet unrest,
Still, still to hear her tender-taken breath,
And so live ever—or else swoon to death.

crossroads A choice between two or more courses of action—usually a critical decision.

Two roads diverged in a yellow wood,
And sorry I could not travel both
And be one traveler, long I stood
And looked down one as far as I could
To where it bent in the undergrowth;

Then took the other, as just as fair,
And having perhaps the better claim,
Because it was grassy and wanted wear;
Though as for that the passing there
Had worn them really about the same,

And both that morning equally lay
In leaves no step had trodden black.
Oh, I kept the first for another day!
Yet knowing how way leads on to way,
I doubted if I should ever come back.

I shall be telling this with a sigh
Somewhere ages and ages hence:
Two roads diverged in a wood, and I—

I took the one less traveled by,
And that has made all the difference.*

ice Coldness, and therefore often death. Also hardness, and therefore the word can imply a personal attitude.

Some say the world will end in fire,
Some say in ice.
From what I've tasted of desire
I hold with those who favor fire.
But if it had to perish twice,
I think I know enough of hate
To say that for destruction ice
Is also great
And would suffice.*

dice Chance, accident, absence of reasonable plan.

moon Peace, serenity, romantic love.

The use of such symbols as these adds much to the emotional tone of any piece of writing. Sometimes they serve to reënforce an impression which is produced by other means. At other times they are used for ironic contrast, as when, for instance, a novelist who has just described a sordid occurrence in the London slums suddenly shifts the reader's vision to the stars shining tranquilly in the skies, and thus intensifies, by contrast, the evil quality of what he has just been talking about.

While the general import of a symbol is fixed, its precise emotional connotation varies with the tone of the passage in which it occurs. And thus symbolism and tone—the part and the whole—interact one upon the other. Take for example three abiding symbols of death—the words *sleep, grave,* and *worm.* Each word implies a different sort of attitude toward the fact of

* From Robert Frost, *Collected Poems,* Henry Holt & Company.

death. *Sleep* is almost wholly favorable in its attitude; it connotes relief from physical and mental pain, welcome oblivion. *Grave,* however, is more ambiguous; it has less of the warmth, the comfort, that *sleep* suggests. It implies, above all, silence, lack of motion, coldness. *Worm* is the least pleasant of the symbols, with its grisly suggestion of the physical disintegration of the body after death.

But note how, in the following passages, the precise feeling we are expected to adopt toward death is determined, not alone by the selection of one symbol rather than another, but by the context, which subtly modifies the connotation of the symbol:

> From too much hope of living,
> From hope and fear set free,
> We thank with brief thanksgiving
> Whatever gods may be
> That no life lives forever;
> That dead men rise up never;
> That even the weariest river
> Winds somewhere safe to sea.
>
> Then star nor sun shall waken,
> Nor any change of light:
> Nor sound of waters shaken,
> Nor any sound or sight;
> Nor wintry leaves nor vernal,
> Nor days nor things diurnal;
> Only the sleep eternal
> In an eternal night.

Here the poet—Swinburne—plainly regards death as a narcotic sleep. It is welcomed, not because it promises anything positive, but because at least it will blot out all the disappointed hopes, the frustrations and uncertainties, of life. The meaning of *sleep,* then, is colored by the lines that lead up to it.

Our revels now are ended. These our actors,
As I foretold you, were all spirits, and
Are melted into air, into thin air;
And, like the baseless fabric of this vision,
The cloud-capp'd towers, the gorgeous palaces,
The solemn temples, the great globe itself,
Yea, all which it inherit, shall dissolve
And, like this insubstantial pageant faded,
Leave not a rack behind. We are such stuff
As dreams are made on, and our little life
Is rounded with a sleep.

To Shakespeare, in these lines, the sleep of death promises nothing more than it promised to Swinburne; but death is viewed not as a release from life, but as a natural culmination of an existence which is itself unsubstantial and illusory. The meaning of *sleep* in the last line is compounded of the meanings of many words that preceded it, all to the same effect—*spirits, melted, thin air, baseless, vision, cloud-capp'd, dissolve, insubstantial, faded, rack* [cloud fragment], *dreams*. Death and life are two parts of a perfectly harmonious whole.

To die; to sleep;
No more; and by a sleep to say we end
The heart-ache and the thousand natural shocks
That flesh is heir to. 'Tis a consummation
Devoutly to be wish'd. To die; to sleep;—
To sleep? Perchance to dream! Ay, there's the rub;
For in that sleep of death what dreams may come,
When we have shuffl'd off this mortal coil,
Must give us pause. There's the respect
That makes calamity of so long life.

Here Shakespeare uses the same basic idea that Swinburne sets forth. But note how he finds in the symbol of sleep elements that Swinburne did not consider. Mention of dreams as a part of sleep in effect nullifies the usual meaning of the symbol. And be sure to compare the total effect of this passage with the preceding one, which also speaks of dreams. What is the difference?

EXERCISE 4. Here is a further group of passages in which the idea of death is represented by one or another of the symbols we have just mentioned—sleep, grave, and worms. By weighing the emotional tone of the whole passage, including the connotation of the other metaphors, try to decide just what attitude each writer wishes us to adopt toward death:

1. Is not short pain well borne, that brings long ease,
   And lays the soul to sleep in quiet grave?
   Sleep after toil, port after stormy seas,
   Ease after war, death after life does greatly please.

2. I must go down to the seas again to the vagrant gypsy life,
   To the gull's way and the whale's way where the wind's like a
   whetted knife;
   And all I ask is a merry yarn from a laughing fellow-rover,
   And quiet sleep and a sweet dream when the long trick's over.*

3. Wherever literature consoles sorrow or assuages pain; wherever it brings gladness to eyes which fail with wakefulness and tears, and ache for the dark house and the long sleep,—there is exhibited in its noblest form the immortal influence of Athens.

4. Sleep is a death; oh make me try,
   By sleeping, what it is to die,
   And as gently lay my head
   On my grave, as now my bed.

* From *Poems,* by John Masefield. By permission of The Macmillan Company, publishers.

5. Let's dry our eyes; and thus far hear me, Cromwell,
   And when I am forgotten, as I shall be,
   And sleep in dull cold marble, where no mention
   Of me more must be heard of, say, I taught thee.

6. Your worm is your only emperor for diet. We fat all creatures else to fat us, and we fat ourselves for maggots. Your fat king and your lean beggar is but variable service, two dishes, but to one table; that's the end. . . . A man may fish with the worm that hath eat of a king, and eat of the fish that hath fed of that worm. . . . [and thus] a king may go a progress through the guts of a beggar.

7. He'd have the best, and that was none too good;
   No barrier could hold, before his terms.
   He lies below, correct in cypress wood,
   And entertains the most exclusive worms.

8. The place and the object [Rome viewed from the Capitoline hill] gave ample scope for moralising on the vicissitudes of fortune, which spares neither man nor the proudest of his works, which buries empires and cities in a common grave; and it was agreed that in proportion to her former greatness the fall of Rome was the more awful and deplorable.

9. *Romeo* [to Mercutio, who is badly wounded]:
   Courage, man; the hurt cannot be much.
   Mercutio: No, 'tis not so deep as a well, nor so wide as a church-door, but 'tis enough, 'twill serve. Ask for me tomorrow, and you shall find me a grave man.

EXERCISE 5.

1. What is the usual meaning of the following symbols?

   Sunrise, noon, twilight, autumn, April, seed, tear, tinsel, drum, tide, wine, poppy, white, purple, red, gray, green, lion, nightingale.

2. Read Ivan Bunin's short story, "The Gentleman from San Francisco," and compile a list of the many symbols it contains.

EXERCISE 6. Explain the symbolism of the following quotations:

1. [Of Dickens's *Pickwick Papers*] The thing is aimed at the diaphragm, and, by ricochet, touches the heart.

2. After all, what laws can be laid down about books? . . . To admit authorities, however heavily furred and gowned, into our libraries and let them tell us how to read, what to read, what value to place upon what we read, is to destroy the spirit of freedom which is the breath of those sanctuaries.* [What is the symbolic meaning of "furred and gowned"?]

3. Snow falling and night falling fast oh fast
In a field I looked into going past,
And the ground almost covered smooth in snow,
But a few weeds and stubble showing last.

The woods around it have it—it is theirs.
All animals are smothered in their lairs.
I am too absent-spirited to count;
The loneliness includes me unawares.

And lonely as it is that loneliness
Will be more lonely ere it will be less—
A blanker whiteness of benighted snow
With no expression, nothing to express.

They cannot scare me with their empty spaces
Between stars—on stars where no human race is.
I have it in me so much nearer home
To scare myself with my own desert places.†

---

* From *The Second Common Reader,* by Virginia Woolf. By permission of Harcourt, Brace & Co., publishers.

† From Robert Frost, *Collected Poems,* Henry Holt & Company.

Allusions

In Chapter One we said, "Often a single line or two may contain a wealth of suggestiveness. To one who knows the story of the fall of Troy, Marlowe's lines

> Was this the face that launched a thousand ships,
> And burnt the topless towers of Ilium?

contain all the emotional values implicit in the story of a beautiful woman for whose love a civilization was almost destroyed." This was an anticipatory example of another important source of tone: the allusion, which is a reference to specific places or persons or literary passages that, like metaphorical symbols, have come to "stand for" a certain idea. Every writer of anything more complicated than a comic strip relies to a greater or less extent upon the device of allusion. The degree of understanding with which anyone reads is directly proportional to the readiness with which he recognizes allusions when he encounters them—and recognizes not only their bare, literal meaning, but also their emotional connotation. And this readiness depends, in turn, upon the fund of general knowledge which he has at his command. The more familiar he is with the history of our culture, with mythology, with famous literary works, the better prepared he is to receive the full message which the writer intends for him. And the only way to cultivate such a familiarity is to read and read and read—and then to remember. It is possible, of course, to identify some allusions by going to books of reference, like Brewer's *Reader's Handbook* and the same compiler's *Dictionary of Phrase and Fable*. But only a few conscientious souls will go to the trouble of constantly interrupting their reading to "look things up," and too frequent recourse to reference books is a dismal business anyway. The only genuinely satisfactory way to handle allusions is to be prepared for them when they come—so that one may have the justifiable pride of recognizing the already familiar. Perhaps we can emphasize the importance of allusions by referring to an entertaining essay by Wallace Stegner, called "Turtle at Home," which appeared a few years ago in a national magazine. "Turtle at Home" is an intimate report of the life of a turtle named Achilles, which survived innumerable encounters with trucks in the street but in the end was crushed (metaphorically if not literally) by the irresistible force of Love in the person of another turtle. Unless we know who the Achilles of Homeric story was and what he represents, we miss the appropriateness of the turtle's name.

In the essay occurs this paragraph:

> But strawberries were his real fleshpots. They left him giddy, speeded up his reactions, put him almost in a frenzy of bliss. I shall cherish to my last hour the picture of Achilles munching large Marshall strawberries with the juice running down his rhythmic jaws and his whole face beatific. He was Greek, he was Dionysiac, he was young Keats bursting Joy's grape against his palate fine, he was a Rabelaisian monk with his robe tucked up, glutting himself with pagan pleasures. What reflections of a like charm could one get from the sight of a dog wolfing his carnivorous meals, or a cat washing her face after meat with a fussy, old-maid, New England nasty-neatness? *

Here is a whole series of allusions, and the humor of the passage is completely lost if the reader cannot interpret them. Remember that Mr. Stegner is describing the sinful appetite of a pet turtle. "His real fleshpots": the dictionary may define the word, but it may not recall the historical association—the fleshpots of Egypt, with their place in Biblical story (*Exodus* XVI:3). "He was Greek, he was Dionysiac": an allusion to the festivals of ancient Greece in which the physical senses, particularly those connected

* Reprinted by permission of Mr. Stegner and *The Atlantic Monthly.*

with eating and drinking, were indulged to the point of frenzy. "He was young Keats . . .": we must recall Keats's "Ode on Melancholy":

> Ay, in the very temple of delight
> Veil'd Melancholy has her sovran shrine,
> Though seen of none save him whose strenuous tongue
> Can burst Joy's grape against his palate fine . . .

"He was a Rabelaisian monk . . .": an allusion to Friar John, that celebrated figure in Rabelais who took a healthy delight in the pleasures of the flesh.

Thus we have, in a single paragraph, a series of four allusions, drawn from the Old Testament, the history of ancient Greece, early nineteenth-century English literature, and Renaissance French literature: all of them connoting indulgence in the joys of the table and the cup. Mr. Stegner might have said, in sentences devoid of metaphor and allusion, that Achilles went wild over strawberries; but how much more vivid is this allusive paragraph—*if* the reader fully reacts to the allusions! Each symbol (because many allusions are just that) summons up, in the well-read man's consciousness, a whole complex of associations. He remembers the story that lay behind the fleshpots of Egypt; he recalls from his miscellaneous reading the story of the Dionysiac revels; he knows that young Keats was enamored of physical beauty, of which the pleasure of the palate is a phase; he sees again Rabelais' robust descriptions of the far from ascetic monk. In effect, therefore, Achilles' strawberry debauch is the sum of all the palatal orgies in human history.

But all this of a *turtle!* What can the gargantuan appetites of a pleasure-loving monk have in common with the quantitatively minute strawberry consumption of a turtle? Nothing, except the gusto. And that is the point. Mr. Stegner has carefully chosen his allusions for a particular purpose. First, they translate Achilles' unrestrained sensuality into a series of human equivalents, and thus induce the reader to regard Achilles in human terms. Secondly, the patent exaggeration and incongruity of the allusions have the ultimate effect of kindly humor. The reader's attitude toward Achilles' gormandizing has been determined by the connotative quality of the allusions.

Probably you think that this explanation has been laborious; and it has. But the very fact that we have labored in trying to explain the function of a few simple allusions in a contemporary essay has its own point, which is that allusions, like metaphors and symbols, are not meant to be analyzed; when they are thus examined, much of their power evaporates. They are meant to be apprehended automatically. The truly intelligent reader, when he encounters such a paragraph as we have quoted, does not stop to wonder what each allusion means; his acquaintanceship with literature and history enables him spontaneously to react as the writer intends him to. In a word, he *knows.*

There are three major sources of allusions, together with lesser sources which are as numerous as the fields of knowledge themselves. Those three major sources are mythology, literature (including the Bible), and history.

One of the most regrettable shortcomings of modern education is that it does not provide for some knowledge of mythology. In the twentieth century it is hard for us to realize how important a part mythology played in the imaginations of writers and readers down through the ages. The gods and goddesses of Olympus, the heroes of ancient legend, were as familiar to the people who created English literature as a popular movie star is to us. Their very names—Juno, Hercules, Prometheus, Vulcan, Jupiter—had the power to evoke rich emotions which sprang from recollection of the wondrous stories in which these figures had their being. Unless you can somehow recreate for yourself the emotional experience which a mythological reference involved for readers in older generations, your reading of much non-contemporary literature is bound to be a dry, unexciting business. One practical way to remedy your ignorance of mythology is to go to the fountainhead of a great many of the myths and legends we have received from ancient Greece and Rome—the poems of Ovid, of which there are many translations. Another way is to browse in such collections as Bulfinch's *Age of Fable*. And in any event, you should read widely in English poetry; if you do, the individual attributes of the mythological figures, and the stories in which they occur, will gradually become familiar to you.

The main reason why modern men and women know so little about mythology is that so few of them ever have, or take, the opportunity to read classical (*i.e.* Latin and Greek) literature, in which these myths are embodied. But even apart from its connection with mythology, a little knowledge of classical literature can be of tremendous help in equipping you to understand allusions even in everyday reading. The *Iliad* and the *Odyssey* of Homer, for instance, are full of episodes and personages that are frequently referred to in ordinary journalism, to say nothing of the permanent monuments of our literature. If we read of a certain political figure who is "sulking in his tent" because he has not got what he wanted, the meaning is far clearer if we recall the episode of Achilles (the fighter, not the turtle) sulking in his tent because he had captured in battle a beautiful girl whom his general, Agamemnon, would not let him keep. Or if someone's prophecies of doom have earned him the name of a Cassandra, it means much to know just who Cassandra was—and to do that we must have read Greek tragedy. (What is the difference in implied attitude between "Cassandra" and "Jeremiah"?)

It is true that since all writers must keep constantly in mind the limitations of their audience, contemporary writers are using fewer and fewer allusions to classical story. The only ones which remain are those which have been used so often that they have become established as part of the common tongue. But no intelligent reader will limit himself to contemporary writing, and he therefore needs to be prepared for the free allusiveness that is characteristic of the writing of earlier ages.

Naturally, allusions to our own English and American literature are more frequently encountered nowadays than classical allusions. Not the least of the functions of a college survey course in literature is to show how a knowledge of older writing is essential to a full comprehension of present-day writing. Mr. Stegner, in the essay about the turtle, speaks of Achilles, after "he" has been discovered to be a "she," as "that Rosalind in boy's clothing." Obviously he expects his reader to recognize the allusion to the disguised heroine of *As You Like It,* and to enjoy the implied incongruity. And he concludes his essay with the simple statement, *"Amor vincit omnia."* One misses much if he does not recollect that this motto was also inscribed on a brooch worn by the Prioress in Chaucer's *Canterbury Tales.*

Thus literary allusions add their not inconsiderable influence in determining the precise effect of any piece of writing. In the case of references to characters in literature, we must know just what part they play in the poem or drama or novel in which they appear, and how their creator wished his readers to regard them in the first place. We then transfer this attitude to the new situation. If a man is called "a veritable Micawber," we are expected to react toward him as we react toward Dickens's Micawber himself: our attitude is expected to be a mixture of annoyance and amused tolerance. If, in his description of a woman, a writer refers to Becky Sharp or to Scarlett O'Hara, we know we are to look upon her as a selfish, willful woman. We could multiply instances almost indefinitely. We often run across references to Mr. So-and-so's "Man Friday." The allusion, of course, is to the friend and servant of Robinson Crusoe, and originally it connoted only helpfulness and devotion. Today, however, the implication has changed, and "Man Friday" has something of a derogatory tone; it suggests not only man-of-all-work but also someone akin to a stooge. Similarly the term "young Lochinvar" ("Young Lochinvar came out of the west"—Scott's *Marmion*) has suffered a change of connotation. Whereas it originally symbolized manliness, nowadays it carries a suggestion of priggishness and unpleasant precocity—as when it is used of a new and untried political leader whose virtues have been proclaimed with suspicious fervor.

Quotations imbedded in the text are a type of allusion. The pleasure and profit of our reading are vastly increased if we are trained to recognize such stray phrases and recall their full meaning in their original context. In his classic description of a prize fight, William Hazlitt uses both simple allusion and direct quotation to good purpose to emphasize the attitude which he maintains throughout the essay—that this is no ordinary prize fight, but an encounter worthy of Homeric epic. And so he draws into his narrative echoes both of Homer and of Milton, whose *Paradise Lost* is closely modelled upon Homer's epics.

> He [Tom Hickman, the "Gas-man"] strutted about more than became a hero, sucked oranges with a supercilious air, and threw away the skin with a toss of his head, and went up and looked at Neate, which was an act of supererogation. The only sensible thing he did was, as he strode away from the modern Ajax, to fling out his arms, as if he wanted to try whether they would do their work that day. By this time they had stripped, and presented a strong contrast in appearance. If Neate was like Ajax, "with Atlantean shoulders, fit to bear" [*Paradise Lost,* II, 306] the pugilistic reputation of all Bristol, Hickman might be compared to Diomed, light, vigorous, elastic, and his back glistened in the sun, as he moved about, like a panther's hide.

And then Hazlitt gives a wonderful blow-by-blow account of the epic encounter, which continued until

> The Gas-man went down, and there was another shout—a roar of triumph as the waves of fortune rolled tumultuously from side to side. This was a settler. Hickman got up, and "grinned horrible a ghastly smile," [*Paradise Lost,* II, 846] . . .

But although "all one side of his face was perfect scarlet, and his right eye was closed in dingy blackness," the bout went on.

> The wonder was the half-minute time. If there had been a minute or more allowed between each round, it would have been intelligible how they should by degrees recover strength and resolution; but to see two men smashed to the ground, smeared with gore, stunned, senseless, the breath beaten out of their bodies; and then, before you recover from the shock, to see them rise up with new strength and courage, stand ready to inflict or receive mortal offence, and rush upon each other "like two clouds over the Caspian" [*Paradise Lost,* II, 714–16]—this is the most astonishing thing of all:—this is the high and heroic state of man!

"This is the high and heroic state of man": and the quotations from *Paradise Lost* admirably underscore that theme. A reader of Hazlitt who remembers his Milton will transfer to his witnessing of the great fight the same feelings of awe with which he watched the titanic encounter between Satan and Death at the gates of hell. And that is exactly what Hazlitt intended.

The third major source from which writers draw their allusions is history. When the WPA sponsored low-priced theatrical performances in the middle 1930's, critics of the New Deal referred caustically to "bread and the circus." They did so because they believed that most of their readers would recognize the allusion to the device by which the Roman Emperors tried to keep their rebellious subjects' minds off their woes. The use of free food and free entertainment as a sop to popular discontent was a symptom of the decline of Roman power; it was followed in time by the complete collapse of Roman civilization—and the anti-New Dealers trusted that people would complete the analogy. That is one of the uses of historical allusions—to suggest a parallel (however incorrect it may be) between a present situation and a historical one, for the purpose of proving a point. In the months following the end of World War II, the air was filled with allusions to Harding, "normalcy," and Teapot Dome, as well as with some to Andrew Johnson. Can you explain why?

But even when it is not a question of argumentation, historical allusions often have powerful connotations to those who understand them. A whole library of romantic stories—or, to be more prosaic, a whole year's college course in history—is summed up in Stephen Vincent Benét's lines, at the beginning of *John Brown's Body,* which refer to the motley crowd who founded America:

> Stepchild of every exile from content
> And all the disavouched, hard-bitten pack
> Shipped overseas to steal a continent
> With neither shirts nor honor to their back.
>
> Pimping grandee and rump-faced regicide,
> Apple-cheeked younkers from a windmill-square,
> Puritans stubborn as the nails of Pride,
> Rakes from Versailles and thieves from County Clare,
>
> The black-robed priests who broke their hearts in vain
> To make you God and France or God and Spain.*

We shall not stop to discuss the main allusions, which should be obvious to every high-school graduate; but we should call your attention to one or two points which are overlooked by all except the most alert readers. Assuming that you know who the regicides were among America's founders, what about "rump-faced"? In addition to the visual image which the epithet suggests, there is also a punning allusion to the Rump Parliament which figures prominently in the history of the English civil war; and in "the nails of Pride" there is an allusion to the leader of the *coup* which resulted in the Rump Parliament.

Exercise 7.

1. What is the meaning and effect of the mythological allusions in the following quotations?

(a) So excellent a king; that was, to this,
Hyperion to a satyr; so loving to my mother
That he might not beteem the winds of heaven
Visit her face too roughly . . .
Frailty, thy name is woman!—
A little month, or e'er those shoes were old
With which she followed my poor father's body,
Like Niobe, all tears,—why she, even she—
O God! a beast, that wants discourse of reason,
Would have mourned longer—married with mine uncle,
My father's brother, but no more like my father
Than I to Hercules . . .

(b) The world is too much with us; late and soon,
Getting and spending, we lay waste our powers:
Little we see in Nature that is ours;
We have given our hearts away, a sordid boon!
The Sea that bares her bosom to the moon;
The winds that will be howling at all hours,
And are up-gathered now like sleeping flowers;

For this, for everything, we are out of tune;
It moves us not.—Great God! I'd rather be
A Pagan suckled in a creed outworn;
So might I, standing on this pleasant lea,
Have glimpses that would make me less forlorn;
Have sight of Proteus rising from the sea;
Or hear old Triton blow his wreathèd horn.

2. What is the symbolic or connotative meaning of the following names from mythology or ancient literature?

Narcissus, Arcadia, Aphrodite, Nestor, Pan, Tantalus, Maecenas, Phoebus Apollo, the Lotus Eaters, Penelope, Mercury, Parnassus, Lethe, Cerberus, Atalanta, Elysium, Hydra.

EXERCISE 8. Suppose you encounter each of the following words or phrases in a contemporary magazine article or book. What is the original source of the allusion? In what sort of modern context would it be found? What sort of event or person or situation might be described? What attitude (if any) is implied? (For example: An allusion to the lion and the lamb lying down together [*Isaiah,* XI:6] might today be found in a discussion of the reconciliation of two hostile factions of a political party.)

1. David and Bathsheba; thirty pieces of silver; Solomon; bringing down the pillars of the house; Jeremiah; pillar of fire; the promised land; Philistines.

2. Playing Boswell to so-and-so's Johnson; Mephistophelean; Utopia; like the wedding guest, he could not choose but hear; Enoch Arden; Babbitt; Izaak Walton; Jeeves; the seacoast of Bohemia; a real-life Horatio Alger story; Falstaffian wit; a pound of flesh; tilting at windmills; Simon Legree.

3. Waterloo; the Medicis; Brutus; the big stick; strength through joy; Puritanical; Nero; Diogenes; Rasputin; Magna Carta; Benedict Arnold; a house divided against itself.

Exercise 9. What is the meaning of the following stanza from Gray's "Elegy Written in a Country Church-Yard"? (It would help to have the whole poem at hand, to show the context in which these lines occur.)

> Some village-Hampden, that with dauntless breast
> The little Tyrant of his fields withstood;
> Some mute, inglorious Milton here may rest,
> Some Cromwell guiltless of his country's blood.

Plainly it is impossible, in a book of this scope, to acquaint you with all the ways in which writers communicate their attitudes to their readers and thus influence the readers' own attitudes. One cannot become a truly intelligent reader simply by remembering a few rules and principles; rather, as we said earlier, one reaches reading maturity only through long and well-directed practice. In the rest of this chapter we shall try to suggest the general direction of that practice by selecting for discussion and illustration a few more common means by which tone is determined. But remember that these in no way exhaust the list; a whole book the size of this one would be inadequate for that task.

Deviations from "Normal" Style

First, what about that particular type of writing that almost every college freshman condemns as "flowery"? It presents so frequent a stumbling block to the immature, and is so intimately associated with the question of tone, that we should devote some space to it.

Precisely what the adjective *flowery* means, the average student cannot tell, any more than a certain immortal writer could specify why he did not like Dr. Fell. But patient cross-examination often will reveal that writing is regarded as "flowery" when it is over-decorated, contains many figures of speech and other rhetorical devices, and, perhaps most important of all, is characterized by language peculiar to older (*i.e.,* pre-twentieth century) poetry. The question is, What is the reader to make of such writing?

You must remember, to begin with, that tastes and fashions in writing change from generation to generation. What once was thought to be "fine writing," today seems unbearably stiff and artificial, full of unnecessary flounces and furbelows. On the other hand, the plain, relatively undecorated style in fashion among most contemporary writers, whether of prose or poetry, would undoubtedly have been called "low" and "vulgar" by people in some other ages. In every epoch there is a "norm" of diction just as there is of sentence-length. And so when you read certain Elizabethan poems, for example, or De Quincey's elaborate flights of prose, or some of Tennyson's verse, it is completely unfair for you to dismiss such masterpieces as "flowery," simply because they do not conform to our contemporary standards of diction. You have a very definite obligation to learn what criteria of style prevailed when these pieces were written—to understand exactly what sort of effects their writers were striving for. You must, in a word, put yourself in the place of the audience for which each work was originally composed. If, by thoughtful study of books about literature and of representative poetry and prose from various epochs, you begin to understand that different ages have different literary fashions, you will see that your wholesale condemnation of unfamiliar styles of writing as "flowery" is unjust.

But what about contemporary writing that has the same "flowery" manner? To discover what the writer means by thus deviating from the present-day norm of diction, consider all that we have already said about the function of words in setting the tone of writing, and recall also, from Chapter Four, the function of rhythm. Here is a sample of writing that is both contemporary and "flowery":

Isolt the abandoned one, fair princess of Brittany, stands forlorn on her native strand. Her wide eyes linger long on the empty horizon of the gray North Sea, where last she has seen her beloved Tristan, dropping over the rim of the world and out of sight.

The good King Howel, fond father of Isolt, stands silent on the headland, watching. His great heart swells with compassion, and as he turns away to his castle, he knows that he will never forget this poignant picture of her loneliness. It had been etched indelibly in his memory.

And yet, as the years unfurl, he remembers much more than her dejection. In his mind's eye he sees her standing there, with white birds circling in the sunlight overhead. He sees the majestic roll of the waves on the eternal sea. He sees the fleecy clouds drifting aloft in the blue, and the blossoming heather blowing in the wind. And so the magnificence of Nature surrounding the lonely Isolt tempered the melancholy of his memory with a glow of enduring beauty.

Plainly the author of those paragraphs wishes to stir his reader's emotions. In attempting to do so, he has pulled out all the stops: he has used connotative words galore, and he has manipulated the sentence rhythms to try to induce the contemplative feelings that are associated with poetry. Perhaps the trick succeeds with the untutored reader; but what about your own reactions? Probably you have marvelled at the lavish array of clichés that are spread out before you: clichés which obviously expect you to respond in a certain way, but to which you, as a critical reader, refuse to respond. You may remember what we said in Chapter Two about the implications of cliché language. And so you will not be surprised to discover that this lantern-slide effusion was written for a crass purpose:

Such is the comfort, the blessing, the benediction, that beauty bestows on memory. The provision of such beauty has ever been the goal of our earnest endeavors at G—— Funeral Homes. To invest a beauty of memory in our every deed, sparing no conceivable effort in providing services of immaculate refinement, always has been our ideal.

In that example, as in the radio-phonograph advertisements quoted on pages 177–78 and 182–83, the writer plainly wanted to achieve a serious tone. His purpose was to hypnotize his uncritical reader into believing in the superiority of his employer's mortuary arrangements. And that is one frequent present-day use (or abuse) of the deliberately "poetic" tone, against which it is not at all hard to be fortified.

The use of language that is inappropriately elevated and "poetic" is one aspect of the general topic of incongruity; another is the use of language that is too colloquial or too earthy for the subject and occasion. A funeral sermon, for instance, should not be "flowery"; it is most effective when its language is simple, unpretentious, and above all unhackneyed. But on the other hand, it should not contain slang or other language which is suggestive of distinctly different occasions. When an incongruous word or phrase suddenly intervenes to break the prevailing tone of the passage, we have a form of bathos (anti-climax), as in Joaquin Miller's poem "Myrrh," on the anguish of his parting from his wife Minnie:

> And you and I have buried Love,
> A red seal on the coffin's lid;
> The clerk below, the court above,
> Pronounce it dead: the corpse is hid
> And I who never cross'd your will
> Consent . . . that you may have it still.
> Farewell! a sad word easy said
> And easy sung, I think, by some . . .
> . . . I clutch'd my hands, I turned my head
> In my endeavour and was dumb;
> And when I should have said, Farewell,
> I only murmured, "This is hell!"

The contemporary American writer H. L. Mencken is a past master of the use of both kinds of incongruities—the pretentious and the colloquial—for comic effect. His three volumes of autobiography (*Happy Days, Newspaper Days,* and *Heathen Days*) can teach the observant reader more about the function of word-connotations than can volumes of commentary:

> Today the fear of cops seems to have departed teetotally from American boys, at least on the level of the bourgeoisie. I have seen innocents of eight or nine go up to one boldly, and speak to him as if he were anyone else. Some time ago the uplifters in Baltimore actually organized a school for Boy Scouts with cops as teachers, and it did a big trade until the cops themselves revolted. What happened was that those told off to instruct the Scouts in the rules of traffic, first aid, the operation of fire-alarm boxes, etiquette toward the aged and blind, the elements of criminal law and other such branches got so much kidding from their fellows that they were covered with shame, and in the end the police commissioner let out the academy *sine die,* and restored the faculty to more he duties.*

Irony

Mr. Mencken's staple device of dead-pan humor brings us naturally to another element of tone—one which causes more trouble to the immature reader than any other. That element is irony, which is an affirmation, written in apparent seriousness, of what one does *not* believe. Irony differs from hypocrisy in that the user of irony expects his reader to see beneath his surface pretensions; he does not wish to be taken seriously. The effect of irony lies in the striking disparity between what is said and what is meant. The most famous example of sustained irony in English literature is "A Modest Proposal" by Jonathan Swift, which you should not neglect to read. In it, Swift describes the economic and social advantages that would accrue to the Irish if

* From *Happy Days,* by H. L. Mencken. By permission of Alfred A. Knopf, Inc., publisher.

they would use a new supply of food—namely, their own children. With all the sobriety and objectivity of a professional economist, he enumerates the benefits of such a practice—the increased income to prolific parents, the lessened demands on public charity, the introduction of a succulent table dish, and so on—and he deftly meets all objections that could be raised to the scheme. Horrified by this cold-blooded advocacy of cannibalism, the reader is forced finally to conclude that Swift could not possibly mean what he says. Only then does the reader realize that Swift is writing in the bitterest vein of irony; that "A Modest Proposal" is really a statement of the terrible poverty which existed in Ireland in the eighteenth century; and that at every point Swift is indicting the political and economic practices that resulted in the plight of his countrymen.

Arthur Hugh Clough's "The Latest Decalogue" (you must, of course, know what the title means) offers a very simple example of irony. Remember that the ironist is a man who writes with his tongue in his cheek:

> Thou shalt have one God only; who
> Would be at the expense of two?
> No graven images may be
> Worshipped, except the currency:
> Swear not at all; for, for thy curse
> Thine enemy is none the worse:
> At church on Sunday to attend
> Will serve to keep the world thy friend:
> Honour thy parents; that is, all
> From whom advancement may befall;
> Thou shalt not kill; but need'st not strive
> Officiously to keep alive:
> Do not adultery commit;
> Advantage rarely comes of it:
> Thou shalt not steal; an empty feat,
> When it's so lucrative to cheat:

Bear not false witness; let the lie
Have time on its own wings to fly:
Thou shalt not covet, but tradition
Approves all forms of competition.

In this sardonic poem, Clough expresses some very profound social criticism. If you can explain, on the basis of these lines, how he feels about the morality of his age, you have made a long step toward understanding how irony functions.

EXERCISE 10. How does the diction of each of the following passages deviate from the "norm" of present-day diction? How does that difference affect the reader's attitude toward what is said?

1. It was a proud and thrilled audience who heard Elizabeth Ann (Betty) Bollinger last evening, sing in the completely filled auditorium of North Idaho Teachers College, giving a program of French, German, Italian, and English compositions, varied in theme, difficult, and musically exquisite. Equal to the demands of each number, Miss Bollinger and her pianist accompanist, Elsa Petersen Hughes, gave a concert of high artistry.

   Miss Bollinger is a mixed bouquet of orchids, primroses and buttercups. She is the sophistication of well guided, obediently earned technique, and the naivete of youth at its first party. She is the headiness of a luxurious perfume, and the stamina of a glass of milk. She is the handclasp of a loyal, good friend, and the hesitant smile of a shy infant. She is the blush of dawn's sun on a hilltop field, and she is the glow of a sparkling gem in a Cartier case. She is Elizabeth Ann Bollinger whom the leading musicians of the country have welcomed into their sacrosanct realm with brilliant praise and prophesies. She is Betty Bollinger, Lewiston's daughter, whose head is unturned by the successes and adulation bestowed upon her by the largest cities of the west.

She is Betty Bollinger who loves better than anything to come to her home town, to her family, and her childhood friends. She is Betty Bollinger who will obligingly stand for hours singing difficult arias for her mother's friends while her own friends are gathering at the coke fountain for chatter and juke box music. She is Betty Bollinger modern as the "Samba," ancient as music, and as far into the pathway of tomorrow as the volume of her luscious voice, singing on and on into the stars.

2. Has it been duly marked by historians that the late William Jennings Bryan's last secular act on this globe of sin was to catch flies? A curious detail, and not without its sardonic overtones. He was the most sedulous fly-catcher in American history, and in many ways the most successful. His quarry, of course, was not *Musca domestica* but *Homo neandertalensis*. For forty years he tracked it with coo and bellow, up and down the rustic backways of the Republic. Wherever the flambeaux of Chautauqua smoked and guttered, and the bilge of Idealism ran in the veins, and Baptist pastors dammed the brooks with the sanctified, and men gathered who were weary and heavy laden, and their wives who were full of Peruna and as fecund as the shad (*Alosa sapidissima*)—there the indefatigable Jennings set up his traps and spread his bait. He knew every country town in the South and West, and he could crowd the most remote of them to suffocation by simply winding his horn. The city proletariat, transiently flustered by him in 1896, quickly penetrated his buncombe and would have no more of him; the cockney gallery jeered him at every Democratic convention for twenty-five years. But out where the grass grows high, and the horned cattle dream away the lazy afternoons, and men still fear the powers and principalities of the air—out there between the corn-rows he held his own puissance to the end. There was no need of beaters to drive in his game. The news that he was coming was enough. For miles the flivver dust would choke the roads. And when he rose at the end of the day to discharge his Message there would be such breathless attention, such a rapt and enchanted ecstasy, such

a sweet rustle of amens as the world had not known since Johann fell to Herod's sardonic ax.*

EXERCISE 11. How much irony is there in each of the following selections? How does what the writer says differ from what he really means?

1. The clear brown eyes, kindly and alert, with 12–20 vision, give confident regard to the passing world through R. K. Lampert & Company lenses framed in gold;
His soul, however, is all his own;
Arndt Brothers necktie and hat (with feather) supply a touch of youth.

With his soul his own, he drives, drives, chats, and drives,
The first and second bicuspids, lower right, replaced by bridgework, while two incisors have porcelain crowns;

(Render unto Federal, state, and city Caesar, but not unto time;
Render nothing unto time until Amalgamated Death serves final notice, in proper form;

The vault is ready;
The will has been drawn by Clagget, Clagget, Clagget, and Brown;
The policies are adequate, Confidential's best, reimbursing for disability, partial or complete, with double indemnity should the end be a pure and simple accident)

Nothing unto time,
Nothing unto change, nothing unto fate,
Nothing unto you, and nothing unto me, or to any other known or unknown party or parties, living or deceased;

* From *Selected Prejudices,* by H. L. Mencken. By permission of Alfred A. Knopf, Inc., publisher.

But Mercury shoes, with special arch supports, take much of the
wear and tear;
On the course, a custombuilt driver corrects a tendency to slice;
Love's ravages have been repaired (it was a textbook case) by
Drs. Schultz, Lightner, Mannheim, and Goode,
While all of it is enclosed in excellent tweed, with Mr. Baumer's
personal attention to the shoulders and the waist;

And all of it now roving, chatting amiably through space in a
Plymouth 6,
With his soul (his own) at peace, soothed by Walter Lippmann,
and sustained by Haig & Haig.*

2. Sir Charles Adderley says to the Warwickshire farmers:—"Talk of the improvement of breed! Why, the race we ourselves represent, the men and women, the old Anglo-Saxon race, are the best breed in the whole world . . . The absence of a too enervating climate, too unclouded skies, and a too luxurious nature, has produced so vigorous a race of people, and has rendered us so superior to all the world."

Mr. Roebuck says to the Sheffield cutlers:—"I look around me and ask what is the state of England? Is not property safe? Is not every man able to say what he likes? Can you not walk from one end of England to the other in perfect security? I ask you whether, the world over or in past history, there is anything like it? Nothing. I pray that our unrivalled happiness may last."

. . . [But consider] this paragraph on which I stumbled in a newspaper immediately after reading Mr. Roebuck:

"A shocking child murder has just been committed at Notingham. A girl named Wragg left the workhouse there on Saturday morning with her young illegitimate child. The chld was soon afterwards found dead on Mapperly Hills, having been strangled. Wragg is in custody."

* From *Collected Poems,* by Kenneth Fearing. Copyright, 1940, by Random House, Inc. Reprinted by permission of Random House, Inc.

Nothing but that; but, in juxtaposition with the absolute eulogies of Sir Charles Adderley and Mr. Roebuck, how eloquent, how suggestive are those few lines! "Our old Anglo-Saxon breed, the best in the whole world!"—how much that is harsh and ill favoured there is in this best! *Wragg!* . . . And "our unrivalled happiness";—what an element of grimness, bareness, and hideousness mixes with it and blurs it; the workhouse, the dismal Mapperly Hills,—how dismal those who have seen them will remember;—the gloom, the smoke, the cold, the strangled illegitimate child! "I ask you whether, the world over or in past history, there is anything like it?" Perhaps not, one is inclined to answer; but at any rate, in that case, the world is very much to be pitied. And the final touch,—short, bleak, and inhuman: *Wragg is in custody*. The sex lost in the confusion of our unrivalled happiness; or (shall I say?) the superfluous Christain name lopped off by the straightforward vigour of our old Anglo-Saxon breed!

3. [Written in England, September, 1938: just after Neville Chamberlain returned from Munich with the assurance of "peace in our time"]

> Now we are back to normal, now the mind is
> Back to the even tenor of the usual day
> Skidding no longer across the uneasy camber
> Of the nightmare way.
> *We* are safe though others have crashed the railings
> Over the river ravine; their wheel-tracks carve the bank
> But after the event all we can do is argue
> And count the widening ripples where they sank.
> October comes with rain whipping around the ankles
> In waves of white at night
> And filling the raw clay trenches (the parks of London
> Are a nasty sight).*

---

* From *Autumn Journal,* by Louis MacNeice. Copyright, 1941, by Louis MacNeice. Reprinted by permisson of Random House, Inc.

Sentimentality

So much for a few of the ways in which humor, conscious or unconscious, is related to the total tone of writing. Now we want to devote some space to the subject of sentimentality, which, in its extreme manifestations, can also be funny.

Many situations in life are always fraught with emotion, no matter who participates in them—innocent childhood viewed by an adult, young love, betrayal, married happiness, pathetic accidents, poverty, old age, death. And they are the situations which form the basic material of literature; they include, indeed, most of the important things in life. Everybody wants to write about them; but, obviously, since they have been written about over and over, few people have anything new to say concerning them. Those who rework the old themes often take refuge in sentimentality.

Sentimentality can be defined most simply as shallow and exaggerated emotion. Taking an emotional symbol or situation—home, mother, death of a pauper, return of a wanderer—the sentimentalist, perhaps from the most sincere of motives, extorts more feeling from it than a reasonable person would find there, and dwells upon it longer and more insistently than he should.

Furthermore, the sentimentalist, lacking fresh ideas, depends heavily upon the cliché in all its forms—upon the tried-and-true devices by which too many preceding writers have stirred their readers' feelings. But those images and phrases are now emotionally dehydrated; they have been used so often that they have lost their power to affect. And so the effect of sentimentality, to the reader who has a sense of fitness and freshness, is the opposite of what is intended. Depending upon the precise quality of the passage, the reader is either exasperated or amused. But he is not touched.

We can illustrate the nature of sentimentality by quoting two accounts dealing with the same material but differing radically in point of view. Not long ago a social worker, after visiting a "case" in a large eastern city, wrote a report from which the following excerpts are made, all proper names having been changed. The tone, whatever else it may be, is not sentimental:

The unfinished frame summer-kitchen addition to the dilapidated farmhouse Mrs. Denby occupies on the outskirts of Birchdale is a mute reminder of the ambition Mr. Denby had entertained to remodel the property and make it more habitable: an ambition interrupted last autumn by his fatal three-month illness. He left his family in quite sorry straits. There are five children, the youngest only fourteen months old. They must live on their Mothers' Assistance Fund grant of $55 a month. Mrs. Denby, a no more than moderately intelligent woman, mingles a somewhat vulgar streak with strong Baptist religiosity. Her house is kept clean, but, with the exception of a shining new electric refrigerator in one corner of the kitchen, it is poorly furnished.

One of Mrs. Denby's elder sons was badly burnt in an accident some years ago and missed a year and a half of school. His sister, Elizabeth, is now living with Mr. Denby's relatives nearby, an arrangement which Mrs. Denby is willing to tolerate at least temporarily, although she has no truck with her numerous "in-laws."

Mr. Denby, the oldest of fifteen children, left school to go to work. He held various jobs, but none for long. He was constantly chasing the will o' the wisp of "more money," and as a result got nowhere. He was a notoriously poor provider, Mrs. Denby says, but despite this shortcoming her life with him was serene.

Their son George is said by his teachers to be retarded in his school work. He has not yet had an intelligence test, but his native ability seems possibly lower than average. He will have some difficulty in keeping up with his age-group.

Not long after the social worker's visit, the Denby house burned down, and one of the city newspapers ran the following story:

WIDOW SOBS AS FLAMES DESTROY ALL

A 38-year-old widow, mother of five children, poked aimlessly through the fire-blackened ruins of her little home at Center Road and Delaney Street yesterday and wept bitter tears of utter hopelessness.

"What are we to do?" Mrs. Hannah S. Denby sobbed. "The fire took everything except the clothes on our backs. It even burned my picture of my husband . . . and he died only six months ago."

And for Mrs. Denby, the loss of that picture seemed even harder to bear than the destruction of all but a few pieces of their furniture in the blaze which broke out Sunday afternoon shortly after the family had returned from church.

For her tow-headed, five-year-old daughter, Beth, the fire had meant another heart-rending loss, for her only doll and her doll coach were consumed by the flames.

And for 17-year-old Frank, now the man of the family, for 11-year-old James and seven-year-old George, the fire meant the end of the happiness they had just started to recapture in family life since the death of their father.

Only 16-month-old Robert was unaware of the feeling of family tragedy. He cooed gaily in his mother's arms.

For the time being the widow and her children have found a home with her sister. "But she is very ill," Mrs. Denby said, "and it is hardly fair for us to stay there. I wish I knew what we could do, where we could turn. Perhaps the good Lord will find a way. . . ."

Compare the two accounts, and you will have a good notion of the elements of sentimentality: the selection of detail to maintain a certain impression, whether wholly or partly false; the use of cliché symbols (*e.g.*, the little girl and the burned doll coach); and the trite language itself ("bitter tears of utter hopelessness").

Do you think the writer of the newspaper account was sincerely moved by the Denbys' plight?

What is sentimental to one person may not be sentimental to another; it all depends upon how fine a sense of fitness the reader has. A reader who is ready to respond to any appeal to emotion, merely because it has something to do with babyhood or the first stirrings of pure young love, will not discriminate between the sentimental and the genuinely emotional. To him it is the subject that counts, not the treatment or the motives behind the treatment. But a more mature reader will instinctively reject an appeal which applies a pressure pump to his lachrymal glands. What do you think of this poem?

> She knelt upon her brother's grave,
> My little girl of six years old—
> He used to be so good and brave,
> The sweetest lamb of all our fold;
> He used to shout, he used to sing,
> Of all our tribe the little king—
> And so unto the turf her ear she laid,
> To hark if still in that dark place he play'd.
> No sound! no sound!
> Death's silence was profound;
> And horror crept
> Into her aching heart, and Dora wept.
> If this is as it ought to be,
> My God, I leave it unto thee.*

Do not think for a moment that we mean to depreciate the expression of emotion in literature. Our point is simply that writing which expresses emotion in hackneyed and excessive terms not only is far inferior to writing which expresses that same emotion with dignity and restraint, but also can give us

* From *Collected Poems,* by T. E. Brown. By permission of The Macmillan Company, publishers.

valuable warning that our generous and warm-hearted natures are about to be imposed upon.

Restraint

The word "restraint" brings us to one final aspect of the subject of tone. We have saved it for this place because to understand it you must have understood all that we have said in the preceding pages of this book.

If there is one lesson which we have preached, over and over again, it is this: The real meaning of writing that matters most is not found on the surface, in the actual, literal significance of the words. It hovers beneath the surface, in the delicate shadings of connotation and rhythm, in the precise effect of metaphor and symbol and allusion. Now sometimes that surface is so highly decorated, so full of a certain kind of meaning, that we are content with its own delights, and neglect to pierce beneath it to the deeper undercurrents. But often (and this is what we mean by restraint) writers leave the surface comparatively bare; the meaning on that level is plain and simple. And the untrained reader in all probability will consider this to be the *only* meaning. But underneath that simple exterior of restraint there lies a rich hidden treasure of suggestion and implication, which the mature reader will appreciate the more because it has not been publicly advertised. It is his reward for being a perceptive and sensitive reader.

Thus the ultimate test, as well as the final reward, of the critical reader is his ability to grasp the implications of any piece of writing: to receive the message that is left unsaid but that is just as real as what is said and very often more important. The most satisfying part of the experience of reading is just that.

The best place to try out your ability to read deeply—to get out of a passage everything that the author packed into it for you—is a poem that describes a situation or a state of mind: not a narrative poem, in which things happen, but a poem in which someone is seen before or after events. If no events are described, then you are confronted with the problem of telling what the poem is "about." Almost any good lyric poem can test your reading faculty. Some of Browning's shorter dramatic monologues also are admirable for this purpose: "A Soliloquy in a Spanish Cloister," "My Last Duchess," "Fra Lippo Lippi," and "The Laboratory." And so too are A. E. Housman's poems, one of which we select for illustration.

On moonlit heath and lonesome bank
 The sheep beside me graze;
And yon the gallows used to clank
 Fast by the four cross ways.

A careless shepherd once would keep 5
 The flocks by moonlight there,
And high amongst the glimmering sheep
 The dead man stood on air.

They hang us now in Shrewsbury jail;
 The whistles blow forlorn, 10
And trains all night groan on the rail
 To men that die at morn.

There sleeps in Shrewsbury jail to-night,
 Or wakes, as may betide,
A better lad, if things went right, 15
 Than most that sleep outside.

And naked to the hangman's noose
 The morning clocks will ring
A neck God made for other use
 Than strangling in a string. 20

And sharp the link of life will snap,
  And dead on air will stand
Heels that held up as straight a chap
  As treads upon the land.

So here I'll watch the night and wait 25
  To see the morning shine,
When he will hear the stroke of eight
  And not the stroke of nine;

And wish my friend as sound a sleep
  As lads' I did not know, 30
That shepherded the moonlit sheep
  A hundred years ago.*

To begin with, the reader must take full advantage of whatever small hints the poet offers outside the poem itself. In this case, Mr. Housman appended a note to the poem, saying simply, "Hanging in chains was called keeping sheep by moonlight." And this brief sentence really sums up the irony, or bitter contrast, which underlies the whole poem—the association of sheep-watching by moonlight (the most peaceful and inoffensive of occupations and the most tranquil of settings) with the gruesome practice of hanging convicted criminals† *in chains* (an especially severe punishment). It is the interplay of these two sets of completely diverse associations that gives the poem its dominant tone.

The basic contrast of the poem is brought out in the first two stanzas. Consider the implications of *moonlit heath, sheep,* and *graze* as against *gallows* and *clank* (what is the effect of the sound of the word?); and of *careless* (carefree), *shepherd, flocks, moonlight,* and *glimmering sheep* as against the *dead man stood*

* From A. E. Housman, *A Shropshire Lad,* Henry Holt & Company.

† Or, perhaps, specifically sheep-stealers. But whichever was in Housman's mind, the poem's impact is unaffected.

on air. The language is very simple; but the clashing associations of those two groups of words give us a key to the very intense emotions that lie beneath the surface. What is the effect of the grotesque image suggested by "The dead man stood on air"?

With mention of Shrewsbury jail, the whistles blowing, and the trains groaning all night, a new note enters—another contrast, this time between the stillness of the old rural setting at the crossroads and the new conditions under which condemned criminals are executed. Does the speaker approve or disapprove of the new system?

In the fourth stanza the precise situation is made clear: the speaker, the sheep-herder, is thinking of someone in particular who is awaiting execution in Shrewsbury jail. What is the attitude implied in the *us* of line 9, the *lad* of line 15, the *chap* of line 23, and the *lads'* of line 30? What do the lines "A better lad, *if things went right,* / Than most that sleep outside" do to clarify that attitude?

In the fifth stanza there is a pun (*ring* in two senses). Is a pun usually found in a poem about someone about to be hanged? Is it a humorous pun? —Housman selected the word *string* in the last line of the stanza for a special reason: not merely because of the rime-scheme. What is the difference in implication between *rope* and *string,* and how does the effect of *string* harmonize with the tone of the whole?

The sixth stanza recalls to mind the earlier image of the criminal "standing on air." The earlier reference was to the gallows at the crossroads; here it is to the modernized gallows in the jailyard. But the effect of hanging is the same under both conditions. And that is a point Housman wishes to make.

Suddenly, at the beginning of the seventh stanza, we are taken back to the original setting—the moonlit heath and lonesome bank, with the sheep peacefully grazing beside the speaker. The idea of death is now conceived of as the difference between hearing the stroke of eight o'clock and not hearing the stroke of nine. Of all the ways in which Housman might have epitomized the fact of death, why do you think he chose that one?

Finally, the speaker alludes to the men who were hanged long years ago and thus "kept sheep by moonlight." And we realize with a shock—if we have not done so before—that he too is "keeping sheep by moonlight." In other words, the ultimate effect of the poem is centered in the double meaning of the phrase. If the phrase can be applied with equal accuracy to both the speaker and the condemned man, as the speaker implies, what, in the last analysis, is the speaker thinking?

One other note. The rhythm of this poem is as incongruous to the subject as is the highly colloquial diction: instead of having a measured, grave tempo, it fairly skips along. The short line is aided by the simple rime-scheme (*a-b-a-b*). The stanza sounds almost like something children memorize in kindergarten.

And so to the superficial reader, the poem seems, perplexingly enough, to be a more or less flippant treatment of a serious subject. There is some sort of humor in the image of the dead man standing on air, in the pun on *ring,* in the familiar *lad* and *chap,* in the offhand way in which death is imaged in the seventh stanza. But the careful reader will realize that the humor is of a peculiar and significant sort: it is humor without the faintest suggestion of a smile; on the contrary, it is grim, bitter humor. And the lightness suggested by the colloquial diction and the lilting rhythm is just as deceptive.

The effect of Housman's poem lies in the complete incongruity between what is said, for anyone to read, and what is left unsaid, for the attentive reader to discover. The flippancy, the offhand manner, point not to any callousness on the part of the speaker. On the contrary, they are simply camouflage for very deep and bitter feelings. The truth about the speaker's emotions resides almost completely in the implications, rather than the external meaning, of what he says. And the half-humorous tone makes the actual subject of the poem—the impending execution—all the more terrible.

We have said by no means all that could be said about this poem; but we have tried to suggest in a fashion the supreme importance of reading for implication as well as for meaning. Most poetry and a great part of imaginative prose are in a very true sense unintelligible unless the reader considers the tone.

Even the most conscientious and intelligent reader finds it difficult to put into words the impression which a poem or an essay or a scene in a novel makes upon him. That is why such vague and meaningless words as "flowery" (which in any event refers to style and not to tone) are so often called into use. And so we shall end this chapter by offering you a short list of serviceable adjectives by which tone may be described. There is no rule of thumb by which you can learn how to use them with accuracy and discrimination; but you can begin by learning their dictionary definitions, and from then on you should be careful to observe how other writers use them. But above all, try your hand at fitting them to a wide variety of selections from writing, old and new. After you have read a short poem, for example, try to find the descriptive adjective which you think most closely conveys the tone of the poem as it strikes you. In Exercise 13 we give you a small assortment of passages for practice. Here are some of the terms you should know and train yourself to use:

> Whimsical, grave, fanciful, bantering, rhapsodic, ironical, devotional, intemperate, fervent, tender, dejected, compassionate, cynical, indignant, meditative, indulgent, bitter, wry, sentimental, satirical, light-hearted, solemn, patronizing, didactic, flippant, reminiscent, sardonic, elegiac, eulogistic, resigned.

These adjectives do not exhaust the possibilities by any means, but they will be of great aid to you in your efforts to put into words your sense of the emotional tone and intention of what you read. From now on, make it a point of pride never to say, "I know what my impression is, but I can't find the right words to express it!"

EXERCISE 12. How sentimental do you think each of the following selections is?

1. Her lips met the press of mine, and, by what strange trick of the imagination I know not, the scene in the cabin of the *Ghost* flashed upon me, when she had pressed her fingers lightly on my lips and said, "Hush, hush."

   "My woman, my one small woman," I said, my free hand petting her shoulder in the way all lovers know though never learn in school.

   "My man," she said, looking at me for an instant with tremulous lids which fluttered down and veiled her eyes as she snuggled her head against my breast with a happy little sigh.

   I looked toward the cutter. It was very close. A boat was being lowered.

   "One kiss, dear love," I whispered. "One kiss more before they come."

   "And rescue us from ourselves," she completed, with a most adorable smile, whimsical as I had never seen it, for it was whimsical with love.*

2. How do I love thee? Let me count the ways.
   I love thee to the depth and breadth and height
   My soul can reach, when feeling out of sight
   For the ends of Being and ideal Grace.
   I love thee to the level of everyday's
   Most quiet need, by sun and candle-light.
   I love thee freely, as men strive for Right;
   I love thee purely, as they turn from Praise.
   I love thee with the passion put to use

* From Jack London's *The Sea Wolf;* by special permission of Charmian Kittredge London.

In my old griefs, and with my childhood's faith.
I love thee with a love I seemed to lose
With my lost saints—I love thee with the breath,
Smiles, tears, of all my life!—and, if God choose,
I shall but love thee better after death.

3. Close the book now. Peter Rabbit was fun to hear about (even if it was the tenth, or twentieth, time for that story!)—but now Mr. Sandman has taken over. O.K. Lights out. Sleep tight there, fella, with that plump little hand clutching the teddy bear's right ear. Pleasant dreams. Tomorrow's another big day—and the day after that . . . You won't worry about the future—and beginning right now, I won't either. I saw my life insurance counsellor today and mapped out a program that will take care of your growing up, even your college years. . . .

4. Sweet is the hour that brings us home,
Where all will spring to meet us;
Where hands are striving, as we come,
To be the first to greet us.
When the world hath spent its frowns and wrath,
And care been sorely pressing:
'Tis sweet to turn from our roving path,
And find a fireside blessing.
Oh, joyfully dear is the homeward track,
If we are but sure of a welcome back.

What do we reck on a dreary way,
Though lonely and benighted,
If we know there are lips to chide our stay,
And eyes that will beam love-lighted?
What is the worth of your diamond ray,
To the glance that flashes pleasure;
When the words that welcome back betray,
We form a heart's chief treasure?
Oh, joyfully dear is our homeward track
If we are but sure of a welcome back.

5. When do I see thee most, beloved one?
   When in the light the spirits of mine eyes
   Before thy face, their altar, solemnize
The worship of that Love through thee made known?
Or when in the dusk hours, (we two alone,)
   Close-kissed and eloquent of still replies
   Thy twilight-hidden glimmering visage lies,
And my soul only sees thy soul its own?

O love, my love! if I no more should see
Thyself, nor on the earth the shadow of thee,
   Nor image of thine eyes in any spring,—
How then should sound upon Life's darkening slope
The ground-whirl of the perished leaves of Hope,
   The wind of Death's imperishable wing?

Exercise 13. Here is a group of passages of very diversified tone. How would you characterize the tone of each, and what specific means (diction, metaphor, allusion, etc.) does the writer use to create that tone?

1. Just for a handful of silver he left us,
   Just for a riband to stick in his coat—
Found the one gift of which fortune bereft us,
   Lost all the others she lets us devote;
They, with the gold to give, doled him out silver,
So much was theirs who so little allowed:
How all our copper had gone for his service!
   Rags—were they purple, his heart had been proud!
We that had loved him so, followed him, honoured him,
   Lived in his mild and magnificent eye,
Learned his great language, caught his clear accents,
   Made him our pattern to live and to die!
Shakespeare was of us, Milton was for us,
   Burns, Shelley, were with us,—they watch from their graves!
He alone breaks from the van and the freemen,
   —He alone sinks to the rear and the slaves!

We shall march prospering,—not thro' his presence;
Songs may inspirit us,—not from his lyre!
Deeds will be done—while he boasts his quiescence,
Still bidding crouch whom the rest bade aspire;
Blot out his name, then, record one lost soul more,
One task more declined, one more footpath untrod,
One more devils'-triumph and sorrow for angels,
One wrong more to man, one more insult to God!
Life's night begins! let him never come back to us!
There would be doubt, hesitation and pain,
Forced praise on our part—the glimmer of twilight,
Never glad confident morning again!
Best fight on well, for we taught him—strike gallantly,
Menace our heart ere we master his own;
Then let him receive the new knowledge and wait us,
Pardoned in heaven, the first by the throne!

2. I perceive the deluge fell upon you before it reached us. It began here but on Monday last, and then rained near eight-and-forty hours without intermission. My poor hay has not a dry thread to its back. I have had a fire these three days. In short, every summer one lives in a state of mutiny and murmur, and I have found the reason. It is because we will affect to have a summer, and we have no title to any such thing. Our poets learnt their trade of the Romans, and so adopted the terms of their masters. They talk of shady groves, purling streams, and cooling breezes, and we get sore throats and agues with attempting to realize these visions. Master Damon writes a song, and invites Miss Chloe to enjoy the cool of the evening, and the deuce a bit have we of any such thing as a cool evening. Zephyr is a north-east wind, that makes Damon button up to the chin, and pinches Chloe's nose till it is red and blue; and then they cry, "This is a bad summer"—as if we ever had any other! The best sun we have is made of Newcastle coal, and I am determined never to reckon upon any other. We ruin ourselves with inviting over foreign trees, and make our houses

clamber up hills to look at prospects. How our ancestors would laugh at us, who knew there was no being comfortable, unless you had a high hill before your nose, and a thick warm wood at your back! Taste is too freezing a commodity for us, and, depend upon it, will go out of fashion again.

3. The stately Homes of England,
How beautiful they stand!
Amidst their tall ancestral trees,
O'er all the pleasant land;
The deer across their greensward bound
Through shade and sunny gleam,
And the swan glides past them with the sound
Of some rejoicing stream.

The merry Homes of England!
Around their hearths by night,
What gladsome looks of household love
Meet in the ruddy light.
There woman's voice flows forth in song,
Or childish tale is told;
Or lips move tunefully along
Some glorious page of old.

The blessèd Homes of England!
How softly on their bowers
Is laid the holy quietness
That breathes from Sabbath hours!
Solemn, yet sweet, the church-bell's chime
Floats through their woods at morn;
All other sounds, in that still time,
Of breeze and leaf are born.

The cottage Homes of England!
By thousands on her plains,
They are smiling o'er the silvery brooks,
And round the hamlet-fanes.

Through glowing orchards forth they peep,
Each from its nook of leaves;
And fearless there the lowly sleep,
As the bird beneath their eaves.
The free, fair Homes of England!
Long, long in hut and hall,
May hearts of native proof be reared
To guard each hallowed wall!

And green forever be the groves,
And bright the flowery sod,
Where first the child's glad spirit loves
Its country and its God!

4. On a starred night Prince Lucifer uprose.
Tired of his dark dominion swung the fiend
Above the rolling ball in cloud part screened,
Where sinners hugged their spectre of repose.
Poor prey to his hot fit of pride were those.
And now upon his western wing he leaned,
Now his huge bulk o'er Afric's sands careened,
Now the black planet shadowed Arctic snows.
Soaring through wider zones that pricked his scars
With memory of the old revolt from Awe,
He reached the middle height, and at the stars,
Which are the brain of heaven, he looked, and sank.
Around the ancient track marched, rank on rank,
The army of unalterable law.*

5. Out upon it! I have loved
Three whole days together;
And am like to love three more,
If it prove fair weather.

* From *Poetical Works,* by George Meredith. By permission of Charles Scribner's Sons, publishers.

Time shall moult away his wings,
  Ere he shall discover
In the whole wide world again
  Such a constant lover.

But the spite on 't is, no praise
  Is due at all to me;
Love with me has made no stays
  Had it any been but she.

Had it any been but she,
  And that very face,
There had been at least ere this
  A dozen dozen in her place.

6. Milton! thou should'st be living at this hour:
England hath need of thee: she is a fen
Of stagnant waters: altar, sword, and pen,
Fireside, the heroic wealth of hall and bower,
Have forfeited their ancient English dower
Of inward happiness. We are selfish men;
Oh! raise us up, return to us again;
And give us manners, virtue, freedom, power.
Thy soul was like a Star, and dwelt apart;
Thou hadst a voice whose sound was like the sea:
Pure as the naked heavens, majestic, free,
So didst thou travel on life's common way,
In cheerful godliness; and yet thy heart
The lowliest duties on herself did lay.

7. And did those feet in ancient time
  Walk upon England's mountains green?
And was the holy Lamb of God
  On England's pleasant pastures seen?

And did the countenance divine
  Shine forth upon our clouded hills?
And was Jerusalem builded here
  Among these dark Satanic mills?

Bring me my bow of burning gold!
  Bring me my arrows of desire!
Bring me my spear! O clouds, unfold!
  Bring me my chariot of fire!

I will not cease from mental fight,
  Nor shall my sword sleep in my hand,
Till we have built Jerusalem
  In England's green and pleasant land.

8. Wilt thou forgive that sin where I begun,
  Which is my sin, though it were done before?
Wilt thou forgive those sins, through which I run,
  And do run still: though still I do deplore?
    When thou has done, thou hast not done,
      For I have more.

Wilt thou forgive that sin by which I have won
  Others to sin? and made my sin their door?
Wilt thou forgive that sin which I did shun
  A year, or two: but wallowed in, a score?
    When thou hast done, thou hast not done,
      For I have more.

I have a sin of fear, that when I have spun
  My last thread, I shall perish on the shore;
Swear by thyself, that at my death thy sun
  Shall shine as he shines now, and heretofore;
    And, having done that, Thou hast done,
      I fear no more.

CHAPTER SIX

On Reading Newspapers

IN THE PAST FEW YEARS many thoughtful observers have commented upon the amazing political illiteracy of the American public. Although the public opinion polls are always discovering that the man-in-the-street is ready with an opinion on any subject under current discussion, a follow-up poll by a group of cross-examiners would reveal that the overwhelming majority of the people who have expressed an opinion are almost completely ignorant of the background of the subject, the issues involved, and the implications of their expressed stand. The scanty knowledge they have of that subject would prove to be derived from incomplete information, hearsay, wishful thinking, and prejudice. Yet not only are they ready with an opinion when the Gallup poll man asks them; they are ready to talk others into believing as they believe; and—most serious of all—they will vote on the basis of that frail tissue of error and bias.

We are including this chapter on the reading of newspapers because we think it shows the way to the most immediately practical application of the principles discussed in the preceding pages. Not the least of the ironies of our present American civilization is the fact that our undoubted ignorance of what is really going on in the world is a phenomenon of an age that sees news carried to every man and woman with a speed and volume unthought of a few years ago. In the midst of "news"—bulky newspapers, incessant commentaries on the air, documentary news films in the theaters—we are starved for truth.

Every college instructor is depressed, whenever he refers to a topic currently talked about in the papers, to discover that many of his students seldom read newspapers. Nevertheless we have chosen to discuss the critical reading of newspapers rather than the critical hearing of radio newscasts because it is quite plain that the newspaper is still the chief source of what the public knows, or thinks it knows, about current events. The radio is an increasingly powerful instrument of information, and people who listen regularly to radio coverage as dependable as that of, for instance, the Columbia Broadcasting System, are probably better informed than those who depend upon the coverage of all but the very best newspapers. Yet radio journalism has many of the shortcomings of newspaper journalism; and though we shall say little specifically of radio in the pages that follow, it would be profitable at every point for you to consider whether what we say of newspapers is not true also—with allowances made for the different medium—of radio.

What will be said here will undoubtedly seem to give aid and comfort to those who make a virtue of not reading the papers because they are sure the papers are composed largely of lies. Yet such an attitude is scarcely appropriate to one who desires to be educated. It is an evasion born of indolence and too easy cynicism. How else can one begin to learn what is happening in the world, if not by regularly reading newspapers? Radio listening is only a partial substitute, and in any event one who neglects the newspapers will scarcely be very diligent in his attention to commentators and forums. Our remarks on the ways in which newspapers largely fail to report objective truth must not be taken as rationalization for failure to read them. Rather, we intend what follows to be a guide for the *critical* reading and analysis of what the newspapers contain. An intelligent reader can penetrate through the jungles of distortion and suppression at least to the environs of the truth. And, what is more important, he can insist that the papers which he buys *give* him more truth. For a newspaper is at the mercy of its readers. Without readers, it can attract no advertisers. Without advertisers, it cannot stay in business. If the readers do not insist upon their right to have the truth, so much the worse for them—and for the world.

Although the defined purpose of a newspaper is to distribute accurate information concerning current events, so that a reader may have a reasonably comprehensive view of the world in which he lives, actually there is no newspaper in the world which completely achieves that ideal. For this failure there are two main reasons, which we shall examine in order. The first is the fact that newspaper publishing, like any other business, is a profit-making venture. The second is that in the actual writing and editing of newspapers, there are certain practices—traditional if not absolutely necessary—which militate against a dispassionate, well-balanced presentation of the news.

Although the mottoes of many newspapers deny it, newspaper publishing is a business first and a public service second. This is an observation that springs not from cynicism but from practical realism. How may the press of any nation be supported financially? There are but two alternatives: governmental subsidization and private ownership. In a society such as ours, which jealously prizes the principle of freedom of the press, few people would seriously advocate the first, with its ever-present danger of bureaucratic control and censorship. There remains the second alternative: private ownership, which implies the profit motive. There have been a few cases in which some wealthy individual or group sought to underwrite a newspaper without expectation of profit and thus to enable it, in theory at least, to present news without restraint or bias. The most recent example has been Marshall Field III's underwriting of the New York *PM* and the Chicago *Sun*. But even such privately subsidized papers find it difficult to be completely independent; they are, after all, obligated to *someone*. *PM* is as biased, in its own special way, as any newspaper in the country. And in any event, the cost of operating a newspaper is so great that only a few of the very richest men in the country can afford to sink money indefinitely into a paper which shows a deficit each year. The only way in which a newspaper can exist is as a profit-making business.

A paper depends upon two sources for its revenue: its readers and its advertisers. Financially, the advertisers are far more important than the readers, because the sales receipts, from subscribers and newsstand buyers, do not come even close to covering the cost of production. The biggest source of revenue is the sale of advertising space. But no paper can sell advertising space if it has no readers; the only way in which it can attract advertisers is to show them imposing statistics about its wide circulation. ("In Philadelphia nearly everybody reads the *Bulletin*." "The [Atlanta] *Journal* covers Dixie like the dew.") And so in the last analysis it is the reader who counts most heavily with the men who put out the newspaper, and it is his tastes and capabilities that every editor and reporter must keep constantly in mind.

The assumption which guides nearly all journalistic practice (there are a few notable exceptions, mainly in the largest cities) is that the average reader has the mentality of a ten- or twelve-year-old. Everything that the paper prints must, therefore, be adapted to this level of intelligence. The writing must be simple and snappy. The range of vocabulary used in news-writing is rigidly limited to the capabilities of the dullest reader; the sentences are short, the paragraphs limited to two or three sentences—and we have already seen (in Chapter Four) what such limitations imply. Above all, the columns of the paper must be made interesting; and by "interesting" is meant non-intellectual and perpetually dramatic. All the news must be presented in terms of men and events, and the deeper issues and concepts and tendencies that shape the news may be neglected without loss. Abstract ideas, according to the newspapermen's theory, never interest the public, because they are not "exciting." Murders, wars, beauty contests, election campaigns, football games, explosions, two-headed calves, unseasonable weather, court trials—all are exciting, in various degrees. The theory is that a newspaper reader is like a playgoer: he demands that he be given something to watch, not to think about. And so, like a play that aims to be a box-office success, the newspaper must keep "talk" down to an absolute minimum, and must on the other hand make a point of supplying as much suspense, action, and spectacle as it can possibly contrive from the day's material. If the events of the day cannot be presented dramatically, there is little point in mentioning them.

This assumption that the average newspaper reader is like a twelve-year-old child at the movies has never been disproved. Many angry words have been written about its supposed fallacy, just as many more have been written about the low intelligence-level of the movies and of radio programs; but the great public that buys the papers, attends the movies, and listens to the radio seems not dissatisfied with what it is given. The newspaper editors, who are intelligent men, cannot be blamed if they continue to be guided by their traditional assumption. Their job is to make up a paper that people will buy. No one would be happier than they if the public did demand a more thoughtful treatment of current events; no one would respond more eagerly to the call for better writing and an adult viewpoint. But they cannot risk taking the initiative. Until their readers concertedly insist upon being treated as adults, the editors will continue to treat them as children.

But putting aside this limitation, it still is not possible for newspapers to provide a clear picture of what goes on in the world. Remember that much of the news is highly controversial. Acts of God, such as tornadoes, or acts of men in their private capacities, such as highway robbery, are about the only staple items of news that do not have an element of controversy in them. If the public is to make an intelligent decision on each issue as it arises, it must be given all the pertinent information, on both sides of the question, which the newspaper can amass. Furthermore, it must be given this information without color, comment, or weighting. This requirement would lay a tremendous responsibility upon any newspaper editor who had a free hand to publish a daily objective account of all that occurred. He would have to be a superhumanly dispassionate man! But actually, under the conditions of newspaper publishing, no editor is either expected or able to be totally unbiased in his reporting of the news.

From the beginning of journalism, it has been recognized that if the press is important as a means of spreading information, it is even more important as a means of influencing public opinion. And there are few men who, if they control a paper, can resist the temptation to use that paper as a mouthpiece for their own sentiments. This in itself is not to be deplored, so long as men of all parties and persuasions are allowed equal freedom to control papers. But there is a difference between expressing opinion, plainly labelled as such, and screening and coloring the news so that the public's reaction is based, not on a knowledge of all the facts, but on only a selected and weighted segment of them. Unfortunately there are few, if any, papers which limit to the editorial page their attempt to sway public opinion. The "policy" of the paper, openly expressed in editorials, covertly influences the treatment of news on every page. And it is this silent selection and coloration of the news, the specific methods of which we shall discuss later, that every intelligent reader must constantly be on his guard against.

Who, in particular, controls a newspaper's attitude toward the news it reports? First, the advertisers, whose influence usually takes the form of a threat to withdraw their advertising if the newspaper takes a stand, either in its editorials or in its reporting of the news, that is inimical to their interests. Advertisers are business men, and they therefore will not help support a paper which advocates measures that they think will "hurt business." In many cases they will urge that the paper present in an unfavorable light such issues as labor movements, government control over prices, profits, and trade practices, and attempts to lower the tariff. Because of their influence, many papers will suppress or mutilate the news of a campaign for more stringent pure food laws or of the exposure of poor working conditions in a certain industry. They will see that political candidates advocating "anti-business" measures of one sort or another receive a "poor press." Their influence will be felt also in the reporting of incidental news. If the local Department of Health finds the dining room of a large department store to be a wholesale distributor of disease, the news, though it is a matter of prime public interest, may be kept from print; and if a proposal is made to remove the transit lines from a main thoroughfare, the business houses along that street, whose customers may go elsewhere as a result of the change, will see that the newspaper's publicity of the scheme is properly colored.

This exertion of pressure upon newspaper editors by advertisers is not to be thought of as necessarily constant or universal. There are some business firms which consider such tactics as a form of blackmail, and will never stoop to it; and there are some papers which try valiantly to resist such pressure as is brought to bear on them. Papers which hold a virtual monopoly in their territory are in a much more favorable position that those which are faced with keen competition. If there is no other paper in the area, the advertiser must choose between advertising in a paper of whose policy he may disapprove, and not advertising at all. But the presence of advertising pressure is a constant danger, to which many editors and publishers, who after all must make a living, succumb.

A much more formidable source of influence is the publisher himself, together with the groups with which he is associated. The policy of every paper may be traced to the people who directly or indirectly own it. The papers owned or controlled by William Randolph Hearst, Colonel Robert McCormick, and Eleanor M. Patterson are thoroughly conservative journals because of the views of these persons. Similarly the *New York Times,* the New York *Daily News,* the Scripps-Howard papers, the members of the Gannett chain, and the St. Louis *Post-Dispatch* (to mention a few at random) reflect, both in their editorial opinions and in their treatment of the news, the attitudes of their owners. Often—usually, indeed—the publishers of newspapers have other financial interests. If a family which controls a certain metropolitan daily also has a large interest in the local transportation system, it may be expected that their paper will seldom publish news that would hurt the transit system, nor will it give anything but meagre or unfavorable publicity to a movement to improve traffic conditions in the city, because this movement, if successful, might tempt more people to drive their own cars instead of riding the buses. And in general, a publisher with other business connections will see that his editors soft-pedal news and opinions which would "hurt business."

This influence is not confined to the men and women whose names appear in the paper's formal statement of ownership.

Often the financial control of a paper is shared, through various arrangements such as loans, with other individuals or groups. They are said to have "bought into" the paper—either as a business venture or for the actual sake of having some voice in the paper's policy. They too will bring pressure to bear on the editor to insure that nothing harmful to their various interests will be printed, and that, on the other hand, full publicity, appropriately slanted, will be given to everything that they specifically advocate and oppose.

A newspaper's treatment of the news, therefore, is to a considerable extent at the mercy of the people who supply the money, whether they be advertisers, publishers, or the financial backers of publishers. Nevertheless, the reader cannot be forgotten. Although he cannot do anything about the actual way in which the news is colored and weighted, he can and will stop buying the paper if it seems too patently a tool of certain interests. As a result, its policies must be expressed in such a way as to persuade the reader that the paper has only the public's interests at heart. In its editorials it may straddle the issue (the glittering generalities and weasel words we discussed in Chapter One are immensely useful here); or it may attempt to "educate" the public to accept the other side's viewpoint. Somewhat less frequently, it may adopt the cause of the public and openly campaign against "the interests." This last alternative is usually confined to cases in which the public welfare is affected directly and dramatically, as in transportation or other public utilities, and in which the paper's financial backers have no great stake.

A moment ago we mentioned a situation in which a newspaper exercised a virtual monopoly over its territory. In recent years there has been a serious tendency toward monopolization. The number of dailies has dropped sharply, and the fewer the papers that are available for comparison and for mutual criticism, the smaller is the chance that the reader will be able to piece together the truth. In many large- and medium-sized cities the papers are all in the hands of one interest, even though they may pay lip-service to different political creeds. Journalism stagnates, and public ignorance deepens, when there is no healthy competition among a number of papers.

So much for the outside influences which affect a newspaper's ability to present all the news objectively. We turn now to the question of just what happens to the objective facts of the news as they pass through the reporter's typewriter and under the editor's blue pencil.

A cardinal tenet of journalistic writing, as it is taught in all the schools, is that of objectivity. Ideally, a reporter writing an account of a news event must exclude from his story all suggestion of bias or personal feeling. In practice, however, this principle prevails only under two conditions. The story will be written "straight" if it has no relation to any topic on which the paper has a "policy," and if "dressing it up" would not improve it for popular consumption (four sick children deserted by their widowed mother.) Under ordinary circumstances, the report of a traffic death might begin in this manner:

> Mary V——, 25, was instantly killed at 10:30 a.m. today when the car she was driving collided with another at the corner of 6th and Main Streets.

But if the paper has been sniping at the city administration, which is dominated by the opposite political party, it might neatly turn the story into a not too well concealed attack upon the Department of Public Safety:

> Residents in the neighborhood of 6th and Main Streets this afternoon were planning an organized campaign for a traffic light following the death there today of pretty Mary V——, 25, whose car collided with another at the unprotected intersection. Viewing the

girl's mangled body, which was hurled 75 feet and landed in a gas station driveway, residents recalled that this was the third death at the site within a year. Several petitions to the city government for a traffic light have been fruitless.

In this account, a little subjective detail creeps into the language: *pretty* and *mangled* are words designed to evoke pity, from which, it is hoped, indignation will then spring. But the bias lies not so much in the writing as in the selection of detail. Presumably everything that is said is true; but the details are chosen and emphasized so as to leave but one impression with the reader: the lethargic city government is responsible for this pretty girl's death! Perhaps if the paper had helped elect the administration, it would not have given so much prominence to the state of feeling in the neighborhood.

Now if the paper's "slanting" of this story resulted in the erection of a traffic light and the saving of lives, it was justified. But too often such more or less subtle coloring of the news can do great harm by influencing the reader's judgment before he can form his own opinion on the basis of all the facts:

Another steep cut in the city's budget for next year was revealed today when Homer D. B——, city comptroller, announced that he had slashed by 30% the municipal university's request for funds. This will result in a saving to the taxpayers of about $300,000, and is in line with the ——— Party's pledge last November to balance the city budget for the first time since 1931. The economy will be effected mainly by dispensing with junior members of the instructional staff and the distribution of their work among the other members of the faculty.

Again, every statement in the paragraph probably could be proved correct. But the paragraph is written and weighted so as to imply approval of the transaction. Compare it with this account of the same event, from another paper:

The municipal university today was the newest victim of City Comptroller B——'s campaign to balance the city budget, as it was announced that the institution's request for funds had been cut by 30%. According to Chancellor R—— of the University, the proposed cut will cause a number of teachers to be dismissed at a time when enrollments are soaring to new highs. "We cannot be expected to do a decent job educating the young men and women of this area," Dr. R—— said today, "unless we are given the money to pay teachers. This is a false economy."

Because their subscribing newspapers are of all popular shades of opinion, the material distributed by the great wire services, the United Press, the Associated Press, and the International News Service, is fairly free from bias. Such slanting as it possesses is the result of the use of newspaperese rather than of any deliberate intention on the part of the writer. But in many newspaper offices, "wire stories" are customarily altered to fit the slant of that particular newspaper. The wording may be changed slightly to fit local prejudices; and the story may be tailored so as to omit details which would not fit in neatly with those prejudices. Furthermore, since every newspaper receives much more wire material than it can possibly use in its next edition, it is forced to select a few from a large mass of stories; and those few will inevitably reflect the present preoccupation of the paper. If, for example, a congressman makes a speech attacking the TVA, a paper which opposes public ownership of utilities will probably find room for the dispatch. But if, the next day, another congressman defends TVA and points out several serious errors in the first speaker's facts, the paper may suddenly become too full to permit inclusion of the rebuttal. In a Republican paper, the utterances of orthodox Republicans always will be featured, and those of Democrats neglected or at least played down, except when the paper expects they will invite Republican rejoinders. And the converse is true, of course, of a Democratic paper. It is seldom possible to discover what both sides are saying without reading two papers.

In Chapter Two we looked briefly at newspaperese, a peculiar kind of jargon. Newspaperese, from the journalist's point of view, is indispensable. The words which comprise it are, many of them, the shortest words that will convey their respective ideas—and short words are the headline writer's salvation. They are also pithy and vivid; they not only describe, they dramatize. And finally, they are convenient. Like all clichés, they save the trouble of searching for a fresh word when the presses are waiting. But for all their terseness and availability, they are obstacles in the way of truthful communication. We have pointed out that such stock words as *attack* and *demand* are customarily used whenever someone disapproves of something or asks for something else. The word *clash* is almost automatically called forth whenever there is a disagreement between two persons or factions. *Crisis* is used to describe almost any state of affairs in which harmony is less than complete.

Now such words have consistently dramatic, even violent, connotations. And because they are used indiscriminately of a minor and entirely temporary difference of opinion between two city councilmen and of a genuinely serious break between major nations, they have the effect of placing all news, the trivial and the momentous, on the same plane of interest. A discussion at the city hall or the state capitol, in which Republicans and Democrats air their respective views according to routine, obviously does not have such grave implications for the future of civilization as does a first-class row between the United States and Russia. Yet the language makes no distinction between them, and the reader, accustomed to reading of "crises" and "tongue-lashings" and "battles" on the floor of Congress in every issue of his newspaper, understandably becomes blasé. What is important, and what is not? The newspaper will not help him decide.

Everything is important to the newspaper editor anxious to increase circulation.

This habitual use of intemperate language is simply one solution of a larger problem: that of keeping the reader interested. As we have said, practical newspaper men cannot afford to regard their papers as primarily a means of educating the public. Despite all the pious sentiments which newspaper publishers and editors utter concerning the function of a free press in a democracy, the fact remains that every editor's first job is to attract his readers to the news stories, so that they will be led in turn to the advertising columns. As you may have discovered by this time, education is not necessarily interesting. Information, however vital, may be deadly dull. And if the choice lies between informing the public and giving it something interesting to read, editors unhesitatingly select the second. Recently a reader complained to the editor of a member of a large newspaper chain that his paper neglected to report international happenings except in the barest, most fragmentary form. The editor calmly replied, "A family newspaper has to be edited with the thought that a great deal of important news is not interesting, and a great deal of interesting news is not important." In every case, interesting news (an "attack-slaying," the death of a wealthy hermit, the discovery of a method of reading a woman's character by examining her legs) will take precedence over important news (a debate in Congress over a new trade agreement, new steps in the nationalization of British industry, newly announced results of cancer experimentation).

Of course there is a certain segment of news which is of such unquestionable importance that it must be given space, regardless of its essentially unexciting qualities. Diplomatic interchanges, the discussion of a major phase of governmental policy, industrial problems—these are basically intellectual issues, "thought stuff." If they are to be handled at all, they must somehow be given color and drama. And so the first job of the newspaper writer is to seek tirelessly for a "news angle"—some aspect of the situation that will give him something to write excitedly about, something that a copy editor can put a headline over. It does not matter at all if the "angle" seizes upon some trivial or irrelevant occurrence, an insignificant side-issue; the "story" is the thing. In an international conference, a brief "clash" of tempers between two diplomats will provide fine headlines for the evening papers. No matter that the "clash" is all over in two minutes and someone else made a speech of top importance an hour later; the "clash" is the news of the day. The day-to-day reporting of the work of Congress is a dull affair; somehow it must be livened up. And so every congressman or senator who "hurls a charge" at someone else, however ridiculous and unfounded the charge, is sure of ample newspaper coverage. There are always numerous members of Congress who are ready to provide reporters with copy for the sake of sensational personal publicity; and one of the first responsibilities of the intelligent reader is to single out those men and steadfastly disregard what they say.

Because the newspapers are so preoccupied with whatever is sensational and dramatic, a great deal of the most important news goes completely unreported. In general, the most deeply significant happenings in the world never make the headlines. What really determines the course of events goes on quietly, in the unpublicized routine of the State Department and the offices of great corporations, in the highly private correspondence and telephone talks between the President and his experts, in the laboratories and research libraries. Wherever policy is being determined, wherever knowledge is being applied to the solution of contemporary problems—there the future of men is truly being shaped. But until these proceedings result in a public statement or provoke a sharp controversy, they go unheeded in the press. What one reads in the newspapers is only the most superficial, though momentarily exciting, manifestation of the vast movements beneath the surface. Not that there is, as a rule, any secrecy about these transactions; it is simply that the newspapers are not interested in material which cannot readily be made "newsworthy." And when there is secrecy, it is often because the participants in a discussion fear what will happen "if the newspapers get hold of it." They do not fear publicity itself, but they dread the distortion and sensationalism which too often will be the price of publicity.

If the necessity for "playing up the news angles" of any event is one major reason why newspapers present an unbalanced view of the world, another is the physical limitations of the paper. Each daily has its own normal size, from which it varies considerably only when there is unusually much advertising to be printed (as in the weeks before Christmas) or when there is a supremely interesting news event to be covered, with much background material (as the death of a president, or some sensational local event). The fact that newspaper size remains fairly constant would present no difficulties if the volume and importance of news also remained constant. Unfortunately, however, there are good days and bad days in the newspaper office. On unusually good days there is not enough space; on bad days there is far too much space. Either way, the reader loses.

When big news events are happening all over the world, events which are not only exciting but also genuinely significant, as during a world war, the editor must wield the scissors with great abandon. (In World War II his problem was complicated by the severe rationing of newsprint.) He must choose material from a mass far too great to be printed complete. The result is that he cuts out important phases of single stories—phases which, if included, might give the reader an entirely different view of the subject. A news report built upon a space-saving generalization may often omit qualifications and attendant circumstances which, if fully reported, would completely change the complexion of the matter. Other stories may be omitted entirely.

One particularly dangerous result of this limitation of space is the cutting of quotations from people's utterances. Given a mimeographed "hand-out" of someone's speech, a reporter will quickly scan it to find a sentence or two which he thinks will make the best (*i.e.*, most interesting) story and, if the speech is a controversial one, will fit in best with his paper's policy. It does not matter if the sentences thus selected for quotation are relatively unimportant—a mere aside in the speaker's main discourse; nor does it matter if, when wrenched from context, they represent the speaker as saying something entirely different from what he meant. The truly critical reader will never base an opinion upon the exceedingly fragmentary press report of someone's public utterance. He will withhold opinion until he can see the full text.

But there are also days when there is not enough news to fill the customary space. What then? The paper cannot let its readers down. Somehow it must find enough excitement to make them believe they are getting their money's worth. And now, instead of being faced with the evil of incomplete and therefore distorted coverage, we are faced with the no less serious one of exaggerated importance. The editor, confronted with the problem of putting out his daily edition, can do two things: he can "blow up" such news as he possesses, and he can create news. Usually he does both. The result in both cases is still further loss of perspective.

When an editor "blows up" a news story, he takes one which on normal days would merit a three-hundred-word coverage and allots it a thousand words instead. The reader, who understandably is in the habit of judging the importance of a news item by the amount of space devoted to it, thus concludes that the story is much more important than it actually is. A case in point occurred while this chapter was being written. For a while early in 1946 the biggest news stories concerned widespread labor troubles in America, such as the General Motors, General Electric, and New York tugboat strikes. Because these stories were of much more immediate interest to readers and because they touched upon topics of basic concern to the newspapers' publishers and their backers, they occupied the front pages, and the first meeting of the United Nations Organization in London received inadequate coverage except when there were dramatic encounters between diplomats. But then most of the strikes were settled, and a vacuum was left on the front page. At that moment there occurred a series of sharp verbal interchanges between Russia and the other two members of the "Big Three." If these had occurred during the period of strikes, they would have received limited coverage; but now, in the dearth of other news, they were given a play completely out of proportion to their real significance. The result was that the public received an exaggerated notion of the "crisis" among the great powers, and opinion concerning Russia was decidedly altered.

The tone of public opinion, then, is often determined by a totally irrelevant and fortuitous circumstance—the condition of the "news market" at the moment. During the doldrums, events and statements which have relatively little significance in the total pattern of affairs are magnified far beyond their true value. It is now a matter of history that the Spanish-American War was caused to no small extent by the eagerness of the Hearst press to have something to put into flaming headlines, as well as by the personal political ambitions of its owner. And although newspapers seldom deliberately mold history in this way, their solution to the problem of what to write about on dull days often has that eventual effect.

The editor's device of actually creating news to fill gaping spaces in his next edition is usually limited to local affairs. Many newspaper "crusades" have their origin in this way. The paper suddenly discovers that there are wretched slums in the heart of the city, or that the police department is lax in its enforcement of traffic laws. Often, of course, such campaigns result in genuine improvements, although they may lose fervor as soon as spontaneous news comes along—or until some powerful "interest" is offended. But often they have the effect of misrepresenting a situation. A certain municipal agency, for example, may be doing its work as honestly and efficiently as conditions permit; and then, on an unlucky day, a reporter, desperate for a story, discovers some isolated case of injustice or graft and emblazons it on page one. Although to any disinterested observer a mountain has been made out of a molehill, the resultant publicity may seriously weaken and demoralize the agency thus embarrassed.

One final source of distortion is the physical makeup of the paper. Page one is what sells every paper on the newsstands. Page one must, therefore, contain the most exciting material. As should be abundantly clear by now, the most exciting material is not necessarily the most significant; but the reader, unconscious as always of the confusion, automatically places most value upon what is given physical prominence in his paper. Often the events which will prove transcendently important later on are relegated to an obscure column on an inside page.

Similarly with headlines. Many people, pressed for time, follow the news exclusively through the headlines, never bothering to read even the fragmentary reports which follow them. Yet the headlines cannot possibly give an accurate summary of the news. For one thing, they are so limited in space that it is a definite art to compose any headline, accurate or not; for another, they represent the ultimate refinement of the dramatic device which we have noted as being the essence of news writing. Furthermore, many papers have the definite rule of always appearing with a block-letter streamer headline all the way across page one. Logically that would mean that every day there is one news story, and only one, which deserves such prominence. Yet who would maintain that STRAY DOG BITES THREE IN SUBURBS should arrest the attention and preoccupy the mind to the same extent that BRITAIN OFFERS INDIA FULL INDEPENDENCE should? We are back once more at the same complaint—that the exigencies, real or imaginary, of newspaper production give the reader a most dangerously distorted view of what is going on in the world.

Why *dangerously?* For these two reasons, which actually are different sides of the same coin. In their unremitting attempt to make their newspapers interesting, not once in a while, but every day without exception, editors and writers grossly exaggerate the true importance of many of the events they report. Probably the gravest danger this involves is in the supremely vital field of international relations. By being constantly led to believe that every small disagreement among nations not only is fraught with danger to world peace but also is evidence of the evil intentions of all countries but our own, the public is given anything but a true picture of world affairs. When it is kept in a state of excitement and suspicion, it cannot possibly develop the calm clarity of mind which is essential to the making of critical decisions.

Furthermore, the newspaper and its public are very much like the boy who was always crying "wolf" and the people who soon learned not to pay any attention to him. When a newspaper pumps artificial excitement into its every item, eventually the public catches on to the trick and becomes blasé. The reader sees a scare headline, and he thinks, "Just another newspaper story." Once in a while a story comes along which is a hundred times more important than its predecessors; one which should command the instant attention and thought of every reader. But the newspaper has no means of showing this unusual importance; it has been so much in the habit of using sensational language and headlines that those devices no longer have any special force. The reader finds that the present story is dealt with in the same terms in which hundreds of other stories have been dealt with; those earlier alarms had meant nothing; why should this one? And so he refuses to consider the latest news worthy of any special consideration. Yet this may be a moment that calls for the exercise of every modicum of intelligence which the nation can muster.

What is the answer? Complete disregard of the newspapers is certainly *not* the answer. A partial one is steadfast refusal to be guided in your thinking by a single newspaper, for even the best and most honest papers have their prejudices. If in your city there is a genuinely Republican paper and another that is genuinely Democratic, you can make a start toward finding out the truth about local and national affairs by habitually playing one against the other. For international affairs, the best policy is to read one of the great metropolitan dailies which have seasoned staffs of foreign correspondents and commentators: the *New York Times,* the New York *Herald-Tribune,* the Chicago *Daily News,* the *Christian Science Monitor*. A quite well-balanced summary of each week's news, both international and national, is found in the "News of the Week in Review" section of the Sunday *New York Times.*

But the daily press as a whole, even including the *New York Times,* which has perhaps the best reputation for fairness and comprehensive coverage, still is conservative. While there is no widespread "conspiracy of silence" on certain matters, such as radicals love to accuse the newspapers of fostering, it is undoubtedly true that for one reason or another some important sidelights and fragments of news stories do fail to appear in even the most conscientious papers. The intelligent reader who insists upon knowing as much as can be known before he makes up his mind must also, therefore, have recourse to one of the responsible organs that specialize in publishing what the others omit to print. One is *PM,* which is an everpresent gadfly at the flank of its more august New York contemporaries. It not only prints much material that they omit but also takes constant delight in pointing out their inaccuracies and biases. Others are the weekly liberal journals, the *Nation* and the *New Republic.* These periodicals are frankly edited from a certain "point of view"; they are as biased in their own way as the large dailies are in another way. One can take their editorial opinions or let them alone. But like *PM,* they do supply some significant material which other papers fail to print.

The intelligent citizen-reader, in a word, must maintain the scientific attitude toward information which will enable him to make up his mind: in the first place, he must seek to accumulate all that he can, and in the second place, once that material is accumulated, he must test it for accuracy. He must take into account all the various means by which objective truth may be distorted in its passage through the news-making process. When he makes up his mind, he must be as sure as any reasonable man can be that his data are free from prejudice of whatever sort—that they represent things as they are, not things as publishers and editors and the people behind them wish him to believe they are. Honest search for the truth of the news is an arduous and often most disheartening labor; but no one can be an intelligent American citizen without committing himself permanently to that quest.

EXERCISE I.

1. Suppose the following is true of the leading newspaper in your city: Its publisher is a member of a family long prominent in

Democratic politics and, in addition to his newspaper holdings, is financially interested in a large textile mill and in local real estate operations. His wife, who also owns a share of the paper, is prominent in the Daughters of the American Revolution. The city itself is the center of an important industrial area, which is not especially well organized by the unions. What sort of treatment is it likely that the newspaper will give to each of the major topics in the news at this moment?

2. Find out all you can about the actual interests of the publishers of the local newspapers, and then, examining their handling of the news over a short period, try to conclude how that handling has been influenced by each newspaper's "policy." (If possible, compare their treatment with the treatment given to the same news by a larger, perhaps more independent, paper in another city.)

EXERCISE 2. Comb current newspapers for examples of the coloring of news by newspaperese. Try to find instances of the use of such words as *plot, hit* ("disapprove of"), *fear, flay, decry, assail, menace, smash, deadlock, expose, grave* (adj.), *cloud* (in "diplomatic skies"), *storm* (of disapproval), etc. Substitute words with less dramatic connotation and determine how far such substitution affects the objective meaning of the news.

EXERCISE 3. In a commencement address at a certain college, a distinguished general of the United States Army said the following things. The time after each item suggests the relative importance the general attached to that subject:

1. A liberal education is the best safeguard of democracy. (8 minutes)
2. The suppression of the universities was one of the greatest mistakes Nazi Germany made. (5 minutes)
3. But the universities had to be ruthlessly suppressed, because the

strongest anti-Nazi feeling was concentrated there. (3 minutes)

4. In fact, certain German scholars did valuable spy work for the Allies. (1 minute)
5. Colleges and the Army should work hand-in-hand for a strong American defense system. (10 minutes)

Which of the following headlines do you think will be used by a newspaper editor eager to sell his papers? Which do you think contains the most significant point General Jones made?

1. LIBERAL EDUCATION GUARDS DEMOCRACY, SAYS GEN. JONES
2. SAYS SCHOOL CLOSING LED TO NAZI DEFEAT
3. GERMAN SCHOOLS HARBORED ANTI-NAZIS, JONES AVERS
4. JONES DISCLOSES ALLIED SPY RING IN NAZI COLLEGES
5. RECOMMENDS ARMY, SCHOOLS JOIN FOR DEFENSE

EXERCISE 4. On a certain day in Congress:

(a) Member A made a thoughtful speech about our foreign policy. (He is not a spectacular figure.)
(b) Member B exposed a case of discrimination against war veterans in industry. He read a letter, received from one of his constituents, describing the case.
(c) Member C (Republican) "hit" the Democratic administration's tariff policy.
(d) There was a vote on a bill for aiding technical research in the Navy.
(e) Member D (Democrat) said that the Republican party was being underwritten by big business interests.
(f) There was a row in a committee hearing when two Democratic members exchanged sharp words.

1. Rank these occurrences in ascending order of what you consider their true importance as they affect the nation's welfare.

2. Rank them in ascending order of news value as viewed by an editor.
3. If you take into account the political bias of the paper, what changes must be made in (2)?

EXERCISE 5. Assuming that you have room to feature only one item from each group, which item would you, an experienced reporter, select for your story?

1. You have covered a meeting of building contractors from all over the United States. From the talks and discussions you learn:
   (a) Prefabricated houses have been over-publicized; they will not be nearly as popular or numerous as the public has been led to believe.
   (b) Public low-cost housing projects, sponsored by the government and by large private interests like insurance companies, are not a threat to the smaller real-estate and building interests.
   (c) New, revolutionary designs have been introduced by which glass ceilings are used in bedrooms, thus permitting indoor sunbaths.
   (d) A study by scientists shows that houses built in the past twenty years are deteriorating twice as fast as houses built twenty to forty years ago.
   (e) The public should be "sold" on the advantages of single houses over apartments, in order to stimulate the construction of single units and thus increase the profits of the builders.
2. You have covered a convention of distinguished American historians, who read papers on the following topics:
   (a) The influence of the Grange upon national politics in the latter part of the last century has been exaggerated.
   (b) The growing bitterness between North and South in recent years strikingly resembles the feeling between the two sections in the years 1830–1860, and steps should be taken to avoid the mistakes made then.

(c) Aaron Burr's lovely daughter, Theodosia, was not lost at sea, as everyone has thought. Records have just been discovered of her having lived as a recluse in New Orleans as late as 1852.

(d) American commercial interests in the Far East have caused the nation far more trouble than the actual dollars-and-cents profit from them has warranted.

EXERCISE 6. What is the difference between the two reports of the same happening in each of the following groups?

1. (a) The flood control measures taken here by the Federal Government, following the disastrous flood in 1936, received their crucial test last night when Callahan Dam broke, spilling 2,000,000 gallons of water into the Joralemon River. Although the flood crest in the downtown section reached within two feet of the all-time high recorded in 1936, little damage was reported. The flood waters were carried safely between the concrete walls built by WPA labor in 1936–38.

   (b) The city received its worst flood scare since the disaster of 1936 last night when Callahan Dam broke without warning, spilling 2,000,000 gallons of water into the Joralemon River. Although all local emergency relief units were mobilized, their services were not needed. At the height of the flood the waters reached to within two feet of the peak recorded during the 1936 disaster, and engineers for a time expressed anxiety whether the retaining walls, built in 1936–38, could resist the unprecedented pressure. However, the waters receded by 4 a.m. and little damage was reported.

2. (a) Before a crowd of 2,000 banqueting industrialists at the Hotel Sherman last night, Senator L—— M—— delivered another in his series of attacks against organized labor. Demanding that Congress end the current labor unrest by placing stringent curbs on the activities of union leaders, he

reiterated his often-quoted stand that millions of dollars are being lost by industry every day so long as the strikes continue. "Every stockholder of every firm affected by these totally unnecessary work stoppages," he said, "should insist that Congress take decisive action now."

To enter the hotel, Senator M—— crossed a picket line thrown around State and Armitage Streets by local union organizations. Carrying banners reading "M—— the Tycoons' Friend," "M——'s votes carry us closer to World War III," and "Here lies M——, once more," about 300 men and women, led by William K——, president of the U.A.W. local, paced the sidewalks for an hour before M——'s arrival. Although there was no disturbance, Senator M—— was protected by a flying wedge of city police as he stepped from his limousine and hurried into the hotel.

(b) Braving picket lines thrown around the Hotel Sherman by C.I.O. and Communist organizations, Senator L—— M—— last night delivered a smashing attack on the irresponsibility of labor, demanding that Congress pass a law to make union leaders as legally responsible for their acts as corporations now are.

The pickets, whom police estimated numbered 1,000 men and women, tied up sidewalk traffic on State and Armitage Streets for three hours. They carried signs attacking Senator M——'s stand on labor issues and his vote on foreign policy measures. Conspicuous among them was William K——, U.A.W. organizer now out on $5,000 bail following his arrest last month for inciting to riot in connection with the strike at the National P—— Company. Police had difficulty clearing a path for Senator M—— at the entrance to the hotel as the pickets and others attempted to prevent him from crossing the sidewalk.

Before a cheering gathering of 2,000 business executives in the hotel's Ebony Room, Senator M—— declared that if there were strong regulatory laws now on the statute books, the present wave of strikes and other labor disturbances would have been averted and millions of dollars saved to labor, the consumer, and industry.

EXERCISE 7. In view of all we have said in this chapter, what are the recognized shortcomings of daily newspapers which the weekly "news magazines," such as *Time* and *Newsweek*, attempt to supply? Exactly what are the virtues and defects of these magazines? Do they give any clearer picture of the week's news than the best newspapers? Do they have any editorial bias?

EXERCISE 8.

1. How much of what we have said of the newspapers' handling of their material is also true of radio news reporting? Specifically, what about over-dramatizing news events? suppression and coloring of news because of the private interests of sponsors or of the owners of the radio stations? the problem of filling up space (remember the newscast has an unvarying time to fill—five, ten, or fifteen minutes)?
2. Discuss the difference between news announcers and news commentators. Are the news announcers always objective? What about the most influential news commentators: do they pretend to objectivity? Of those who you think are prejudiced, which freely admit having a certain bias, and which conceal that bias under a pretense of objectivity?

EXERCISE 9. Why are there so many syndicated columnists, especially in Washington, who specialize in "filling in the background" (*i.e.,* reporting rumors, "secrets," and "hidden trends") of the news? Is this a silent commentary on the shortcomings of their papers' formal coverage of the news? What actual value have the reports of these columnists? Do they actually broaden one's view of daily affairs? Who are the most reliable? Which are the professional crystal-gazers?

Appendix A

In the following pages we have printed, for the convenience of the teacher and the explorative student, additional illustrative material of various sorts. Believing that each teacher will wish to use this material as his own preference and the needs of individual classes direct, we give only the bare texts, without commentary. Some of the quotations bear on certain specific passages in the main body of the book, and may be used in addition to, or in place of, the exercises and illustrations given there. Others, because they illustrate several points at once, could well be used as summary and review material. Several could form good starting points for student themes.

1

A word is not a crystal, transparent and unchanged; it is the skin of a living thought, and may vary greatly in color and content according to the circumstances and the time in which it is used.

2

It cannot at this time be too often repeated,—line upon line, precept upon precept,—until it comes into the currency of a proverb:

to innovate is not to reform. The French revolutionists complained of everything; they refused to reform anything; and they left nothing, no, nothing at all *unchanged*. The consequences are *before us*, —not in remote history; not in future prognostication;—they are about us; they are upon us. They shake the public security; they menace private enjoyment. They dwarf the growth of the young; they break the quiet of the old. If we travel, they stop our way. They infest us in town; they pursue us to the country. Our business is interrupted; our repose is troubled; our pleasures are saddened, our very studies are poisoned and perverted, and knowledge is rendered worse than ignorance, by the enormous evils of this dreadful innovation. The revolution harpies of France, sprung from Night and Hell, or from that chaotic Anarchy which generates equivocally "all monstrous, all prodigious things," cuckoo-like, adulterously lay their eggs, and brood over, and hatch them in the nest of every neighboring state. These obscene harpies, who deck themselves in I know not what divine attributes, but who in reality are foul and ravenous birds of prey (both mothers and daughters), flutter over our heads, and souse down upon our tables, and leave nothing unrent, unrifled, unravaged, or unpolluted with the slime of their filthy offal.

3

[*From a newspaper dispatch*]

Mr. Halleck portrayed the Republican party as:

"The party of forward-looking wisdom, opposed to the party of reckless experiment . . . the party of Americanism, opposed to a party riddled and inoculated with foreign, left-wing un-Americanism . . . the anti-radical party, opposed to the radical party . . . the anti-regimentation party, opposed to the party that would put a nation in a tyrannical production line or under the thumbs of political top-sergeants . . . the anti-bureaucratic party, opposed to the party that would fasten the dry rot of a vested bureaucracy upon every phase of American life."

In a paragraph that set the keynote for much of his speech, Mr. Halleck said:

"The Republican party is the anti-Communist and anti-left-wing party, in opposition to the party that conciliates and fraternizes with Communists and revolutionists. The Republican party is affirmatively the party of competition and the right of the individual to carry on his business subject to fair regulation but without improper governmental meddling."

4

Dear Brother Alumnus:

Thanks a million, loyal brothers who so kindly responded to last year's appeal. You encouraged and helped at a most critical time in the history of our grand old Fraternity. Praise be! to those who became Life Honor Key Men, in Sigma Phi Sigma.

This annual letter to all our alumni brothers, and also for the information of our younger active brothers, is important. We have been asked to put dynamite in it that our negligent brothers may realize their duties directly following a depression cycle of the most exhausting nature. My personal feeling is that our Fraternity is too profound in our lives to confuse it in high pressure tactics for loyal support. True, we have reached a day of dire need for personal interest and earnest assistance of every good Sigma Phi Sigma brother.

What shall we say? It is not easy to write one letter for so many diversified minds. We wish you would lean back and think, then say it all for us. Surely you know the answer. You can admit that the Fraternity is one of the gems in your social background, like old lavender, old lace and old gold in the family treasure chest of traditions. You may call it a buoy, a memory through a mist to days of youth, happy days; and you can admit that it is a real treasure of your life; something of pride and satisfaction in your cognition of accomplishment as an individual of standing in the academic social world. You may admit that old Sigma Phi Sigma has passed through its many years of service with but little, fractional help from you, except if you have remained on the firing line. You can act on these material factors by giving some personal interest to the old love, and a little financial support each year. You can thus help preserve the traditions and service of a truly noble, academic, social organization, of far reaching significance, by deciding you will do better in future, if you have failed in past. It is an opportunity, an honor to be a loyal brother in Sigma Phi Sigma.

In merry whirl of life, oft take fallacy for truth. Somehow, there is an ever present confidence, almost gloriously inept, that the old Fraternity will go right on, that your Active Chapter will pay off the property debt, keep up taxes, replacements and repairs and the demanding running expenses; get new pledges, stand high scholastically and continue safely onward without your personal interest or help. A proud realization of security appears to obtain in some quarters that our ennobled Grand Chapter, with its national administrative responsibility for leadership stability of our system of chapters, can plough through each year without deficit, regardless of alumni assistance. Our National Headquarters, home of our Grand Chapter, becomes most heavily burdened of any activity in our National Fraternity system, as the executive branch of a far flung organization. Save for generous sacrifices of Grand Officers in freely going forth in the ever demanding interests of Sigma Phi Sigma, the System would soon be lost to account. Close, detailed supervision is necessary at all times. There has been good sportsmanship, big sentimental, old play boy enthusiasm in the spirit of our workers, together with an earnest and sincere brotherhood. . . .

5

On Saturday afternoon, January 11, a gay group of YM and YW cabinet members trekked via automobile and Cecil Thomas' lorrie to a quaint spot about due north of Columbus, known as Verbeck's lodge. After everyone who rode with Cecil thawed out before the crackling log fire, a short business meeting was held. Then the entire group enjoyed and exhausted themselves square-dancing with Mr. Verbeck directing.

After a delightful luncheon the group participated in several games. Of these, the most fascinating was one called "Concentration." Following the games, there was more dancing, both round and square. Later on, marshmallows were toasted, and cokes were served. After the farewell ceremony, the group returned in Cecil's "fresh-air taxi."

6

THE MAN WHO BROUGHT THE PRICE OF TOMMY GUNS DOWN FROM $250 TO $45 IS THE MAN WHO BRINGS GIMBELS RADIO PHONOGRAPH DOWN FROM DIZZY HEIGHTS TO $79

Gimbels went searching for something lots of people thought was unfindable—a really fine radio phonograph to sell under $80. It's no surprise to anyone who knows the Maguire Industries that the radio-phonograph we found was the Maguire. The Maguire people acquired the manufacturing rights to the Thompson sub-machine gun (tommy gun) in 1938. When they started producing, tommy guns cost $250. After they rolled up their sleeves, did some fancy calculating on their cuffs, did an imitation of a new broom in every department, tommy guns cost $45! *That* kind of production engineering, combined with Gimbels 4-store buying and price-peeling genius, brings you a superb radio-phonograph at $79. (The Maguire people are more than just price lowering experts—they've made all sorts of electronic equiment, including the radar equipment used by the B-29's that bombed Tokyo.) This new Maguire radio phonograph has one of the fastest automatic changers made—only 4 seconds between records. The "push-pull" audio output gives you console-tone record and radio reproduction. (Push-pull means 2 audio tubes instead of the usual 1, hooked to the speaker. It's like the extra engine the train takes on to push it up a mountain.) Use our easy payment plan. You pay as little as ⅓ down, the balance monthly, including service charge. Write, phone. We'll ship your radio phonograph as soon as your order gets to Gimbels.

7

NOW THEY CAN BE TOLD: Behind the Scenes Dramas of the Navy!

NOW YOU CAN SEE THEM: Hitherto Secret Photos Never Before Released!

"BATTLE STATIONS!" The ship's loud speaker sounds the alarm! It's "Mae Wests" for all hands! Then all Hell lets loose! Orange flames from crashing Zeros! Pin-pointed bombings! Terrific salvos! Flaming, smoking beachheads! . . . Death . . . agony . . . glory . . . break over our men as the world's mightiest fleet goes into action!

Now hear this! Turn to! for this big new book—for the first uncensored story of our modern Navy . . . Complete in one volume . . . Told by the great admirals . . . Pictured in hundreds of startling, never-before-published action photos, maps, documents (many in full color) right from the Navy's confidential files!

Astounding photos after photos reveal glorious epics of our Seabees, Marines, Coast Guards, the Fleet, the Air Arm, Amphibious Forces and the Armed Guard! Thrill to this authentic photo-drama of your Navy's cruise to VICTORY, actually written by the men who charted that cruise! Feel a new pride in every branch of our Navy sweep through your being!

See the outbreak of war in September 1939, when the Navy convoyed American cargo ships; through the American invasions of the African, Mediterranean and Channel Coasts; through the decisive sea battles in the Pacific!

Learn from none other than Admiral of the Fleet Ernest J. King, Chief of Naval Operations, the secrets of the Navy's strategy that won for America such amazing triumphs. See Navy guns knocking hundreds of Jap Zeros from the sky . . . See mad Kamikazes crashing the flight decks of Carrier Bunker Hill . . . See the Navy ferrying our armies to invasion shores, even across the Rhine! . . . See Halsey's Third Fleet blasting Jap battleship Yamato!

Page after page, many in full color, bring to life, with the breathless continuity of an action film, many epical achievements . . . the huge naval bases erected on Bermuda, Newfoundland, Trinidad, Nova Scotia, and many other far-flung areas for the protection of our homeland . . . the campaign which wiped out the U-boat packs that all but halted our shipping . . . the strategy against V-1 and V-2 bombs marked for American cities . . . the Navy's powerful Squadron 58 in full battle-action in the Philippine Seas . . . the signing of the Japan surrender on the USS Missouri—shown in full color! Over 500 pictures, mostly full page!

Here is the dramatic account of our Navy, not only in war, but as a guardian of world peace and of American interests on the seas.*

8

Every man speaks and writes with intent to be understood; and it can seldom happen but he that understands himself might convey his notions to another, if, content to be understood, he did not seek to be admired. But when once he begins to contrive how his sentiments may be received, not with most ease to his reader, but with most advantage to himself, he then transfers his consideration from words to sounds, from sentences to periods, and as he grows more elegant becomes less intelligible.

It is difficult to enumerate every species of authors whose labors counteract themselves: the man of exuberance and copiousness, who diffuses every thought through so many diversities of expression, that it is lost like water in a mill; the ponderous dictator of sentences, whose notions are delivered in the lump, and are, like uncoined bullion, of more weight than use; the liberal illustrator, who shows by examples and comparisons what was clearly seen when it was first proposed; and the stately son of demonstration, who proves

* Copyright, 1946, by William H. Wise & Co.; reprinted by special permission.

with mathematical formality what no man has yet pretended to doubt.

There is a mode of style for which I know not that the masters of oratory have yet found a name; a style by which the most evident truths are so obscured that they can no longer be perceived, and the most familiar propositions so dignified that they cannot be known. Every other kind of eloquence is the dress of sense, but this is the mask by which a true master of his art will so effectually conceal it, that a man will as easily mistake his own positions, if he meets them thus transformed, as he may pass in a masquerade his nearest acquaintance. This style may be called the *terrific,* for its chief intention is to terrify and amaze. It may be termed the *repulsive,* for its natural effect is to drive away the reader. Or it may be distinguished, in plain English, by the denomination of the *bugbear* style, for it has more terror than danger, and will appear less formidable as it is more nearly approached.

9

HOTSPUR

Where is his son,
The nimble-footed madcap Prince of Wales,
And his comrades, that daff'd the world aside
And bid it pass?

VERNON

All furnish'd, all in arms;
All plum'd like estridges that with the wind
Bated like eagles having lately bath'd;
Glittering in golden coats like images;
As full of spirit as the month of May
And gorgeous as the sun at midsummer;
Wanton as youthful goats, wild as young bulls.
I saw young Harry with his beaver on,
His cuisses on his thighs, gallantly arm'd,
Rise from the ground like feathered Mercury,

And vaulted with such ease into his seat
As if an angel dropp'd down from the clouds
To turn and wind a fiery Pegasus
And witch the world with noble horsemanship.

HOTSPUR

No more, no more! Worse than the sun in March,
This praise doth nourish agues. Let them come.
They come like sacrifices in their trim,
And to the fire-ey'd maid of smoky war
All hot and bleeding will we offer them.
The mailed Mars shall on his altar sit
Up to the ears in blood. I am on fire
To hear this rich reprisal is so nigh,
And not yet ours. Come, let me taste my horse,
Who is to bear me like a thunderbolt
Against the bosom of the Prince of Wales.

10

Come sleep! O sleep, the certain knot of peace,
  The baiting place of wit, the balm of woe,
  The poor man's wealth, the prisoner's release,
  Th' indifferent judge between the high and low;
With shield of proof shield me from out the prease
  Of those fierce darts despair at me doth throw;
  O make in me those civil wars to cease;
  I will good tribute pay, if thou do so.
Take thou of me smooth pillows, sweetest bed,
  A chamber deaf to noise and blind to light,
  A rosy garland and a weary head;
And if these things, as being thine by right,
  Move not thy heavy grace, thou shalt in me,
  Livelier than elsewhere, Stella's image see.

11

(a)

The grey sea and the long black land;
And the yellow half-moon large and low;
And the startled little waves that leap
In fiery ringlets from their sleep,
As I gain the cove with pushing prow,
And quench its speed i' the slushy sand.

Then a mile of warm sea-scented beach;
Three fields to cross till a farm appears;
A tap at the pane, the quick sharp scratch
And blue spurt of a lighted match,
And a voice less loud, thro' its joys and fears,
Than the two hearts beating each to each.

(b)

Round the cape of a sudden came the sea,
And the sun looked over the mountain's rim:
And straight was a path of gold for him,
And the need of a world of men for me.

12

(a)

Thus fenced, and, as they thought, their shame in part
Covered, but not at rest or ease of mind,
They sat them down to weep. Nor only tears
Rained at their eyes, but high winds worse within
Began to rise, high passions—anger, hate,
Mistrust, suspicion, discord—and shook sore
Their inward state of mind, calm region once

And full of peace, now tost and turbulent:
For Understanding ruled not, and the Will
Heard not her lore, both in subjection now
To sensual Appetite, who, from beneath
Usurping over sovran Reason, claimed
Superior sway. From thus distempered breast
Adam, estranged in look and altered style,
Speech intermitted thus to Eve renewed:—
"Would thou hadst hearkened to my words, and stayed
With me, as I besought thee, when that strange
Desire of wandering, this unhappy morn,
I know not whence possessed thee! We had then
Remained still happy—not, as now, despoiled
Of all our good, shamed, naked, miserable!
Let none henceforth seek needless cause to approve
The faith they owe; when earnestly they seek
Such proof, conclude they then begin to fail."
To whom, soon moved with touch of blame, thus Eve:—
"What words have passed thy lips, Adam severe?
Imput'st thou that to my default, or will
Of wandering, as thou call'st it, which who knows
But might as ill have happened thou being by,
Or to thyself perhaps? Hadst thou been there,
Or here the attempt, thou couldst not have discerned
Fraud in the Serpent, speaking as he spake;
No ground of enmity between us known
Why he should mean me ill or seek to harm.
Was I to have never parted from thy side?
As good have grown there still, a lifeless rib.
Being as I am, why didst not thou, the Head,
Command me absolutely not to go,
Going into such danger, as thou saidst?
Too facile then, thou didst not much gainsay,
Nay, didst permit, approve, and fair dismiss.
Hadst thou been firm and fixed in thy dissent,
Neither had I transgressed, nor thou with me."

To whom, then first incensed, Adam replied:—
"Is this the love, is this the recompense
Of mine to thee, ingrateful Eve, expressed
Immutable when thou wert lost, not I—
Who might have lived, and joyed immortal bliss,
Yet willingly chose rather death with thee?
And am I now upbraided as the cause
Of thy transgressing? not enough severe,
It seems, in thy restraint! What could I more?
I warned thee, I admonished thee, foretold
The danger, and the lurking Enemy
That lay in wait; beyond this had been force,
And force upon free will hath here no place.
But confidence then bore thee on, secure
Either to meet no danger, or to find
Matter of glorious trial; and perhaps
I also erred in overmuch admiring
What seemed in thee so perfect that I thought
No evil durst attempt thee. But I rue
That error now, which is become my crime,
And thou the accuser. Thus it shall befall
Him who, to worth in woman overtrusting,
Lets her will rule: restraint she will not brook;
And, left to herself, if evil thence ensue,
She first his weak indulgence will accuse."

(b)

"Madam, if my advice had been of any authority with you when that strange desire of gadding possessed you this morning, we had still been happy. But your cursed vanity, and opinion of your own conduct, which is certainly very wavering when it seeks occasions of being proved, has ruined both yourself and me who trusted you."

Eve had no fan in her hand to ruffle, or tucker to pull down; but with a reproachful air she answered: "Sir, do you impute that to my desire of gadding, which might have happened to yourself with all your wisdom and gravity? The serpent spoke so excellently, and with so good a grace, that— Besides, what harm had I ever done him, that he should design me any? Was I to have been always at your side, I might as well have continued there, and been but your rib still; but if I was so weak a creature as you thought me, why did you not interpose your sage authority more absolutely? You denied me going as faintly as you say I resisted the serpent. Had not you been too easy, neither you nor I had now transgressed."

Adam replied: "Why, Eve, hast thou the impudence to upbraid me as the cause of thy transgression, for my indulgence to thee? Thus it will ever be with him who trusts too much to a woman. At the same time that she refuses to be governed, if she suffers by her obstinacy she will accuse the man that shall leave her to herself."

13

England has been in a dreadful state for some weeks. Lord Coodle would go out, Sir Thomas Doodle wouldn't come in, and there being nobody in Great Britain (to speak of) except Coodle and Doodle, there has been no Government. It is a mercy that the hostile meeting between these two great men, which at one time seemed inevitable, did not come off; because if both pistols had taken effect, and Coodle and Doodle had killed each other, it is to be presumed that England must have waited to be governed until young Coodle and young Doodle, now in frocks and long stockings, were grown up. This stupendous national calamity, however, was averted by Lord Coodle's making the timely discovery, that if in the heat of debate he had said that he scorned and despised the whole ignoble career of Sir Thomas Doodle, he had merely meant to say that party differences should never induce him to withhold from it the tribute of his warmest admiration; while it as opportunely turned out, on the other hand, that Sir Thomas Doodle had in his own bosom expressly booked Lord Coodle to go down to posterity as the mirror of virtue and honour. Still England has been some weeks in the dismal strait of having no pilot (as was well observed by Sir Leicester Dedlock) to weather the storm; and the marvellous part of the matter is, that

England has not appeared to care very much about it, but has gone on eating and drinking and marrying and giving in marriage, as the old world did in the days before the flood. But Coodle knew the danger, and Doodle knew the danger, and all their followers and hangers-on had the clearest possible perception of the danger. At last Sir Thomas Doodle has not only condescended to come in, but has done it handsomely, bringing in with him all his nephews, all his male cousins, and all his brothers-in-law. So there is hope for the old ship yet.

14

The past, as it were, rises before me like a dream. Again we are in the great struggle for national life. We hear the sound of preparation—the music of the boisterous drums—the silver voices of heroic bugles. We see thousands of assemblages and hear the appeals of orators; we see the pale cheeks of women, and the flushed faces of men; and in those assemblages we see all the dead whose dust we have covered with flowers. We lose sight of them no more. We are with them when they enlist in the great army of freedom. We see them part with those they love. Some are walking for the last time in quiet, woody places with the maidens they adore. We hear the whisperings and the sweet vows of eternal love as they lingeringly part forever. Others are bending over cradles kissing babes that are asleep. Some are receiving the blessings of old men. Some are parting with mothers who hold them and press them to their hearts again and again, and say nothing; and some are talking with wives, and endeavoring with brave words spoken in the old tones to drive away the awful fear. We see them part. We see the wife standing in the door with the babe in her arms—standing in the sunlight sobbing—at the turn of the road a hand waves—she answers by holding high in her loving hands the child. He is gone, and forever.

We see them all as they march proudly away under the flaunting flag, keeping time to the wild grand music of war—marching down the streets of great cities—through the towns and across the prairies—down to the fields of glory, to do, and to die for the eternal right.

15

I can look a whole day with delight upon a handsome picture, though it be but of a horse. It is my temper, and I like it the better, to affect all harmony; and sure there is music even in the beauty, and the silent note which Cupid strikes, far sweeter than the sound of an instrument. For there is a music wherever there is a harmony, order, or proportion; and thus far we may maintain the music of the spheres; for those well-ordered motions, and regular paces, though they give no sound unto the ear, yet to the understanding they strike a note most full of harmony. Whosoever is harmonically composed delights in harmony; which makes me much distrust the symmetry of those heads which declaim against all church music. For myself, not only from my obedience, but my particular genius, I do embrace it: for even that vulgar and tavern-music, which makes one man merry, another mad, strikes in me a deep fit of devotion and a profound contemplation of the First Composer. There is something in it of divinity more than the ear discovers. It is an hieroglyphical and shadowed lesson of the whole world, and creatures of God. Such a melody to the ear, as the whole world, well understood, would afford the understanding. In brief, it is a sensible fit of that harmony which intellectually sounds in the ears of God.

Appendix B

THE CAMPAIGN AGAINST "OFFICIAL" JARGON

(From the "Better Writing" series of the Federal Security Agency, Social Security Board.)

I

DO WE HAVE TO USE SUCH LONG WORDS?

The answers is "Yes"—sometimes. Surely we are justified in using technical terms when writing to others who know their meaning.

But why should a busy regional representative have to puzzle through this kind of language:

> It is requested that the Social Security Board be furnished with three authenticated copies of the deed, in pursuance of which the title to said Grand Rapids National Bank Building was conveyed unto Frank D. McKay Realty Company. The authentication of a written instrument is such official attestation thereof as will render it legally admissible in evidence.

Complex or unusual words make writing harder for anyone to understand. Anyone will understand more quickly if we write "after a careful review of the facts," instead of "After a comprehensive and thorough appraisal of all the circumstances pertaining to the case . . ."

Unnecessarily long, technical, or high-brow words also give readers the impression that we are:

"Legalistic bureaucrats making things more difficult than they are."

"Professionals more anxious to impress than to inform."

"Pompous people trying to show how much they know."

We really are not, so let's try to write—

Not Like This	But Like This
a substantial segment of the population	many people (a large group)
fully cognizant of	know well
interpose an objection	object
comprising numerous agricultural units	made up of many farms
hold in abeyance	wait (postpone action)
promulgate the regulation	issue the regulation
effectuate (implement) the policy	carry out the policy
pursuant to your request	as you requested
prior to . . . subsequent to	before . . . after
secure (ascertain) the data	get the facts
interrogate the claimant	ask (question) him
purports to construe	explain (tries to explain)
encounter difficulty in	find it hard to
precludes the institution of appeals processes	does away with the need for . . .
marked discrepancy	clear difference
initiate (institute) a project	begin . . .
consummate the arrangement	make or complete . . .
in the initial instance	in the first place
of the order of magnitude	about

2

ARE GOVERNMENT WORKERS PEOPLE?

Believe it or not, we too are people, even though we often don't seem so when we write.

We are usually normal when we talk, but put a pencil in our hand or a stenographer at our side and a mysterious change takes place. Some claim that the flesh turns to stone and blood to ice water. No human being would talk this way:

"In further reference to your request, attention is called to the fact that the Social Security Board is concerned only when the matter affects the Federal Social Security laws."

Readers of Government "literature" sometimes get the impression that no human beings exist, anywhere. The world consists entirely of bureaus, boards, policies, grants, benefits, assistance, ideas, and "it"—especially "it." Everything but people. Ours is a program for people, administered by people, yet we often write like this:

"Employment in manufacturing and government recorded increases, while there were declines in trade and domestic services."
(More people were employed in manufacturing and government, and fewer in trade and domestic service.)
"The check is returned so that pay for November 2 may be deducted."
(We are returning the check so that you may deduct pay for November 2.)
"It will be appreciated if this refund is forwarded immediately to this office."
(Please send us the refund immediately.)
"It is strongly recommended that every effort be made to have this matter brought to the attention of the agency."
(We strongly recommend that you make every effort to bring this matter to the attention of the agency.)

When we do admit that people exist, we often treat them as mere appendages to abstract ideas:

"General assistance or relief accounted for nearly all the remaining recipients of public aid."
(Nearly all the other people getting public aid were receiving general assistance or relief.)
"The protection afforded industrial and commercial workers is far from complete."

(Many industrial and commercial workers are not protected.)

To a worker who asks about benefits:—"Because of the many factors which must be taken into consideration in computing the amount of benefits an individual will receive under this program, it is not possible for the Social Security Board to inform an individual of the specific amount of his monthly benefits until a claim has been filed."

(Because many facts must be considered in figuring benefits, we are unable to tell you the exact amount of your monthly benefit until you file a claim.)

Under some circumstances we even appear to take on a god-like form! Our voices come from the mountain top when we say—

"Many risks to family income maintenance are not insurable in that they stem from individual and chance situations or combined misfortunes not common to large segments of the population in normal times. Such disasters, however, are none the less severe for their fortuitous character."

3

YOU DON'T HAVE TO SOUND LIKE A GOVERNMENT OFFICIAL

The Federal government for many years has used a language all its own. Editorial writers and others who wish to ridicule us call it "governmentese."

We don't have to write that way! Oscar M. Powell, Executive Director, has said:

"I understand that many employees and supervisors have the impression that they are supposed to write in the impersonal and stilted style typical of much writing in government. That impression is wrong. I see no reason, for example, why anyone should write, 'It is suggested that consideration be given to the document attached hereto,' when he means, 'We suggest that you consider the attached report.' "

WE CAN FORGET STILTED "GOVERNMENTESE" EXPRESSIONS

Here are a few typical phrases that make our writing stuffy, stilted, "bureaucratic," and hard to read.

Pursuant to your request
Please be advised
  You are advised
  We wish to advise
  Kindly advise
Receipt is acknowledged
Attention is directed (invited)
Hold in abeyance
Reference is made

Pending receipt
Transmitted herewith
  Attached hereto
  Action thereon
(Let's ditch the whole tribe)
At your earliest convenience
Under date of
Deem it advisable
In lieu of
In further reference

WE CAN AVOID UNDESIRABLE IMPERSONAL EXPRESSION

Studied effort to be impersonal is one of the main characteristics of governmentese. We write of things in place of people, and reduce people to "it," like this:

Governmentese	English
The Bureau believes . . .	We believe . . .
The division's view . . .	Our view . . .
It is suggested . . .	We suggest . . .
It is reported . . .	Mr. Blank reports . . .
It is the opinion of the writer . . .	I think . . .

This mistaken tendency to dehumanize writing forces a passive construction that is unemphatic and often obscure:

Revision of this provision is suggested.	We suggest you revise this provision.
The plan was approved . . .	Mr. Blank approved the plan.
It is requested that the Social Security Board be furnished with three copies . . .	Please send us three copies . . .
Attention is called to . . .	We call your attention to . . .

Index

1. SUBJECTS

2. SOURCES OF QUOTATIONS